Hugh McManners joined the British
missioned into the Royal Artillery. I
him to read Geography at Oxford U
Boxing Blue, a Half-Blue for Modern
was awarded a 'Mention in Despatches' for his part in the Falklands
War; *Falklands Commando*, his account of his experiences in the
war, was published to considerable acclaim in 1986. He is now
leaving the Army to embark on a career as full-time writer and
broadcaster.

By the same author

Falklands Commando

HUGH McMANNERS

Crowning the Dragon

Adventures in the Chinese Karakoram

GRAFTON BOOKS

A Division of the Collins Publishing Group

LONDON GLASGOW
TORONTO SYDNEY AUCKLAND

Grafton Books
A Division of the Collins Publishing Group
8 Grafton Street, London WIX 3LA

Published in paperback by Grafton Books 1990

First published in Great Britain by
Grafton Books 1989

Copyright © Hugh McManners 1989

A CIP catalogue record for this book is available
from the British Library

ISBN 0-586-20425-3

Printed and bound in Great Britain by
Collins, Glasgow

Set in Sabon

All photographs are by the author

CONTENTS

ACKNOWLEDGEMENTS

There are many people without whom I would not have been able to make this trip.

Foremost are June Han and Hamish Blyth, who backed my enthusiasm with financial guarantees. My 'rear party' in Britain was headed by the capable Susie Scott, of Scott Tinsley, and Major Chris Coats, together with Barbara Levy, my literary agent, Alice Ilich of Christie's, and Justin Samuel, my solicitor. Michael McCarthy of *The Times*, now the paper's Environment Correspondent, covered the story from start to finish with all his usual humour and panache.

I was particularly fortunate in having been supplied with Agfa Gevaert film – for both the cine and still photography. Despite extremes of temperature, varying from well over 140°F in the noonday sun to below −40° on the mountain, the film was not affected. At very low temperatures film often snaps, but this never happened and the colours, particularly the reds, remained fast.

I had to dump a quarter of my exposed film under piles of stones for six weeks; the extreme temperature fluctuations made the canisters hot to handle by day, and as cold as ice at night. I used Agfa Professional 35mm stock and their XT 125 colour negative cine film. I am very grateful to Agfa Gevaert for all their expert help.

I am indebted to the BBC's Graham Pass for his interest and support; to Cliff Kitney for taking me on as a budding broadcaster, entrusting me with expensive sound equipment; and to producer Louise Swan for her perseverance in reducing ten hours of high altitude puffing and panting into a one-hour radio programme.

Dr Marjorie Sweeting, an experienced China traveller and much-invited guest of the Chinese People's Republic, checked my rather rusty geomorphology and confirmed that our less fortunate experiences at the hands of Chinese bureaucracy were not abnormal.

I would also like to thank my editor Richard Johnson for his invaluable encouragement and guidance; Janice Robertson for her expert, exact and always helpful comments and suggestions; and Katherine Everett for choosing my photographs to their best advantage. My thanks also must go to Dr Richard and Mary Fargher for their accurate and perceptive comments on the text.

Alan Stephenson of Graph Techniques made possible the very high standard of colour printing. Agfa provided all the film, with especial thanks to Hans Lodders of Agfa Hong Kong. The Services Sound and Vision Corporation, in particular Ann Eva, provided cine cameras and much practical advice and support.

As with everything in this book, despite all the expert help and advice I have been given, any mistakes it might contain are mine alone. And, in trying to be honest, I hope I have not caused offence.

Finally, without Henry Morgan's vision and hard work, and the comradeship, expertise and good humour of 'the team', nothing could have been achieved. I am deeply grateful to them all, for a remarkable experience that I will remember, and draw upon, for the rest of my life. I could not have asked for a more capable group of people with whom to travel.

PREFACE

As a small boy, I saw the film of Sir Edmund Hillary's first ascent of Everest in 1953. Since then I have always been interested in big mountains. Suppressing an equally strong urge to become a deep-sea diver, I joined the Army and was paid to throw myself from aeroplanes, slide down ropes from hovering helicopters and tramp happily for days across rain-swept heathland carrying rifle and rucksack. I learned to climb rocks, to ski and to survive in the arctic conditions of Norwegian mountains, but never had the time for proper mountaineering.

To me, mountaineers had always seemed a race apart from normal humans, as big as the mountains they conquered and as tough as the conditions they endured. To them, being so close to the gods, the squabbles of us mere mortals must seem petty, unworthy of souls cleansed by clear air, cutting winds and the rays of an unmasked sun.

Although in reality mountaineers are a tough breed, I should have realized that the inescapable and incalculable dangers of mountaineering would eventually bring out all the usual human frailties in them. If a family holiday by car to the South of France were afforded the number 3 on a Richter Scale of Conflict Potential, then high altitude mountaineering scores 6 or 7 (I reserve the figure 8 for voyages to other planets).

People who climb mountains are very highly motivated. If they are to have any will-power left by the time they approach within striking distance of the summit, their reservoirs must be deep and full at the beginning. High altitude drains will-power subtly and irresistibly away.

The reasons for individuals exposing themselves to the high risks of big mountains are as various as the people who do it. All are ambitious, some for themselves alone, others for the team as a whole. The team spirit of each individual varies greatly, too; the most highly motivated mountaineer may easily be the least team-spirited.

When it comes to the crunch on a mountain, everyone is on his own, and only the most determined gets to the top. The weak fall by the wayside – sometimes literally, being left behind by comrades who have only just enough strength to save themselves. It is a hard business; technical, individualistic, and very dangerous. I wonder now whether the most effective mountaineers might also be the most selfish.

I told an interviewer from Capital Radio that I was joining Henry Morgan's expedition 'to escape the boredom of peacetime soldiering' – a rather negative reason. Although I had no technical mountaineering expertise, I was swept up by Henry's enthusiasm and vision, and by his assurances that I could learn all I needed as we went along.

Henry needed a properly-qualified team as well as the financial backing of others in order to climb the Crown in the Chinese Karakoram and achieve his vision. His optimism was infectious. By the time we left Britain, he had co-opted two more novices onto his team, while the doctor with Himalayan experience proved unable to come. So, although we had some top-grade climbers, no-one had climbed at high altitude. Were we taking on too much?

Team spirit in the face of hardship and danger is vital. Everything conspires against the individual. The physical dangers are difficult to gauge; avalanches are unpredictable, rivers vary, and accidents happen. This uncertainty leads to stress and fear, and in turn to tiredness. High altitude causes sickness, and is always debilitating. Isolation from the outside world increases the fear; anxiety goes hand in hand with exultation; irritation grows.

The most splendid scenery may be laid out before you; the highest mountains in the world swathed in blue-trimmed cloud, the glaciers cracked and glistening, the snow perfectly white. Yet in that moment all you can think about is the unreasonableness of the pair in the next tent who ate more than their fair share of the biscuits.

There is a statistically significant comparison between the dangers of mountaineering and those of war. A 1 in 25 chance of someone being killed is a figure often quoted in connection with Karakoram climbing expeditions. For a ten-man team, this could mean an almost fifty per cent chance of someone not coming home at the end.

I began the expedition thinking that in the face of these odds, we would establish the kind of team spirit I had experienced during the Falklands War. As it turned out, we did not.

The concept of danger in the mountains turned out to be different to the military evaluation of risks in battle. Skilled climbers take few risks, so in their minds there is no danger – save from unpredictable avalanche. Apart from avoiding avalanche areas and knowing what to do if one hits you, there is little point in thinking about it. The mountain – the source of the danger – is implacable. It does not care if you are there or not; it is unaware and inscrutable. At times I found myself becoming frightened of it, as if it were alive and even vindictive. Perhaps this feeling was an attempt to cut the mountain down to the size of something I could understand.

In a war the enemy is personal, a body of men into whose minds you try to think, and over whom you feel you have superiority. Of course, if the bullet or shell has your name on it, regardless of your expertise or professionalism you will go down. Also, in war nobody knows what they are in for. One noticeable characteristic of combat veterans is their reluctance to expose themselves in a second battle; they have already seen what happens. Once they get going, experience makes veterans very effective; but they are understandably cautious at the outset.

A mountain to climb is a fortress under siege, throwing down avalanches of snow instead of boiling oil. Any death, however, is incidental and not deliberate – the fundamental difference that separates mountains from battlefields.

Danger is nevertheless integral to the thrill of mountaineering, the spice that makes the dish special. And everyone is there because they want to be, not because of the dictates of duty. They have personal ambitions to fulfil. Again the military analogy has parallel here; it would be as if every soldier had the winning of a gallantry medal as his aim in war. A selfish, kamikaze chaos would ensue, destroying team spirit and thus losing the battle.

I have persisted with this military analogy because our group were soldiers acting as mountaineers. The expert mountaineers in the team were able to play that role convincingly, but we novices were not; we were just soldiers learning as fast as we could. Nevertheless, when things were really difficult, the discipline stamped upon us all by the bizarre, time-honoured and peculiarly effective British Army parade ground got us through.

One aspect that remained in everyone's minds throughout the expedition was finance. Henry had assured us that sponsorship would be found, so when we were all asked to take out personal bank loans for sums varying from £2,350 to £5,200 (depending upon Army pay), some of us were taken aback. Unfortunately Henry's unquenchable optimism alone could not induce hard-headed businessmen to part with large enough sums.

I am not certain exactly what pressures this situation put upon each team member. We were all loyal to Henry, and apart from a bit of initial muttering everyone got on with the job. I decided that as no professional camera crew could be persuaded to come with us I should shoot a film, then use it to try to recoup money on our return. Unfortunately for me, the film replaced the mythical sponsor who would solve all our financial problems. Worse, an unworthy suspicion grew that I was intending to profit personally from the time, money and efforts of my comrades. No-one really believed this, but it was easier to shift the general anxiety over money into this area. Anything was better than asking difficult questions about our leader's judgement before we were even within sniffing distance of the camels. Instead, the devil of our anxiety nibbled away at me.

At the climax of the mountaineering, just below the very summit of the Crown, the dark question of money re-emerged as a factor in the life-or-death decision of whether or not to abandon the climb. The lives of two men, held by a sitting belay and a length of rope, were balanced against the potential for sponsorship. Money is another of the harsh realities of mountaineering.

From the top of the Crown you can see far into Pakistan, past K2 to India and north to Afghanistan, a truly beautiful place to be tempted . . .

MAPS

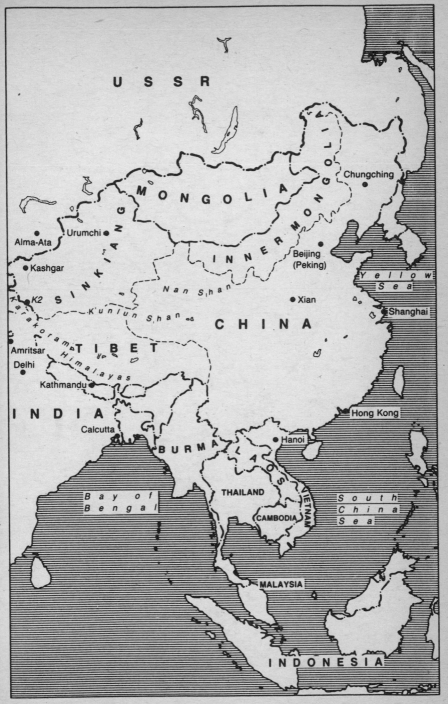

Map 1 China and Tibet

Map 2 The Journey by Road

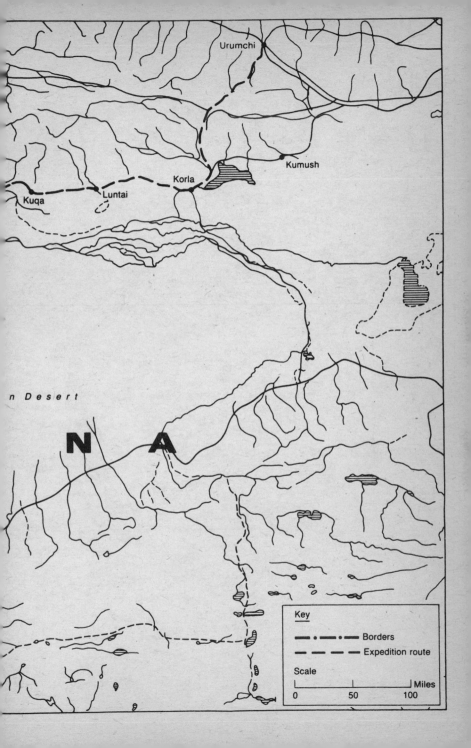

Map 3 The Journey on Foot

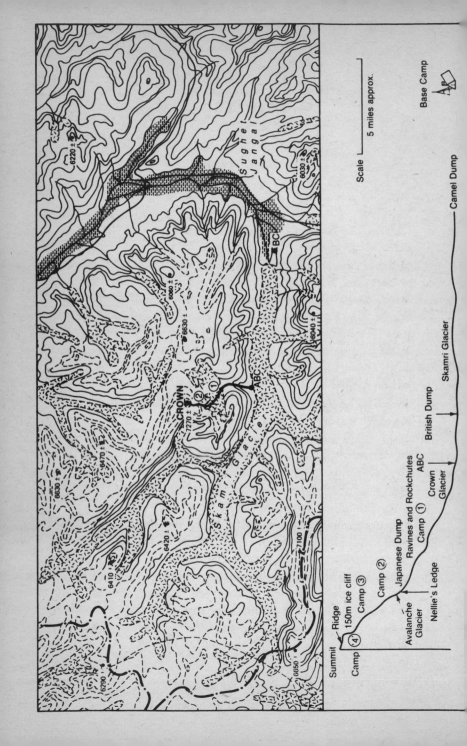

CHAPTER 1

A Need for Dragons

At first light I eased out of my sleeping bag and started boiling water for the breakfast. K2 Base Camp was uncharacteristically busy that morning. A caravan had pulled in late the previous night, Turki camel drivers and some Chinese Army soldiers escorting a group of Chinese scientists. The officer, his red-star peaked cap tilted backwards at a jaunty angle, emerged from a tent (his companions still sleeping) carrying a long stick ringed red and white (a survey stadia rod) and a fire bucket. Army officers the world over seem to do the same things and the Sarpo Laggo river looked like a good place to fish.

The camel drivers, wearing dusty, dark suits with flat caps or battered fur-trimmed hats, came over from their makeshift canvas shelter, squatted on their haunches ten metres away and stared, blankly and without comment, as if we were from another planet. The sun was now upon us, removing all the chill of the early morning, feeling hot against the skin.

We found a small cairn on the hilltop above the camp, with an inscribed metal plate bolted down with ice screws commemorating a Japanese climber killed on K2 a few years earlier. Beyond the cairn, the path continued up the valley, past lesser (but nevertheless massive) mountains towards the beginning of that terrifying peak.

The four of us, on foot without the strong backs of camels to carry our heavy loads, packed up and left the Chinese Army, who had started cooking appetizing-looking noodles in a large black cauldron.

We walked south along the Sarpo Laggo river for the next two hours, looking for a place to cross. The waters were grey with silt, and even this early in the day, before the sun had melted the ice on the massive glaciers from which it issued, were raging and powerful. The place where our expedition's camels were supposed to have dumped our equipment, and where we hoped our base camp would be set (at the foot of the Skamri Glacier), was to the west, a couple of hours' walk on the other side of the river. As our food was running out, we were anxious to cross.

Captain John Day attempted crossings at several places, entering the water without his heavy bergen rucksack, leaning on a bamboo pole for some degree of stability. The water surged up from his thighs, wetting his chest before swirling away downstream. It seemed vicious, far too powerful for us to do more than test the edges.

Weighed down with heavy bergens, we continued south, across loose boulders and through the smaller streams of cold water. We walked past the entrance to the Skamri Glacier valley and our base camp.

Hidden in grey cloud twenty miles west, further up the valley, the angular rock and ice tower of the Crown (the third highest unclimbed mountain in the world) lurked unseen. We, with the others, were in the Chinese Karakoram to make the first ascent of this most inaccessible and difficult mountain. The other six should now be marking routes up the glacier and carrying equipment from the camel dump up towards the higher camps that would have to be established as the climbing proceeded.

The others, as far as we knew, had made it across the river on the camels over a week earlier, or at least we hoped they had. For the previous fortnight, having left them marching with the camels and the equipment, the four of us had gone south-east, to explore the massive Upper Shakesgam Valley. We had taken two camels, the other twenty-four carrying the rest of our food and equipment to the mountain.

On our way back, emerging from the end of the Shakesgam Valley, we had met the twenty-four, with their drivers, on the long walk back to the outside world. The driver of our two camels could not walk out on his own (one hundred miles over high passes to the nearest habitation) and so had rejoined his comrades. This left us camel-less on a five-day walk to catch up with the others under our own steam. Without the strength and height of the camels to get us across (and after having already made several very cold, wet crossings), this, the Sarpo Laggo river, seemed the most serious problem of many we had overcome so far.

One hundred metres across, the river was too strong and wide to rope our way over. The water was likely to swing the first man back, as if on a huge pendulum. We walked up and down the banks for several hours, getting wet and numb from many fruitless attempts to cross.

We next decided to continue south up to the snout of the glacier (several miles on our very rough map), hoping to be able to scramble onto its ice and rubble, then across to the other side. Unfortunately, half a mile on, the river cut into a cliff on our side barring further progress upstream. We were walking across large, round boulders and down into deep, dry water courses two and five feet deep, which was very tiring.

After more discussion we returned downstream to where the valley widened and where the force of the water might be dissipated laterally. The afternoon was drawing on. This late in the day the river would be approaching its maximum volume from glacier melt-water. We might have to camp and try again first thing in the morning when the glacier had frozen up and the water level had dropped.

John Day was very anxious to cross, striding down the side of the torrent, his thick black beard and bamboo pole making him look like Moses on the banks of the Red Sea (an effect spoiled by tri-colour shorts). He beckoned us all over to a spot I had noticed as we walked up, but had thought dangerous.

He proposed crossing here, in stages; to the islands of boulders in the centre, then working downstream until he reached the last fifteen feet, which were on the outside of a bend and the deepest and fastest part of the river, which he would get across as best he could. It looked even more dangerous now than it had earlier in the day.

The discussion was going very badly. John was having no more talk. He was going to make his crossing attempt here and now. We had discussed it, I had voiced my objections strongly but he was adamant. I looked to the others; 'Rad said nothing and Nick asked John at what point he would enter the water.

'I'm very unhappy about this,' I said. 'Why don't we wait until the morning? It won't make any difference and the chances are that it will be very much safer.'

'I've made up my mind,' said John. 'It's my decision and that is that.'

I wasn't sure what he meant; was it 'his decision' as our self-appointed leader or 'his decision' because he was risking his own life and nobody else's? Nick Moore supported John, saying earnestly to me that it was John's life and therefore I had no say in the matter.

I found this extraordinary. Where was the responsibility to the team who needed John's expertise to climb the mountain? What about parents and loved ones back home?

Did everyone on the expedition feel this way, regarding themselves as individuals, responsible only to themselves, rather than as members of the team? (Several very experienced mountaineers had warned me how selfish mountaineers and mountaineering could be.) With my purely military background (and no mountaineering experience), I couldn't believe people who shared danger and depended upon one another could be anything other than strong team members.

Short of having a fight (with fists) by the river side, or picking up a large rock and smashing John over the head with it, there was nothing I could do to stop him. I had a vision of his being swept away back into China, smashed to a pulp against the rocks (as one of our donkeys had been on an earlier, easier crossing). I sat on my bergen hoping there wasn't going to be a disaster. We would be able to do nothing for him.

As he edged into the first part of the river I decided simply to do my job, and take photographs. Peering through a viewfinder insulates a photographer from the real world to some extent. My main job was to record, which I thought might absolve me from responsibility for whatever might happen.

Conrad Ainsley nudged me, to point out a dust storm whirling around the valley a little lower down. With relief, I was able to take the lens off John for a few frames.

John struggled across the easier parts of the river, rested for a time on the rocks in the centre, then with grim and tottering determination plunged into the last fifteen metres. The water surged over his waist and chest, forcing him to lean heavily on the bamboo pole.

With painful slowness, carefully shuffling his feet lest the current pluck his leg from the rocky river bottom and spin him away downstream, he moved through the grey torrent and into the last and deepest bit. Exhaustion and the redoubled force of the deeper water caused him to waver. He lost his balance and, with his seventy-pound bergen, was spun round like a rag doll by the flood. With a desperate lunge, he grabbed a rock on the far bank and clawed his way to the side, pulling himself slowly from the water.

John was soaked and bitterly cold, but safe. Although extremely relieved, my heart sank as I realized I would now have to attempt the same thing. I immediately set off downstream towards John's crossing place, without waiting for the other two, using a false, enforced jollity and briskness to prevent any further thought. Meanwhile, John dumped his bergen, tied a safety rope to a boulder on the far side and came back with the rope-end.

'Rad was first, choosing a bad line. For a few moments, with the water surging up his legs and body, he looked like a novice water skier struggling to stand up. I crossed next and asked for too much rope so that one side of the loop dragged in the water. I had to wait in the middle of the river until John pulled in the slack. My legs were shaking with cold. The effort of hanging onto the rope and keeping on my feet in the powerful waters was exhausting, making me gasp for breath like a sprinter. John bellowed instructions over the noise:

'Go for it, Hugh. Fight hard NOW. Really fight through the next bit.'

I kept my legs pistoning up, down and sideways until 'Rad grabbed me, hauling me onto the bank like a gaffed fish. The weight of my bergen toppled me sideways onto the stones. At first I could not feel my legs at all, then there was intense pain for several minutes. Nick started across. I dived into my bergen for a camera.

All safely across, we slumped exhausted on the boulders for quite some time, chewing raisins and wringing out our socks.

In July 1982, I returned home from the Falklands War aboard SS *Canberra* to Southampton and an astonishing welcome that seemed to have welled up from the deepest recesses of the nation. I had served with 148 Commando Forward Observation Battery, Royal Artillery, a small, very specialized unit that carries out covert forward reconnaissance, then fires the Royal Navy's guns (as well as field artillery) and directs Royal Air Force jets (with bomb, missile and gun armaments) onto the most important targets. I had fought the war as part of the Special Boat Squadron Royal Marines (the specialists in small boat reconnaissance, demolition and raiding operations). For the final battles around Port Stanley, I had been loaned to the Special Air Service.

With my five-man team, as part of an SBS fighting patrol, we were inserted, twelve hours before the 3 Commando Brigade assault landing to retake the Islands, to locate then neutralize an Argentinian heavy weapons company, preventing them from sinking the troop ships sailing into San Carlos Water. We carried out raids on Argentinian port positions in rubber assault boats and patrolled huge areas of waterlogged heath searching for the enemy (hiding by day in soggy holes under the ground). Preparing for operations on warships, we endured air raids and an Exocet attack.

We finished the fighting living hidden for two weeks in an exposed, wind-swept cleft in the rock on a very open hillside overlooking the Argentinian positions on the north side of Stanley, observing them closely by day and shelling them by night. Throughout the war, all around, friends had been killed and wounded. By some miracle of good fortune, the five of us were untouched.

We found that all our training had been vital: cold winter months in the mountains of Norway, the sweaty discomfort of Central American jungles, months of exercises on Dartmoor, Okehampton, Otterburn, Sennybridge . . . the weather making them amongst the most inhospitable training areas used by any Army in the world, and the best places to make the mistakes and learn.

We found also that our motives, day by day, had very little to do with hatred of Argentinians, patriotism or even regimental pride. We were doing our jobs as well as we could, step by step, taking each moment as it came. We were real people and rank and capbadge faded into insignificance. Our own little team was the most important thing in the world, and the shock of losing a member of the team would have been enormous. If that had happened, the survivors would have continued (ruthlessly) to do the job for the sake of the missing man. Our motivation was the strongest possible; we were doing it for one another.

Returning to Southampton, we were completely unprepared for the welcome; it seemed as I imagined VE Day must have been, a golden moment of collective, joyous abandon. I remember looking out from crowded decks onto that incredible scene with bewilderment; we were still living with the relief of survival, and the memories of friends who were not coming back.

Life flows on. For me, after six weeks' leave, a posting into the Ministry of Defence to work long hours as a personal staff officer for a general who understood my mood: the peculiar anti-climax, frustration and stress of getting back to 'normal' life.

Leaving 148 Battery and the other four in my team so soon after the end of the war had been a mistake. It is essential to talk away the hidden tensions that build up during such an extreme experience. Family and friends, having been so deeply affected themselves, could only be given a rather sanitized version of events, and with so much explanation that meaningful talk was an enormous effort. Their well-meant comments could sometimes be irritating. At other times, by revealing how little they understood, they made me feel isolated and very lonely.

I became a focus of attention at supper parties, the source of a form of entertainment. I was amazed at the way so many people had followed the events of the war through the media. As so few of us had been directly involved in the fighting, I understood their interest in having me to hand, and would answer questions as best I could. This 'Falklands veteran' tag, a phrase so swiftly coined by the newspapers, increased my feeling of isolation. The questions that *I* needed to ask (of myself or of someone who truly did understand) remained unanswered.

I found conversation with fellow servicemen who had also been in the fighting equally or even more frustrating, because every person's experience of a war is so very parochial. Naval officers with whom I had shared moments of great danger had very different memories and feelings from mine. My conclusion was that only the other four members of my team truly understood what we had been through, and that by leaving the unit for the staff job in the MOD, I had missed out on a vital part of the post-combat healing process.

And so I wrote a book, entitled *Falklands Commando*, to explain what the war was really like (a counter to the highlighted versions I had given at supper parties) and to give a soldier's version of events so heavily and swiftly documented by returning journalists. I wrote about the war as I experienced it, escaping from the frustrations of the day by going back through my memories, trying to lay ghosts to rest (for example, why did I have it so easy when others suffered so much?) and examining my conscience, on the kitchen table of my lonely London digs.

The book was finished in the autumn of 1983, when I moved on to the Army Staff College at Camberley. Towards the end of the Staff College course, in November 1984, *Falklands Commando* was published, to much good humoured leg-pulling from my friends, a very formidable assembly of military expertise.

The years from February 1984 to March 1987 were a grim time. Having settled down to work hard at the Staff College, enjoying getting to grips with aspects of my profession of which, as a Captain in a slit trench, I had been blissfully unaware, I was struck down by a virus which gave me symptoms of permanent influenza and caused deep depression, making me a burden to my friends. From being an indestructible runner of marathons, player of rugby and burner of the candle at both ends and in the middle, I became a hesitant, selfish and boringly irritable person. I felt ill most of the time, and very tired all of the time.

I endured the Staff College course but, because of the illness, derived very little benefit from it. At the end I was posted back to London, to another job in the Ministry of Defence. After a year, I was admitted to hospital, and several months later, having been tested for everything – leukaemia, malaria, Hodgkin's disease,

Crohn's disease . . . you name it – the medical profession could find nothing.

The following year I was again admitted to hospital, with the same lack of result. The Ear, Nose and Throat specialist whipped out my tonsils, which helped a little. I was almost wishing something nasty on myself to at least put a name to my suffering. At work my superior was less than sympathetic, and life seemed at times to be hardly worth the effort.

The turning point came when I was admitted to RAF Headley Court to be medically tested prior to taking up command of an artillery battery. In addition to the malaise, I had a form of arthritis (caused by parachuting in my last operational job).

Before putting me back into an operational unit commanding soldiers, the Army had to be assured that I was fit enough. Surrounded by severely damaged people (Headley Court started off as the rehabilitation centre for RAF pilots literally shortened by ejecting from their aircraft), I abandoned all caution and pushed myself to the limits, emerging physically fit and confident that, although I still felt ill, there was not something sinister lurking deep inside.

Today the cause of my suffering is well known: 'ME' (myalgic encephalomyelitis), or 'Post-Viral Disease Syndrome' and nick-named the 'Royal Free Disease'. (It is also sometimes referred to as 'Yuppies Disease', which I hesitate to admit.) The misery can continue for several years or more, and nothing can be done. The virus, and its aftermath, had removed my self-confidence and enthusiasm for life. It had smeared the clarity of my love for the bright skies and perfect beaches of home (Cornwall), and had placed the knife of worry into my stomach, to turn every morning as I tried to escape the new day.

By the spring of 1987, two and a half years later, I had become much better, no longer feeling quite so ill, even enjoying isolated moments of well-being. Deep inside, however, I was still uncertain. I needed to test myself, body and spirit, to be sure that the malaise was defeated.

Ironically it was also my year, The Year of the Dragon, when those born in previous Dragon years (1952 in my case) are supposed to have a bumper twelve months. Dragons are very similar to Sagittarians (of which also I am one), full of ideas that they think absolutely brilliant, and boundless energy for their own wonderful projects.

The Chinese value the dragon most highly of all their mythical animals: strong, brave, capable and loyal. Dragons are also likely to eat anyone who disturbs them while they sleep, a very good reason to let sleeping dragons lie. They represent that unswerving confidence of mind and strength of spirit that is so easily replaced by hesitation, uncertainty and fear, and can, if properly cultivated, bring luck and good fortune.

After all my virally-induced misery, I needed to be certain that my dragon was with me once again, giving confidence, strength and good luck. Also, with my recovering health, and the perversity that makes men reflect on dreadful experiences with peculiar and wistful satisfaction, five years without an adventure seemed rather too long. I needed a test, and by chance in the spring of 1987, my meeting in Portsmouth with Captain Henry Morgan of the Royal Engineers was to be the start of a test and the adventure of a lifetime.

Her Majesty's Ship *Nelson* neither sails, steams nor floats, being a huge Royal Navy training establishment twenty minutes' walk from Portsmouth Harbour railway station. Sailors returning from a run ashore in Pompeii (Portsmouth in Royal Naval argot) must negotiate the watchful eyes of the Regulating Staff (naval policemen) guarding the main gate and stumble past a magnificent twenty-foot figurehead (a gleaming effigy of Admiral the Lord Nelson, his telescope at the ready), before making it to the lifts of the high-rise accommodation blocks, and the safety of their bunks.

HMS *Nelson*'s sickbay and a passport photo machine remain open all night (and at weekends) so that sailors suddenly required to join ships in foreign parts may get inoculations and visas and be swiftly on their way. Notice boards display to those recently returned from long voyages black and white photographs of side, front and rear profiles of the perfect sailor, showing exactly what is permissible by way of haircuts, sideburns and beards. Moustaches on their own are strictly prohibited, a conceit to which only a soldier or airman would succumb. 'Sideburns, if worn, may extend down the face only to a line drawn through the centre of the earhole.'

At the entrance to the Wardroom the sentry was swathed against the drizzle in a dark blue cloak, his black gaiters and boots gleaming in the orange light from the arc lamps above. I showed my Army ID card and received a smart navy salute, hand turned palm downwards as if shielding one eye from salt spray. I knew from a previous visit to HMS *Nelson* not to walk straight up the steps to the front doors of the grey stone Wardroom Mess building. This route was for senior officers only; the two flights at either side were for lesser mortals.

Captain Henry Morgan was waiting for me in the bar. His slight build and conventional, quiet manner was polite rather than piratical. He spoke quietly, had a lively sense of humour and was chirpy, like a small bird on a spring morning. (He was however no light-weight; underneath the feathers and song he was very single-minded and determined.) Henry, no distant descendant of the Elizabethan privateer made good in the Royal Navy, was an Army Captain in the Royal Engineers, working at HMS *Nelson* as the Inspector of Army Diving.

'Dive Army' could easily be a car sticker. Surprisingly, the first military diving was done (in 1838) by the Army rather than the Navy, by Royal Engineers who, in 1839, cleared the wreck of the *Royal George* from the bottom of Portsmouth harbour and accidentally damaged part of *Mary Rose*, an Elizabethan warship raised over a century later by a new generation of Royal Engineers divers.

As Inspector of Army Diving, Henry, at thirty-two years of age, was responsible for the standard of all Royal Engineers diving teams throughout the world, from Northern Ireland (where they search sewers and ponds for weapons and bodies) to the Falklands (where they build underwater moorings, jetty foundations and install ship-to-shore pipelines). His personal expertise ranged from underwater demolition through to planning and executing huge marine construction projects. He was also, in a complete contrast of environments, an expert mountaineer.

Smart Wrens in their elegant black stockings and tight-ish

uniform skirts waited on a scattering of officers at dinner. Above our heads, massive timbers curved up into a high vaulted ceiling; they are the work of an eighteenth-century shipwright for a sixty-foot inverted hull forms the framework to the roof of this superbly gilded and plastered room.

With much manoeuvre of silver salt cellars and drawing of lines on the polished surface of the oaken tables, Henry started telling me about his plans to get up an unclimbed mountain in the wildest, most remote and (to me) completely undreamt-of parts of China. Dragons once more reared their magnificent heads; ancient cartographers inscribed 'Here Be Dragons' to denote those chunks of their map that no-one had ever explored. The route to Henry's mountain went past the mouth of an unexplored valley, from which massive glaciers had produced floodwaters that devastated settlements hundreds of miles away. My geographical instincts took over; what was up there and how could the flooding be predicted? Very soon I was on the list of prospective team members.

Henry's *curriculum vitae* makes him 'a running, jumping and rarely standing still sort of chap' (to quote M. J. McCarthy of *The Times*). He plays most sports, has a private pilot's licence, and joined the Army after 'becoming sick of being a poor architecture student at the London Architectural Association'. His flying start in life sprang from being born and bred in Uganda, getting out into the bush with intrepid parents at every opportunity.

He came to mountaineering relatively late; a Royal Navy doctor friend who kept ropes, 'sticky' climbing shoes and a bag of krabs and chocks constantly in the boot of his car in case he came upon a suitable cliff, passed on the bug. He then acquired all the Army mountaineering, skiing, climbing and canoeing qualifications and had organized eighteen Army expeditions, four of them to the USA and nine to the Alps.

He worked for Colonel John Blashford-Snell on the Army Youth Adventurous Training Scheme and did a tour of duty at the Army Apprentices College at Chepstow. This, and spending virtually every leave and weekend on his own expeditions or simply shinnying up rock faces, enabled Henry to develop his own ideas about why people should risk life and limb in a wild variety of different ways in the great outdoors.

In the absence of any actual combat, the Army uses many outdoor pursuits, such as free-fall parachuting, rock climbing, mountaineering and white water canoeing, to develop leadership qualities and provide challenges for an essentially peacetime force. This 'adventurous training', as well as giving a bit of spice to Army life, provides a wonderful opportunity for those interested in such pursuits to develop their skills without spending very much money.

Henry's military career became dominated by adventure training and he developed a philosophy that became one of his main motivations. He felt that his mountaineering skills had developed to the point where he no longer got quite the same thrill from being exposed to danger, for as he became more expert the danger to which he was exposing himself became less. Being of a generous nature, he began to take more pleasure in helping novices climb hard routes than from the extreme climbs that his skill allowed him to attempt himself.

To give an example, in 1984 Henry took a party of eight climbers to attempt the Salathe Wall of the USA's El Capitan, four of whom were complete novices. The experienced four acted as the lead climbers, and after a day or so of basic tuition, the whole party started on the 3,500-foot sheer rock face. The climb took six days and required bivouacking lashed onto tiny ledges at night. The novices were either experts or nervous wrecks at the end – probably a bit of both!

IAE Engineering's 'Ben Hardwick Memorial Fund' benefited greatly from another Morgan stunt. Scaling a 300-foot Medway factory chimney (an exposed and arduous climb) and a weekend hammering in specially made bolts, enabled thirty IAE employees (all novices) to climb up and abseil down from the chimney lip.

It was thus in the Henry Morgan tradition that I, a complete mountaineering novice (I have never been even to the top of Snowdon; the railway is too expensive), came to be invited to join his team to make the first ascent on the Crown, a 7,400-metre peak in the Chinese Karakoram.

I was to be the geographer and cameraman, and to try to get publicity that would help with the search for sponsorship. I also wanted to get a professional camera crew to make a television documentary of what was certain to be an epic journey: from Hong Kong overland across China into one of the few remaining unexplored regions of the world, returning south through the Kunjerab Pass into Pakistan.

I soon discovered that my role would become as large as I chose to make it. There was a mass of vital jobs which probably would never get done. Most important of all, we needed money, and so I became directly involved with generating publicity and trying to interest firms in sponsoring the trip.

My friends from university, now captains of industry and paradigms of the financial and business world and all a shade green with envy, kindly lobbied the PR departments of their companies and racked their brains for ideas, no doubt wishing that their employers were as enterprising as the British Army, who were letting us do our own thing for over three months. June Han, of County Nat West, whipped in all her contacts in the Hong Kong money market. Simon Clarke, an Army officer, then with the computer company UNISYS and a frustrated sail bum, obtained his Chairman's ear for Henry, and a free lunch at the Army vs Navy match at Twickenham. John Webster, a front-row forward from James Capel, after much effort expressed regret, blaming their expensive sponsorship of a racing yacht.

The Hong Kong and Shanghai Bank eventually decided that we were not really educational enough for them to sponsor; also our plan to perform the first abseil from the top of their futuristic building in Hong Kong may not have been exactly the sort of PR they were looking for – especially as someone chose that time to get out of equities and into the Hereafter via the tenth floor.

Charles Peel, an oarsman and then of the industrial investment bankers 3Is, taught me how to lure bankers (as one of the shrewdest, he knows). His wise counsel enabled me to understand the rejections and polish up my performance for the next attempt, which led on to Colonel Dougie Charles at IMS, General Gus Sinclair at Tarmac . . . and so on.

The message was always the same: 'If only you had come to us earlier.' We were six weeks from departure when I started trying to drum up some support. Two years would have been more realistic.

I did, however, have a number of supreme strokes of luck; through the painter Sophie Macpherson, who conjures up the latent beauty in rock-crushing plants, slum shop-fronts and petroleum storage depots and the like, I met Susie Scott – who runs a PR and design business in Soho. She and an old friend from commando days, Major Chris Coats in the MOD, became the nucleus of my 'rear party' holding the fort back in the UK. Susie, with her experience as a designer, artist and photographer, helped me to use what little time there was left before our departure to best effect.

We had no money and there were only days left before we had to pay the Chinese (who were withholding our visas until the money was cleared into their account). June Han came to the rescue again, with Hamish Blyth, a professional-soldier-turned-stockbroker and an old friend, formerly of Her Majesty's Royal Marines, as guarantors for a £35,000 bank loan. We now had the money, but at seven and a half per cent above base.

Meanwhile inside fortress Wapping, Mike McCarthy was manoeuvring carefully on my behalf with *The Times* features editor to get an 'intrepid explorer, last truly British, pith helmet, cleft stick and camels across the trackless wastes' piece into the paper on a day when news was in short supply. In fact, he got it in the morning of our press reception and farewell at the Royal Geographical Society, complete with map and photograph. Not only was our morale greatly boosted but the Army took an added interest in us as providers of good PR.

I decided I was wasting my time trying to get a professional camera crew to come with us. Tim Slessor at the Beeb (editor of *The World About Us*) wrote to explain that, although the trip was suitably wild and interesting, three months is too long for a crew to be away, and therefore far too expensive. A friend, Sebastian Rich (ITN's award-winning cameraman) had failed to persuade his bosses to allow him to come; the General Election was inconveniently timed and whatever would ITN do about overtime on such a trip? The only solution was to shoot the film myself, in spite of never having handled, let alone used, a movie camera before.

SSVC (Services Sound and Vision Corporation) came to the rescue with a Bolex H16 reflex camera and the user handbooks, which became very dog-eared as the trip progressed. Paul Randolph of the Euro-Foto Centre sold me a set of Nikons at a good price, and I was equipped.

I telephoned as many professional cameramen as were in this country (most seemed to be abroad making films). Few were au fait with 16mm; they tend to use video these days. But the cameraman Jan Peston advised me on the basic filters and answered some basic questions about light levels and the effects of different lenses on shutter speeds and apertures; for example how shutter speeds with a camera shooting moving pictures were likely to be very different from those of a still camera. I dealt with most of my remaining queries by close study of the Bolex handbook on the train to Beijing.

Alan Ravenscroft, with several expeditions-worth of experience, talked me through some of the fundamental differences between moving pictures and stills: 'Don't hosepipe [spray it round], take long shots: you must have movement in your pictures: have people moving on and off camera and include close-ups of faces and hands.'

For the most part, I would have to rely on my knowledge of still photography to get me through. The Bolex had all the same features as any other camera, and the more I talked to the experts, the more I realized that the basic physics of photography still applied.

Panning shots seem to be one of the main differences, and the experts urge caution when using them. I decided that even if nothing else went right, I would at least shoot well framed shots, and when panning would start with a well framed shot and rehearse so that I ended up with another. I knew nothing of how to organize the shoots themselves, making the team parade past the camera without looking wooden and ridiculous, nor how to squeeze the action into the twenty-eight seconds that was all the Bolex's clockwork mechanism would allow.

I was however happier to be using film rather than video; I understand what happens to film in different sorts of light. Video is a complete mystery to me. I took great comfort from Ann Eva at SSVC, who assured me that 16mm film was far more 'atmospheric' than video. Also, as we were going hundreds of miles beyond the likelihood of recharging batteries, a clockwork film camera was the only option.

Nevertheless I was becoming more and more nervous about being both still and movie cameraman. A BBC film crew consists of at least three people (four went on Chris Bonington's first ascent of Everest by the South West Face and one, the high altitude cameraman Mick Burke, died on the summit). If I wanted any help, which would be essential, I would have to train up other team members.

Also, and more terrifying to a photographer, I hadn't managed, in the rush to get ready, to run film through any of my cameras to check that they were working properly and to become confident and used to them. This uncertainty, and the workload of taking all the pictures, was to get much worse as the expedition proceeded, making me irritable, stressed and very anxious.

Finally, the complete team had only got together days before leaving London. We did not know one another. I had only just met one of the team, John Day, and all except two (our leader Henry and an artilleryman Conrad Ainsley from 148 Forward Observation Battery) were really no more than slight acquaintances.

We had a lot of work to do.

CHAPTER 2

Entry to the Middle Kingdom

The lift door opened onto a dirty, dimly lit landing. With Wong Wai Lin (a Hang Seng stockbroker), I stepped out with caution. Emboldened by her lack of concern, I pressed the bell. After a brief pause, the heavily fortified door opened, an eye having first appeared at the peep-hole before heavy bolts were drawn back to reveal a brightly lit room with marble floor, black wall tiles, huge mirrors and the sound of running water flowing from a large and elaborate Chinese-style samovar into a pond.

The tall white-jacketed butler ushered us in. We were greeted by a slender young man dressed in open-necked shirt, cotton trousers and hand-stitched leather slip-on shoes. At the far end of the room a group of people chatted, bright in the concealed spotlights, outlined against the soft darkness of the sheet of plate glass that formed the far wall, silhouetted as they lounged in a cockpit of sofas against the bright, finely etched neon colours of the cityscape.

Below in the advancing evening, the financial power house of Hong Kong Island relentlessly generated wealth from a seemingly unending reservoir of potential, from which some (those with nerve and wit) become millionaires with indecent speed. Unblinking (so as not to confuse the pilots of jumbo jets dodging between the high rise apartments of Kowloon to land at Kai Tak airport) the huge neon advertisements proclaimed capitalism and the entrepreneurial spirit. As our expedition was in dire need of sponsorship (like every expedition), with so many freestyle entrepreneurs per square foot, Hong Kong seemed a good place to find a backer. Unfortunately, as time had run out and we were less than a week from crossing the Chinese border, it looked as though none of this wealth was going to help us.

The dark waters of the harbour reflected the shimmering neon colours. The masthead lights of the ferries (running from Hong Kong Island to Kowloon side) criss-crossed with other vessels sailing parallel to the shore. In bright pools of light, clusters of tenders loaded and unloaded battered cargo vessels, and the private hydrofoils of the very rich sliced through the chaos en route to weekend mansions on the far islands.

Money and luck are very important to the Chinese. They have developed a whole philosophy over the centuries to make wealth (and health) more certain. This philosophy (perhaps it is also a religion and a science) called 'feng-shui', meaning 'Wind and Water', is a vital part of the commercial life of Hong Kong.

No prudent, successful Chinese businessman would plan an office tower block without 'feng-shui' advice. In conjunction with the architect, the feng-shui sage ensures that the building faces a large body of water (the pool from which luck and prosperity is drawn), with a hill to the rear where a dragon lives. Strong, brave, clever and loyal, the dragon will watch over the business and protect it. The rooms of the office block will have their corners rounded or the angles opened up by clever and interesting partitions to prevent evil spirits lurking. Running water at the entrance brings good luck and good business in through the front door. Once the building is in operation, fine tuning ensures that small design errors do not hamper effective and profitable work. The principles of good design have, in Hong Kong, an added dimension which is taken very seriously indeed.

The dining room opened off the huge sitting room, arched doors swinging inwards to darkness in which a huge gilded Buddha presided like an old friend. We ate with knives and forks, elaborate *nouvelle cuisine* dishes beautifully arranged and served, washed down with modest amounts of German Riesling.

From opposite I was questioned about the Army by a languid English stockbroker who proved to have spent several years as a young officer in a cavalry regiment. His pedigree stood out a mile:

'You mean to say that the Army is giving you three months off to go swanning across China? Are they sponsoring you as well?'

'Only in the sense that they continue to pay our salaries. My regiment has given three hundred pounds from a private fund – so no taxpayer's money is going to waste. We've had to borrow the rest – I owe Nat West £5,635 at seven and a half per cent above base. Those more junior in rank owe proportionately less.'

A soft-voiced import/export executive sat beside the elegant former cavalryman. His business took him into China regularly. I told him about the Chinese names we had been given:

'It seemed to me that sophisticated people like the Chinese, faced with difficult European names, would invent Chinese ones. Rather than risk being labelled "Clumsy One With Large and Ridiculous Nose" I thought to pre-empt this and got us all named by a Chinese person in London before we left.'

The import/export man nodded, then explained that, in Hong Kong, until he retires, not even the head of a large company gets to know the Chinese name given him by his employees, and then only if he and the name are liked and acceptable.

Chinese working with Europeans have adopted the same sort of approach with regard to their own names. They resign themselves to the sad fact that few Europeans will be able to pronounce (or even remember) their real forenames; but the English names they adopt are often ridiculous sounding combinations (Sally Yip, Eric Wong, Amy Han . . .).

The keen and ultra polite 'gweilo' (or European, literally 'foreign devil') who carefully learns the Chinese forenames of his Chinese friends can however come seriously unstuck if he tries to use them. The two languages (Cantonese and Mandarin, the former spoken in Hong Kong and in the south of China) are outrageously tonal, to the extent that the same word pronounced in a slightly different fashion, or at a slightly different pitch, can vary in meaning from, using one particular Cantonese word as an example, 'computer' or 'idiot' to 'electric oven'. The scope for accidental insult is enormous.

The Chinese can be very formal, restricting the use of their forenames to close friends and family. They address one another using surnames, and allow us less formal Europeans to use their adopted English first name. In the Chinese People's Republic, however, no outlandish English names are tacked onto the Chinese; instead a person is introduced as 'Mister Wang' or 'Miss Wong'. The formality may be relaxed by the individual offering an English translation of her forename . . . 'But you may call me Yellow Jade.'

Before leaving London I had met a group of Chinese doctors, formerly of Beijing and Lhanzou, now residing in Wandsworth. The odd one out was 'Eric' Peng — a former mountaineer and veteran of many high altitude expeditions including K2 and Everest. On Everest (he called it Chomolungma), frostbite had removed the end of his nose. He was very keen to give advice and hear the plans for our trip to a part of the world he loved very much.

These sympathetic Chinese friends were kind enough to work out Chinese names for us all, based upon my descriptions of the other members. In Hong Kong we had these inscribed in red brushwork onto the pockets of smart white shirts, for the banquet being given in Beijing by the Chinese International Sport Travel Association.

Eric Peng and one of the doctors had gone completely over the top with my name; Sun Dar Shen is the much loved heroic character of legend, 'The Monkey King', provoking the same sort of response as might calling yourself 'Robin Hood' in England. Captain John Day, tall, dark and slightly sinister looking, became 'Sherlock Holmes', who to my astonishment is well known in China. Gunner Conrad Ainsley, a strong, cheerful black man with roots in Jamaica and a mortgage in Poole, became An Pili, a clever play on words which colloquially could mean a sort of break dance, but translated as a quiet, dependable thunderbolt, suiting 'Rad very well. Our Royal Marine, Second Lieutenant Jerry Slack, was named Hi Oh or Seagull (a bird of strength and wisdom), and our man of jokes and wily pranks, Corporal Andy Aspinall, became Wan Jin Yu, a sort of universal remedy for all ills, the strong smelling ointment we call 'tiger balm'. (This last name caused much laughter, a bit like being called 'aspirin'.)

Our leader Captain Henry Morgan had already been given a name on his first visit to Beijing, when he signed the contract which booked the mountain for us and set down the costs of the trip. The Chinese characters that made up his name came out as the phonetic approximation 'Hunglee Morgan' when pronounced in Mandarin. The other four team members, Sergeant Bob Wood the quarter-master, Corporal Ian Roberts his assistant and a medic, Sapper Robert Nelson the youngest member, and Corporal Nick Moore, another medic, also had appropriate names.

The supper party ended and Wong Wai Lin and I walked down the deeply pot-holed access road to the main street. The outside of the apartment block in the Mid-Levels (half-way up the steep slopes of Victoria Peak on Hong Kong Island, close to the financial heart and popular with Hang Seng yuppies) was dark, water stained and in need of paint and repair.

In Hong Kong, there is time only to do what is absolutely necessary for comfort and prosperity. Outside the splendour of the apartment, and the protective influence of the friendly dragons, the reality of Hong Kong, the poverty of those who do not succeed and the strain and fragility of the monetary success of those who do, hit me with my first lungful of damp, warm and slightly fetid non-conditioned air.

The MTR (Hong Kong's subway) took me north from Hong Kong Island to Tuen Mun in the New Territories. Even now, in the early hours of the morning, the wide, clean, well-lit platforms were thronged with chattering people. Silver trains absorbed the crowds into wide, polished aluminium interiors, arriving every few minutes and departing in rubber-muted silence. Inside, the bright lighting reflected from rounded aluminium seats; although hard in appearance they were quite comfortable. The train, to an eye used to the gloom and squalor of London's overburdened Underground, was very wide and, like the stations and platforms, built to cope with huge volumes of humanity.

There were no dividing doors between the carriages, the interior undulating like a gently moving snake as the train flowed around the bends, deep beneath the waters of the harbour and the teeming tenement blocks of Kowloon. There was standing room only, people strap-hanging, wedged closely together. Sideways glances were directed towards me, the sweaty 'gweilo' who was taking up more space than he should with his clumsy over-sized body.

The crush eased as people flooded off at Tsim Sha Tsui, Yau Ma Tei and Hung Hom — to new, vast, vertical cities of tower apartments where large extended families (grandparents, parents and grown-up offspring) are jammed into tiny flats piled inside the chimney-like buildings. Up there, in constant acrid smoke, factories are almost indistinguishable from dwellings; blocks with frosted glass windows, clattering machinery and smoking chimneys stand beside identically depressing blocks with air-conditioners and lines of washing festooned like bunting from every window.

I nodded off, waking as the last passengers hurried from the now deserted train. It was the end of the line. As I leapt for the doors they started to close. Here no railway official goes down the carriages waking the tired and emotional. With cold efficiency, the train waited just long enough for all able-bodied passengers to disembark then sped off into the distance to be cleared of all debris (human or otherwise) and cleaned (no doubt by robotic arms) in a bright computer-powered engine shed.

The taxi driver spoke no English, nor could he recognize the name Perowne Barracks on a map. (The New Territories are very Chinese, the Union Flag flies only for administrative convenience.) Tuen Mun, the nearest town, is huge with a maze of flyovers and dual carriageways that take you twice round the harbour before allowing you to travel in the direction of your destination. The driver seemed to understand the name of a bay two miles east of where I wanted to go and looked as though he was taking the correct route out of town.

I tapped him on the shoulder and motioned him into the layby at the Army camp gates. A chain and padlock secured them but I was able to slip through the gap underneath, hoping that no zealous Gurkha guard armed with iron-shod pick-axe helve and kukri would spot me.

We were relieved to be leaving Hong Kong.

The pace had been frantic; rushing round the shops getting bamboo wands for route markers on the mountain; three of our ten expedition members still had no visa for Pakistan; radio interviews on stations RTHK and BFBS; television sessions on ATV (one of the two English television channels, in which Andy Aspinall, our blond, blue-eyed, team joker, declared that when we left Hong Kong he would miss 'the sun, the beaches and . . . er yes, the beer'); and large needles of gamma globulin in the backside to ward off evil spirits.

We had been living twenty-four-hour days, commuting across Hong Kong harbour in the hoverfoil from Tuen Mun, working through endless lists of tasks in the entrepreneurial jungle of Jordan Road and Tsim Sha Tsui, ending up dancing on the tables at Tokyo Joe's as the sun rose onto chop suey-smelling streets.

I for one was tired out.

On the morning of 5 August 1987 we entered China. We progressed onto the train via a series of queues, our documents carefully examined by each official. My passport was without an entry stamp from Kai Tak (to jump a long queue I had entered Hong Kong on my Army identity card). Much furious computer punching satisfied the official that I was not an illegal immigrant escaping back to China.

As the train slipped past dripping air-conditioning units and the gaunt frameworks of burnt-out neon lights hanging like washing over the jammed streets of Kowloon, a TV screen above the carriage door started a tortuous in-flight briefing, first in Cantonese and then English, showing us how to use the ashtrays.

The busy streets of Kowloon Tong gave way to the paddy fields, steep green hills and the dust-blown flyovers and building sites of the New Territories.

Suddenly the station names were in Chinese, without the English version. In sidings, oily, dark-green diesel locomotives bore dirty brass plates 'Made in Romania'. We had entered China. There were few cars, no taxis and hundreds of cyclists wearing white, wide-brimmed hats. The scrubby green hills through which we were travelling remained the same: we had crossed a political rather than a geographical border.

Farming hamlets flashed past: tile-roofed huts with square fish ponds, the hills behind them sliced up into narrow cultivated terraces. Halfway up, between flooded paddy fields and green hilltops, small whitewashed temples, with bright red arches and pillars, watched over small peasant settlements, huts with mud block walls and tiled or corrugated iron roofs.

The flat bottoms between small, round, red-brown hills were filled with shallow water, divided into rice fields by grassy banks. Beside the track a muscular grey water buffalo strode through the muddy water pulling a single-shared plough, controlled by an equally muscular man, short and squat, with wide-brimmed straw hat, wet grey shirt and shorts. A woman (his wife perhaps) worked bent double in the water picking out fine rice shoots, placing them in a bucket at her side. Where the ground was not low or flat enough to be made into rice paddy, there were rows of orange, lemon and banana trees.

As the hills grew higher and the valley widened, the acreage under rice paddy increased. Narrow winding footpaths had been built above the mud and water, used by lightly clothed farmers in wide-brimmed Chinese hats who bustled from field to field. The men wore shorts and loose shirts, the women long trousers and high-necked, long-sleeved tunics. The older women wore black trouser suits, heads bowed under heavy-looking wicker-woven hats with wide brims like flattened lobster pots. Most of our team were fast asleep. The train radio was on: a competition perhaps, in which individuals from the audience were required to sing as appallingly as possible. Instant rapturous applause greeted the end of each performance. The accompaniment was less easy to classify; perhaps the Portsmouth Sinfonia or a record being played backwards.

Outside, the hills had given way to flat lands, muddy rivers, paddies, ditches, pools and lakes. Pylon lines followed the track, curving off towards villages. We passed through ancient brick and tile-built towns with beautifully decrepit houses, their enclosed courtyards completely surrounded by water and rice paddies, large water lilies floating on the still surface.

A family worked in a threshing yard with high stone walls, the golden grain in lines on a stone floor. Outside the town, laughing children played beside a bridge across a deep red, slow-flowing river; and a water buffalo, shining from head to toe with fresh mud, walked slowly behind a robed woman protecting herself from the sun with a black umbrella.

In the distance there appeared an incredible space-age sports stadium. Beside the track, a football pitch was clumped and overgrown, the goals unpainted and sagging in the middle; an Olympic-sized swimming pool was grey from lack of use with two feet of brackish water in the bottom and stained starting blocks at the far end.

The train pulled into Guanghou (Canton) and we piled out in a heap of confusion, fumbling to fill in customs and medical declarations and counting all our foreign currency. Every item of western origin that might be saleable inside China had to be listed; we were assured that this list would be checked against each item when we came to leave the country. I panicked over the make and model of the cine camera, having visions of being prevented from entering Pakistan in three months' time by twitchy Chinese border guards.

A small round man bustled forward carrying a briefcase, wearing a maroon T shirt as if it were a badge of office. The logo said 'Hallworth Basketball Team'. He was our CIST guide for Guanghou (China International Sport Travel, the agency that was looking after us on our journey).

As we left the customs hall, a slender figure detached himself from the crowd at the ticket barrier, patting Henry enthusiastically on the back and shaking hands all round. Jin Jun, dark-haired, aged twenty-four, about five foot ten (taller than his fellow countrymen) with a boyish face and dimples whenever he smiled, would be our interpreter from now until we travelled south into Pakistan.

Jin Jun had met Henry in Beijing two months earlier when the contract for the expedition had been drafted and signed. Henry had been impressed by his enthusiasm, intelligence and sense of humour. His English was good (although he was inclined to laugh and both nod and shake his head when he couldn't quite understand what was being said to him). He also wore a T shirt with a slogan in English, which seemed to be the fashionable thing. Jin Jun's read, 'Set a Good Example'.

We saw something of Guanghou, our introduction to Chinese driving being somewhat alarming. As the guide lectured us about this being the most modern city in China, chirruping phrases like 'much more modern than Beijing', the driver ploughed straight into a mass of cyclists and motorcyclists on a large roundabout. They swerved and braked sharply but seemed not the slightest bit put out.

I wondered about oriental inscrutability and the need not to show fear or impotent anger lest 'face' be lost. We carved our way up onto a flyover. Death seemed imminent and lane discipline a philosophical concept that passed all understanding.

There were hundreds of people stumbling along in the humid twilight of the concrete tunnel, weighed down with cardboard cartons, boxes and bags, jostling along the wide, dusty concourse underneath the platforms. Huge metal gates, padlocked and chained, prevented access to all but the platform from which the Beijing express would leave.

Weighed down by our very heavy hand luggage (carried to avoid having to pay excess freight charges), we struggled through the crowd. The train was very long indeed, each carriage attended by food trolleys, pretty girl conductresses and policemen. Struggling amid the surge of humanity, the platform seemed interminable.

Each compartment had four bunk couchettes with straw matting, frilled sheets, crimson carpets, chintz net curtains and embroidered towels and tablecloths. An electric table lamp stood in each window with a globe-shaped floral shade giving a distinctive Chinese Edwardian look to the decor.

Every hour (or so), for this first part of the journey, the train stopped. From the intermediate first class (the very top accommodation was air-conditioned) the hard wooden benches of the ordinary sleepers looked grim.

At one station, as twilight turned the fields a deep shade of green and a red sun reflected like blood in the still waters of the rice paddies, Jin Jun introduced us to his grandparents, who had come to see him briefly as we passed through. His grandmother brought presents of nuts, sweets and biscuits and small carved wood masks of opera characters in their traditional white and black makeup.

The next morning, on the platform at Changsha, loud shouts were taken up until a hue and cry developed. A young man seemed to have stolen something from the platform's magazine stall. He dashed down the steps and came up on the next platform, darting about like a cornered animal. A dozen young men caught him and beat him to the ground, kicking him as he lay senseless, face upwards on the warm tarmac. They ran off.

Several people wandered across to peer at him. Eventually someone half-turned him over and he lay still, face covered with his own blood. Two uniformed railway officials carrying track hammers sauntered by, stopped, looked incuriously, then continued along the platform. After ten minutes the man stirred and got slowly and uncertainly to his feet, vanishing unsteadily from view down the steps. No-one seemed interested once justice had been seen to be done.

Henry wished us all to take meals in the train's restaurant, partly because Jin Jun had made special arrangements with the restaurant manager, but also to get everyone used to local cuisine. We had to eat heartily now because in the mountains at high altitude we would lose weight rapidly.

I found out later from Jin Jun that the restaurant manager had originally refused to feed us, although our fares included meals:

'My responsibilities are for the other thousand passengers on this train and not just for you and your party of ten westerners.'

The manager wanted his share of the wealth that western tourists generate when in China. Jin Jun handed over the first of the many bribes that were essential if we were to proceed smoothly. A young progressive, Jin Jun did not approve of this traditional corruption. He was nevertheless a realist and wanted everyone, in this case ourselves and the restaurant manager, to be happy. The bribes were small and came from his own pocket, not from China International Sport Travel who employed him. (He did not tell me of the bribery until our last week in China, by which time he felt able to speak frankly to me. His reticence was prompted not by fear but by pride in his country and his desire not to speak ill of it to foreigners.)

In spite of the experience we had gained in Hong Kong, mealtimes were messy; even the dexterous Chinese get food and sauce all over the table tops. The red tablecloths were covered over with thick transparent plastic, but there were no napkins. The food was tasty if greasy, dishes like prawns in onions and oil, mushroom and pork soup (complete with the odd bit of intestine) and steamed fish in soy sauce.

The world outside the train windows was fascinating. Coolies wearing white wide-brimmed oyster-catcher hats danced along under the weight of heavily loaded web bags suspended on bendy wooden poles. Lorries, small three-wheeled agricultural tractors with trailers (the latter usually with two or more people on board), donkeys pulling grossly overloaded carts (the drivers sleeping soundly, lying stretched out on top of their loads with hats pulled down over their faces), cyclists and pedestrians, the world watching as we clattered by on our way towards the far distant capital city.

We drank jasmine tea from huge thermos flasks of boiling water brought round every couple of hours and ate Jacobs' digestive biscuits, the genuine article from the Friendship Supermarket in Guanghou. Southern China rolled past beneath grey and overcast skies.

At ten past four in the afternoon we passed through Lujiashan, catching tantalizing glimpses of steam locomotives hauling heavy goods trains and being shunted and loaded in sidings. By the time we had finished supper, night had fallen and we were well into Hunan Province.

This journey was a peculiar time. Most high altitude expeditions fly in as close to the mountain as they can, and get on with it immediately. Until a climbing team gets onto the mountain, frustration, worry and irritation generates a lot of stress. Our four-week overland journey was a holiday by contrast to the mountaineering, but the stress was being generated just the same, yet with none of the physical outlet of an approach march. Although the mountain seemed a long way into the future, we had started the process of assessing one another, deciding who to trust for the time when life would depend upon having a good partner.

We did not know one another as a team, although Bob Wood, Andy Aspinall, Nick Moore, John Day, young Robert (Nellie) Nelson and Ian Roberts (Robbo) had climbed together and with Henry in the past. A work-up trip to the Eiger a month before leaving the UK had been useful, but not everyone had been able to make it. (Also, because of bad weather, we had been able to do no more than camp above Eiger-Gletscher cable-car station, drinking many bottles of expensive beer in the café.)

I felt uneasy about the trip and the team. Partly this was the normal process of starting an expedition, but it was also because the atmosphere seemed different from what I had thought it might be, based upon what I had known in my five-man commando team. With only ten, most of us being paratroopers or commandos going to do something physical and dangerous, I had imagined the same sort of camaraderie and closeness would develop.

I shared a compartment with three others; Bob Wood was kind and supportive; Robert Nelson, although very young, was in his way wise, and kind; Andy Aspinall, noisy and slickly witty, was putting up patiently with the impatience and irritation that the constant need to film was causing me. With Conrad Ainsley (whom I knew from my previous commando unit) Andy was working hard on helping me with the filming. The others new to me were in another compartment and I had not yet got to know them, although I judged Nick Moore to be 'absolutely solid and capable' and Robbo 'steady'.

I wondered whether my uneasiness could be a product of officers being together; I was a major and Henry and John were captains. In the Falklands my team had been organized the way I wanted it. Here I was pretty low on the batting order. Maybe I needed to get used to not having things my own way?

Being conditioned to take charge, to command soldiers and be totally responsible (in return for absolute obedience from them) puts an officer on a pedestal, and there is usually only room on the pedestal for one. On this trip, because John and Henry knew each other well and were both respected as mountaineers by the team, the two of them might balance together without falling. The fourth officer on the trip, Jerry Slack, a capable, mature and very amusing man, but a second lieutenant just out of training and not yet fully conditioned to taking charge, was much less likely than myself to inadvertently create friction.

I worried that I was the potential problem, a novice mountaineer and yet the senior officer present. I had made it plain that I was never going to use my rank, that Henry was the leader come what may, but on the other hand I would still always have that rank. Perhaps this created a problem for Henry and John? John certainly seemed uneasy.

For my part, I was unsure of my standing under military law should there be a disaster which could have been avoided and which, as the senior officer, I had done nothing to prevent. I hoped that this worry would prove to be academic, especially as such an accident was most likely to occur in the mountains where my knowledge was slight and where I could therefore not be expected to exercise any authority. While hoping this, I felt uncomfortably close to avoiding responsibility, 'sloping shoulders' in military parlance.

The expedition had been 'civilianized' by Henry; everyone was on first name terms and military ranks were, on the surface, irrelevant. However, regardless of how informal and chummy we might be, I would always be a major, John and Henry captains, Jerry a second lieutenant, Bob a sergeant, Nick, Andy and Robbo corporals and Conrad and Nellie private soldiers.

I wondered about this informal, non-military system. It was irrelevant to me how we addressed one another; in my commando team we used first names and nicknames, but the officer was always 'Boss', which emphasized who was in charge and responsible, and who, therefore, ultimately took the decisions. I was the oldest at thirty-four (Henry was thirty-two and the others ranged from eighteen to twenty-eight) and I was well used to responsibility. Nellie, the youngest and only recently out of basic training, was more used to doing what he was told. Our individual experience of life, let alone mountaineering, varied so much as to make equality rather spurious.

Henry's philosophy was for expeditions to be a sort of 'school for life', with him in charge. We would all find our own levels within the group, and ourselves in the process, while he presided and gave little nudges to the wayward when he felt it absolutely necessary. This approach seemed to have been fine on trips to the Alps as a break from the military routine: a few days in the mountains followed by an evening sampling local Pilsner and disco dancing. However, in a part of the world where one mountaineer in every twenty that enter has been killed, I was not so sure.

For our trip, discipline in the team was vital because the stresses of what we were attempting to do would be so great. We were lucky; being a military expedition we had military discipline as our common denominator, which should give us a tremendous advantage over other groups of mountaineers.

I was worried that 'civilianization' might have weakened the strong military social structure that we all felt comfortable with and understood, a structure developed over the centuries to ensure effective behaviour in dangerous situations. Its removal gave each of us the extra task of finding our own code of behaviour.

At the moment, although we were all edgy, with nothing more life-threatening than Chinese driving to contend with, we were not having any major problems. I hoped that when things did get tough, like some sort of turbo-charger our military common denominator would come into play.

Henry's team selection had been very different from the usual. In general he had gone for people he liked and trusted rather than those of proven mountaineering ability. Several mountaineers with Himalayan or Karakoram experience who had initially been keen to come had cried off late in the day, so we had only text-book information on how high altitude would affect us.

Also, as the team included three novices, Nick, 'Rad and myself, the experienced climbers would have the additional responsibility of teaching and supervising us until we reached an acceptable level of ability. I hoped that the climbers were prepared to do this, under what would be very testing circumstances for each of them without a helpless pupil to look after as well.

The command structure of the expedition was also unusual. Everyone owed their place to Henry, who had selected his team and got the trip off the ground. He knew everyone except Conrad Ainsley (whom I had invited with Henry's approval, to operate the radios, and as a tenth member to share the costs). We all therefore accepted Henry as the natural leader.

When any military unit goes into action, the commander

(whether a corporal in charge of an infantry section or a major general commanding a division of tanks) lays down an order of command; who takes over should he be killed, who from him and so on. We had no clear chain of command, and unless instructions emanated directly from Henry, or whatever had to be done was obvious, there was much un-military (and unnecessary) discussion and debate.

Captain John Day joined the expedition as we left the UK, and in Hong Kong appointed himself Henry's second-in-command. John was respected, as a mountaineer and as a strong personality, but there was no formal devolution of powers to him from Henry.

During these early days, this lack of structure caused only slight problems. Everyone was willing and healthy, cheerfully doing whatever had to be done. I wondered whether the expedition quartermaster Bob Wood, responsible for all the equipment, would have problems getting people to help him when they were tired, or whether Henry (or John) would take over at various times and do his job for him. Bob would have been an ideal third in command, but being a quiet, hard-working, low-key sort of bloke, he was unlikely to thrust this idea forward. Perhaps he knew (from previous trips with Henry) that such a thing as a third-in-command would not be acceptable.

To further complicate matters, Henry had brought along his fiancée Catherine and her friend Ann, who were to leave us at Kashgar as we went on the last part of the road trip to rendezvous with the camels. Until then, Henry was continually distracted. John Day cannot have been entirely at ease either as Ann was a former girlfriend, whom Henry had invited while John was away in Africa, Henry thinking that the two were still close. Although the girls were great fun, they rather inhibited the pre-battle girding up of loins. Several team members privately felt that they should not have been allowed to come.

Perhaps also the filming was a problem. I created difficulties that Henry could do without. (The film and equipment made up one complete camel load, at £500 per camel for the trip.)

The producer Richard Robinson of the BBC had told me that after three days, film crews should expect to be hated by the rest of the expedition. Already people were becoming irritated by retakes; having to walk 'casually' along platforms and onto trains on hot days:

'Go back and do it again but try not to look like Pinocchio without strings if that's possible.'

My own nerves were becoming very frayed. Inevitably I was being difficult as I struggled to do my job, learning as a million beautiful shots rolled past unfilmed.

We reached the outskirts of Beijing on the morning of Friday, 7 August. In the huge echoing station, amid the thousands of Han Chinese, there were members of every Central Asian ethnic group, some wearing exotic traditional clothing, dusty, frayed and certainly not intended to be decorative.

As we emerged from the dimness of the building into the large square outside, speakers played loud Chinese classical music with very good quality sound. In our colourful mountaineering trousers and shirts, and standing head and shoulders above everybody else, we contrasted sharply with the rest of the mass of humanity that milled about the wide open area.

I felt we had arrived at the focus of a vast multi-ethnic nation, at the centre of an enormous yet isolated world of which Beijing was the absolute hub, and that wished, like the Wizard of Oz, to be well regarded. The music, although performing the same function as the Wizard's rose-tinted spectacles, was part of the best of China's culture, of which Beijing, as the ultimate destination of every citizen of the People's Republic, was the custodian.

CHAPTER 3

Bicycles, Beer and Banter

The low buildings and wide streets of Beijing are spread over a very large area. To a western eye, in the dust of summer, with block after block of shoddily built three- and four-storey buildings and the bicycles, it looks like down-town Los Angeles once the oil runs out. There is no sign of the city wall, levelled to build the underground railway and ring road. The Forbidden City and Summer Palace however are glorious, carefully preserved in all their splendour.

The danger of being a tourist in Beijing is that you are circulated at break-neck speed through all the sights, then whipped off to the next city before you have had a chance to draw breath – exactly that happened to us and I found it very frustrating.

As the centre of an enormous bureaucracy that administers 9,597,000 square kilometres and well over one billion people, Beijing city itself is not wildly interesting. Its people, however, are fascinating. They cycle miles to and from work each day, along the extra wide streets in special cycle lanes, thousands upon thousands of chromium-glinting, bell-tinkling bikes that flow and eddy like shoals of silvery fish across every intersection and up every heroic boulevard, transforming the sterility of the modern city that the city fathers would like to see, into a place where real, ordinary people live and work.

The variety of pedal-powered vehicles on the streets of China is astonishing. Apart from the standard pedal cycle, an exact replica of Raleigh's best schoolmistress special, complete with Raleigh badge in Chinese on the front, there are a wide variety of tricycles:

with a bath-chair on the back for transporting mothers-in-law with appropriate decorum, or with a flatbed for carrying everything from mountainous loads of hay, spring onions or melons, from twenty miles or more out of town, to metal pipes or heavy machinery. Several people perch on the sides of unladen flatbeds, swinging legs indolently while the riders labour over the pedals, sweating under large straw hats.

Policemen stand on circular plinths in the centre of the wide intersections, wearing white uniform jackets and ice-cream hats, protected from the hot sun by large, colourful beach umbrellas. Traffic lights on some intersections were operated by second policemen in a glass windowed kiosk on the pavement – which seemed rather to defeat the labour-saving purpose of traffic lights.

However, neither these lights nor the policemen on point duty seemed to have any effect on the traffic. The streams of pedestrians, bicycles and motor vehicles flowed across and through one another with complete abandon.

From the safety of our minibus, each near miss was funny, amusement heightened by the complete lack of concern shown by the blank-faced riders. Margins were slender. Every minute, hundreds of potentially lethal accidents were avoided by fractions of inches. Some riders, starting off from the wrong side of the street, launched directly onto the oncoming traffic rather than waiting to cross. They dodged between the lines of vehicles coming at them, mounted the central reservation, then proceeded with the flow in their intended direction.

To us the bikes seemed amusing and delightful, a colourful anachronism. We did not take them seriously. Yet a brief paragraph in the overseas news section of The Times told of a Beijing man who had stolen seventy-two bicycles, and a further thirty with the aid of an accomplice. The idea of Mafiosi stealing bikes in London would be ridiculous, train robbers raiding sweetie shops. Here it was taken very seriously; the guilty man had just been executed.

From the minibus, we cheered when, quite gently, one man fell off his bike then got up from the ground with an embarrassed smile. After a second accident, a ferocious street fight developed. But the reality of cycling imposed itself upon us during one hot afternoon's sightseeing, as we drove past a small car with its front wing dented, recent blood having run down the passenger door. The poor cyclist had been removed; the bike was twisted at the roadside, and a small crowd of interested onlookers remained.

China presents an enormous problem of comprehension to western visitors. The language is just one of many cultural, intellectual, philosophical and political barriers. As a group, we were ethnically different – obviously so – from the rest of the world in which we found ourselves.

Most of our number had never before experienced this sort of isolation. Our dismissive reaction to bicycles as a serious form of transport was part of our reaction to the pressure induced by this isolation, although John Day and I did not share this particular reaction as we were former bicycle users. John had read Engineering at Cambridge and, like me, had wobbled back from lectures or (in my case) the pub, on lever-braked Oxbridge bone-shakers.

However, we were soldiers on a high-altitude mountaineering expedition, not university students on a cultural exchange. We tended to be xenophobic. As a group, we had closed in on ourselves and were looking outwards at a strange, incomprehensible land and its alien people. We read guide books more out of wonderment and for entertainment than through any desire to understand. Our insularity was entirely natural, and not dissimilar to the reactions of many on package tours of China.

The social organization of our group made this insularity worse than it might have been. The removal of military rank and Henry's letting everyone find their own level meant that socially we became a group that functioned at the level of the majority – who were privates and corporals. They were conditioned by barrack block life, as I had been conditioned for my first years of military service by the public-school atmosphere of the Royal Military Academy, Sandhurst. Our conditioning was in most respects a stabilizing, strengthening factor, to the extent that the cohesion of the group was unlikely to be disturbed by any outside pressure.

Barrack block life creates teams of people who live, work and play together and who tend to share the same aspirations and views.

One becomes of necessity tolerant of noise and lack of privacy, boisterously sociable and concerned if an individual seems not to be joining in with the rest. Constant pop music is the essential backdrop to everything as it drowns out sounds from the next man's bedspace, creating zones of pulsating privacy.

At home some of our team no longer lived in barracks. Ian Roberts roomed in Nick Moore's house in a Plymouth suburb; 'Rad was married, in his own house in Poole; Bob lived in the wilds of Wales, near the Army Outward Bound school, and John, Henry and I had our own houses or flats.

Back in the UK, after work, seven of us lived our own lives, as individuals.

The other three lived in barracks: Jerry in an Officers' Mess in Plymouth and Nellie and Andy in single men's accommodation at their military units. But as most officers start off as officer cadets, living like private soldiers, all ten of us had the barrack block way of life as our common background. It was therefore natural for the team to slip into the social ways of that life, which I (for one) found difficult to cope with.

This adoption of the ways of the majority certainly made our insularity and xenophobia worse than they might have been. Andy Aspinall, working hard at keeping the team amused, energetically maintaining his reputation as 'Jack the Lad', would have seemed to an outsider to be the worst offender as he made jokes that the Chinese would not have found funny. He was expressing the group point of view rather than his own, a view that I hoped no individual who had thought about it actually held. In my darker moments I felt that I was travelling, on this journey of a lifetime, with a group of football supporters – and I resented some of this group behaviour, even though I was part of the group.

As always, the mountain loomed in my mind. Would the majority continue to exert their rather nihilistic influence over the whole trip, with each of us as individuals having to go along with things of which we didn't in our hearts approve? What would be the effect of imposed equality on the leadership qualities of officers and NCOs who had been trained and selected as leaders in exactly this sort of venture?

There were many uncertainties. It seemed to me that without Henry we might have serious problems. No-one knew where they stood regarding rank – in particular between the 'other ranks' and officers. Besides, as rank was very much related to experience and strength of personality, the supposed equality did not actually exist.

Below Henry, as leader, there was no formal command structure, although John Day was forcing himself firmly into the second's slot. Finally, I worried that we might have condemned ourselves to having to abide by the decisions of the majority, which I did not believe were likely to encompass the full consideration of any problem.

I was worried and unsettled.

On our first afternoon in Beijing we 'did' the Forbidden City. The minibus dropped us off on the southern side of Tian'anmen Square amid crocodiles of bright-faced school children and Chinese families gazing about them in wide-eyed wonder. Heroic statues, reminiscent of the classic US Marine Corps picture of the raising of the flag at Iowo Jima, depicted the struggle of the people.

Tian'anmen Square, although the original centre of imperial Beijing, was the creation of Chairman Mao, whose huge portrait dominates the Gate of Heavenly Peace at the northern end. Here, on 1 October 1949, he proclaimed the People's Republic, then removed a clutter of imperial government office buildings to create a vast, paved expanse for parades of a million people.

The square is the heart of the modern Chinese nation, and every day thousands of families have themselves photographed beside one of the seven bridges that cross the stream and lead up to the grey stone of the Gate. On summer evenings the warm air is bright with fluttering swooping kites, the colours of elaborate paper dragons glowing as the sun sinks over low roofed government buildings and the calm waters of Nanhai Lake.

We entered the Forbidden City from Tian'anmen Square through the Gate of Heavenly Peace, passing under the busy road that runs in front via a wide pedestrian tunnel. It was jammed with Chinese sightseers.

In the massive tree-lined Taihemen courtyard, in front of the Hall of Supreme Harmony, there were stuffed donkeys, pandas, camels, and gilded thrones with the elaborate robes of emperors and empresses. Baffled children, thrust into the colourful robes, perched precariously on stunned-looking mounts and stared at a sea of curious faces while the photographer's camera clicked. Proud parents held squirming infants on gilded thrones or urged pretty but embarrassed teenage daughters to smile or look suitably regal.

In the fifteenth century, the populace were kept at bay beyond the walls. Coronations and emperors' birthday parties were held in this courtyard, incense billowing from the mouths of the huge bronze turtle. Particularly well-thought-of criminals were hung from the eaves, and inside, in the Dragon Throne hall, the emperor did business, his courtiers banging their heads on the floor nine times as each decision was irrevocably taken.

Each of the Khan's four wives had her own court. There was a total of 40,000 ladies-in-waiting, cooks, messengers, pages, eunuchs, maids and bottle-washers, with ten thousand Imperial horsemen, five thousand parade elephants and many more camels. They held banquets for six thousand diners, which the populace were permitted to watch from outside, the grandees kneeling every time the great man drank his fermented mare's milk.

The smell, bustle and vitality must have been unbelievable. Today the palace is sadly empty, the vacant, dusty rooms like huge garden pavilions in winter.

After a frustrating sprint through the Forbidden City (I could have spent several days there), Henry looking at his watch and muttering about 'not wanting to hurry me with the filming but we do have to leave here in forty-five minutes . . .' we roared off in the minibus to the Tiantin Sport Hotel to get changed for the banquet into our team 'uniform' – white shirts with Chinese names and off-red cotton trousers.

Andy Aspinall, still very uncertain about the meaning of his Chinese name (Wan Jin Yu – 'Aspirin') and knowing only that people laughed whenever they saw it, was keeping his arms folded across his chest. The Beijing Duck, reputed to be the best restaurant in Beijing, looked like a municipal administration building in two-storey prefab concrete, standing on its own with wide steps up from the large paved carpark.

China International Sport Travel were giving us the banquet so that we would return to Europe and spread the good word about them. Their sister organization, the Chinese Mountaineering Association, had a very bad reputation – for overcharging, putting prices up during expeditions and generally getting things wrong. CIST seemed to be supplanting them in Beijing although, as we were soon to discover, this was just a front and the CMA, with all their warts and carbuncles, would take over once we got near the mountain.

I had never before managed to get drunk in exactly two hours. Our hosts, CIST officials, were three to each table. Henry and John, with Catherine, Ann and three other team members, sat with the head of CIST, Jin Jun and two senior officials on the 'top table'. I sat with 'Rad, Andy, Bob and Jerry with the three junior CIST men.

Our shirts proved the vital ingredient that allowed us to 'converse'. Andy was assured by our hosts, after initial mirth, that Wan Jin Yu was a very good name as it meant the 'Universal Solution', the man with all the answers to all the problems, a sympathetic and diplomatic reaction which cheered him up.

Soon our table degenerated into an international series of debilitating rounds of lethal rice spirit with toasts to each of our names. 'Rad, defending Queen and Country, took on the Chinese single-handed, some of whom (quite sensibly) were not knocking back every slug of the fire water. Soon we were beyond the embarrassment of non-conversation, lost in a welter of noise, back slapping and the fumes of Chinese cigarette smoke.

We had arrived at 6 P.M. At twenty to eight the senior CIST man, who spoke good English, gave a short speech to which Henry replied. At exactly eight o'clock our hosts stood up and ushered us firmly to the door of the banqueting room, wished us well and, like a rugby team after the match, formed a line by the door shaking hands as we left.

We found ourselves outside in the carpark wondering what had hit us.

The team were at flying speed, in a mood to continue the festivities. This meant, in the unalterable timetable of the soldier's night out – now at the equivalent of pub closing time – going to a disco. It was inconceivable that Beijing could be so uncivilized as not to have a discotheque where we could meet some girls, so Jin Jun was asked to take us to one without delay. He looked thoughtful, then said he would take us somewhere – 'no problems'.

To our chagrin, we were dropped off outside yet another Friendship Store, to look at over-priced carpets, cheap silk, coffee tables and marble eggs.

Back at the Sport Hotel, we opened bottles of excellent Chinese beer. I got my guitar out and, watched by a large number of the hotel staff, who crowded into the corridor around our door and listened with amazement, played a selection of rock and roll classics, very badly, but with spirit.

The next morning I felt grim. I had to get up early to film cyclists and the morning rush-hour traffic jam. Andy Aspinall was helping me and we were sharing a room. Like me, Andy was suffering too. After a slow start, I left him to come on with half of the camera gear as I wanted to make the best of the early morning light – before the sun got too high.

Our hotel stood in a quiet concrete courtyard behind a row of anonymous government buildings. Wrought iron gates and a tree-lined promenade led towards the quiet gardens and splendid domed Temple of Heaven, beside a huge, busy roundabout. Outside the Temple gates, the traffic pedalled past an ineffectual policeman with sweaty concentration. Inside the gates, the calmness of quiet thought prevailed as people walked, conversed and pushed aged relatives in wheelchairs.

In the early morning, as sunshine wreathed gnarled cypress trees with a faint mist, figures moved carefully from light to shade in the gentle, stylized movements of Tai Chi. Some formed groups behind a venerable master, following his slow, balanced postures like shadows.

Others practised quietly on their own: old folk with short, limited movements; a solitary young man, stripped to the waist, darted backwards and forwards, bending almost to the ground in uncanny imitation of a fighting bird. Beside a curved stone wall an overweight man in black trousers and a white vest too short to cover a generous stomach manoeuvred a bright, two-handed sword in a slow concentration of medieval combat drills, the broad blade glinting like a mirror in the sunshine. Others less martial played badminton among the trees.

As the working day began, people slipped away leaving the temple grounds to those with the time to use it as a park and meeting place. The covered walkways echoed with the sound of the old men playing cards and chequers, slapping counters onto boards and shouting with the enthusiasm of total concentration at the end of each round. Others crowded round, silently watching, following the game with great care.

Solitary old men, some with bell-shaped cane canary cages, sat smoking reflective pipes as their birds sang, watching with quiet amusement as round-faced toddlers showed off before doting parents. A strange, single-stringed viola was played by a chain-smoking old man with thick-glassed spectacles. He was lost in concentration as he accompanied a thin, younger man in rambling half-toned songs that seemed by the drama of gesture with which they were performed to be from classical Chinese operas.

I filmed for about two hours, staring through my viewfinders with all the enthusiasm of a really good hangover. Andy, in a similar condition, helped me to record events that were fascinating and beautiful – but which we would at the time have swapped for the quiet and comfort of our beds.

For the team, this part of the trip was a sightseeing holiday that several individuals were not really enjoying. Their usual entertainments, as they had discovered the night before, were not to be had, even in the capital city of the People's Republic. Trailing round old buildings and archaeological sites was not their idea of a laugh. There were no English-speaking girls to chat up, which was probably a good thing as the loud comments about 'slopes', 'slitty eyes' and 'chinks' that some of the frustrations of the journey elicited from time to time would not have stood us in good stead.

For me this part of the trip was hard work, having to shoot film rapidly and constantly as China flashed past. The others stopped for filming only with reluctance and constant reference to wrist watches. I was getting up early to take advantage of the clear morning light, working hard all day and becoming extremely tired.

It was therefore a great shock when John Day mounted what seemed to be an attack on me and my thoughts about what should be done with the 35mm stills film on our return to the UK at the end of the trip. John had come to the expedition very late, having just returned from working in the Cameroons. He was unaware of my discussions with Henry over possible future uses of the film. Nevertheless, he tore into the subject, demanding answers to questions I had not had the time even to begin to consider. One effect of this was to create the suspicion that I would make a lot of money for myself out of the expedition. My insistence that, in the event of a TV company buying the film, or my snapping the Abominable Snowman, the majority of the money (less agents' fees, expenses and such like) would go towards settling the overdrafts of the others as well as my own seemed to cut no ice.

This bitter and startling exchange made me feel even more isolated from the group than my existing worries had done. My work seemed to count for nothing, and the impositions that my filming made on the others seemed to be resented.

John's aggressive and disruptive interference with my job seemed like the last straw. I started thinking seriously about leaving the expedition and travelling back to the UK via Hong Kong.

We left the Tiantin Sport Hotel after a late breakfast on the morning of Saturday, 8 August, to see the Great Wall. The city spread itself out into the surrounding countryside for over half an hour of fast minibus travel, the cycle paths filled with strong legged travellers and ridiculously heavily laden tricyclists.

In the distance the hills appeared out of the flat green plain, blue in the morning light. Henry offered a beer to the first person to spot the Great Wall, to be paid for by the last person to see it. Spurious responses led him to institute a forfeit of two beers for false claims. The hangover, the motion of the minibus and the thought of warm beer got the better of Andy Aspinall, who was too busy being ill out of the rear window to compete.

We were well into the hills themselves before the inner wall was spotted, and then after several more miles the Great Wall itself (Nellie winning the beer), with its watch towers and incredibly convoluted course winding up and along the contours and spur lines.

The basic military principles for defence seemed to have been followed. The distance we travelled from the inner walls to the 10,000 Li Wall – as the Chinese call it – would give Depth (the first principle) to the defences. The convolutions of the wall and towers as it snakes along the ridge lines and spurs would make some of the defensive positions Mutually Supportive and would work well today with the long ranges of modern weapons. The last factor, however, Concealment, was never even attempted. The Great Wall stands out in wild-looking hill country with an insane yet well proportioned beauty, the sort of artistic concept for which Californians obtain grants, and construct using rolls of bed linen on bamboo posts. Few walls have ever been militarily successful, the Berlin Wall being an expensive exception. The Great Wall of China, the only man-made object visible from space with the unaided eye, was really only a massive, costly imperial public relations exercise –which could also be marched along by reinforcing troops in times of undue pressure from the north.

In the organized whirlwind of official Chinese sightseeing, you do the Great Wall in the morning and the Ming Tombs in the afternoon. Having nothing at all to do with Flash Gordon, the Ming Tombs lie at Shisanling in quiet scrub-covered hills, an hour's drive from the Wall.

On the minibus trip from the Great Wall, Henry decided to have a general discussion about the arrangements for various aspects of the expedition. It was during this that John Day and I first crossed swords.

John Day, a Royal Engineers captain, is tall, athletic and dark; his eyes, slightly sunk into their sockets, give an intense and hawkish look, hence his Chinese nickname meaning Sherlock Holmes. John had just spent a year in Africa, struggling with what he saw as the corruption and ineptitude of life there, living cheek-by-jowl with a small team of soldiers in very isolated and far-flung places. He had not wanted to come on the expedition, needing to get back to his house in Berkshire and live a normal life, rather than set off with yet another small group of men to wander round another continent and live again in primitive conditions.

Henry, however, had persuaded him to come, appealing to his strongly developed sense of adventure, and to his professional interest as a surveyor. They had been on expeditions together in the past and John knew how Henry operated as an expedition leader. Before we entered China, John had taken upon himself, with my support, the job of second-in-command.

In Hong Kong John had explained to me that on Morgan expeditions, Henry didn't delegate properly, nor did he go into the administration in sufficient detail, having too much on his plate to do everything properly. As the second-in-command, John would go along behind Henry picking up the small but essential tasks that had fallen by the wayside and get them done.

Apart from knowing Henry, John was well qualified for this task, being a very experienced mountaineer, respected by those in the team who had climbed with him. He was also a powerful personality, determined and strong-willed, decisive and confident of his own judgement – but very impatient.

It seemed, from the several disagreements we had suffered already, as though John had decided I was not his sort of person. For my part, some friction between the two of us was inevitable; I was not prepared to agree with everything that John said. I give shelter to a devil who sometimes disagrees simply for the hell of it.

On occasions I found John's cynicism distasteful, even downright depressing. As an example, in Hong Kong, when I was talking about how keen I was to get on with the expedition, John told me that I would soon be longing to be back there. He said that expeditions were lonely, uncomfortable, anxious and at times frightening, cold and miserable; the only good thing about them was coming home at the end. (As the expedition proceeded I was to discover elements of truth in John's pessimism.)

After a time thrown together in a small group, irritations become harder to ignore as you cannot seek other company. The alternative is the loneliness of withdrawal but I needed to learn as much as I could from the experienced mountaineers before it was too late. John, however, seemed to be becoming an adversary rather than a mentor.

That night we went to the theatre. I was drifting along behind the others in the jostling streets trying to take photographs, and was left behind, on my own, with no idea of where our hotel might be and unable to communicate with any of the mildly curious people that streamed past.

After half an hour of intrepid exploration, wandering up and down in what I hoped was the direction that Jin Jun had taken, Jin Jun reappeared, worried in case I had vanished for ever. He was 'responsible' for us whilst in China and would be accountable to his superiors for any difficulties we might get into whilst in his charge.

We strode off through the gathering darkness, dodging across roads through streams of tinkling bicycles, shouldering and elbowing past discussion groups of blue-pyjama'd grandmothers, past young families out for a stroll, finally diving into a long dark alley and the anonymous double doors of the theatre.

I had missed several acts. Apart from our small party the audience were all Chinese, laughing and applauding from bucket seats in the auditorium of an Edwardian music hall, complete with the obviously authentic Chinese-style decor. On stage two pretty girls were lying on their backs balancing solid-looking card tables on their feet, spinning them round until they became a blur, throwing them across the stage to each other, catching them with their feet.

Two huge 'Ming' vases were brought on, larger but as robust as porcelain lavatories. The girls, still upside down but now on the tables, threw them around with their feet, ran to spin them, then threw them across the stage to each other in swirling parabolas.

The finale of the evening, after incredible acrobats, jugglers and a pair of very familiar slap-stick clowns pouring buckets of water down their huge multi-coloured trousers, was a smooth conjuror in dinner jacket and bow tie. He turned out to be a Chinese version of the Egyptian 'Gully-Gully Man', using goldfish where gully-gully men use chicks.

He swallowed and regurgitated live fish, often with several coming from his mouth hooked onto a fishing line. He placed goldfish in bowls at each end of the stage and moved them, under black cloths from one bowl to the other, by means of the appropriate magic words.

For his final RSPCA-award-winning trick, he produced a huge carp – last seen swimming happily in a bowl in the centre of the stage – from the bosom of a woman two seats in front of me, hooked onto a line, flapping furiously.

The Shang-tu Summer Palace of Kublai Khan (a ruin today) was a Mongol paradise on earth; it was stocked with small deer so that the larger of the Khan's birds of prey or trained cheetah that rode to hunt perched on his saddle behind the emperor, could pull them down.

Kublai Khan believed in a Supreme Being, and that all religions were essentially the same. Ecumenical to the extreme, he thought that all the great religions could therefore be amalgamated. In this he was pragmatic, adding to his own Mongol belief those of Buddhists and Christians. He respected the festivals of Christ, Buddha, Mohammed and Moses and asked Marco Polo's father and uncle to send him friars from Europe so that he could learn more about Christianity.

His real reason for wanting friars was to counter the magical powers of the Tibetan and Kashmiri Buddhist monks, who, to an extent, terrorized his court. Surprisingly, he dared not remove them for fear they would kill him through sorcery. They performed tricks; caused wine cups to move from sideboard to table of their own volition. The Polos recorded seeing this sort of thing happening. Friars sent from the Pope, so the Khan's logic went, would be more powerful than these evil men, were they to turn upon him.

On our visit to the Summer Palace we climbed the steep stairways that led from Kunming Lake up through the Hall That Dispels Clouds and the Tower for Incense for the Buddha. The sun was hot, the sky cloudy and sultry and the crowds noisy, cheerful and, as usual, curious about us.

Halfway down the stone steps through the Sea of Wisdom Temple, a group of Chinese punks were leaning against the orange-emulsioned walls, a large chromium ghetto-blaster pumping out Chinese rock music. They stank of unwashed clothing, smoke, garlic and stale alcohol. Herds of similarly clad, but more elaborately coiffured youths were familiar to us – from Oxford Street's Saturday parades and late-night London tube trains.

Holidaying Chinese families and the groups of young, pretty girls that giggled their way through the gardens were not however used to such wildly anti-social elements. They scurried away with alarm and disapproval from the punks' aggressive posturing, which – as we stood our ground – evaporated into an affable interest in our filming. Apart from a bit of yobbish shouting and the noise of *le rock chinoise*, they were quite well-behaved.

Below, the lake was crawling with insect-like rowing boats packed with brightly dressed families basking in the sunshine, trailing languid arms in the calm waters. Fathers, husbands and boyfriends toiled inexpertly over stubby oars, their bustling and indolence all owed to the eighteenth-century Emperor Qianlong, who had dug out the lake as he expanded the existing royal gardens.

Conrad Ainsley, with his black skin and body-builder's physique, was stripped to the waist in the afternoon heat. His presence, so much larger than normal life in Beijing, was causing consternation. Jaws dropped open and people stopped in their tracks to watch him go by.

Although a gentle and very humorous man with great patience, 'Rad became a little fed up with all the attention. (John Day was amused by this, considering it a turning of tables; in Africa John had suffered the same attention in remote villages where all would gather to watch, silently, as he cooked his food, did his work and washed. He would simply strip off and get on with it as his audience refused to go away.)

Conrad Ainsley was very solidly athletic, about five foot ten inches tall with a huge, white-toothed smile and cheerful laugh. I had known him for several years at Royal Marines Poole, although we had never been together in the same forward observation team. In his late twenties, he was very old to be a Gunner (the rank of

Private in the Royal Artillery), but most Gunners in 148 Battery were equally senior in age. Few wanted to leave; the quality of those in the unit was of the very highest, and promotion, into dead men's shoes, was extremely slow. In any other unit, 'Rad would certainly have been an NCO.

'Rad was the only married man in the team, with a young daughter. The marriage was going through a bad patch and he was quite glad to be away to think about it all in peace. Although very much one of the boys, he could be philosophical when on his own, talking reflectively and with a sense of fun.

From what 'Rad said, his mother was an exemplary lady, a staunch gospel-singing Christian who had worked hard to bring her family up properly and who clearly kept good order in the Ainsley household. She was also, I would think, the source of 'Rad's irrepressible good humour and cheerfulness, a light that was rarely dimmed – and then only temporarily.

The Summer Palace closed at 5 P.M. Our breakneck itinerary demanded that we go back to the Tiantin Sport Hotel for supper. Meal times were fixed and immutable; in China the staff arrive late, leave early and under no circumstances, unless money changes hands, can be persuaded or induced to provide late meals – or anything beyond the usual routine. With full employment and no financial incentives to work harder or provide better service, it is only human nature to do the minimum amount of work.

Promptly at five, people left the promenades and ornamental gardens. The boats bobbed empty at their moorings as day-trippers returned on bus and bicycle to suburban apartments. The last sightseers lingered on the steps of Longevity Hill and a father walked hand in hand with his beautiful small daughter, red ribbons in her hair. The sun dropped into calm waters and silent water lilies, touching Seventeen Arch Bridge with fire.

After supper at the hotel, bicycles had been procured for us to ride that evening, if we wished. As an experienced London bicycle commuter, I demurred, with John Day and the eminently sensible Bob Wood. We preferred not to tempt Providence more than absolutely necessary.

This night cycle ride to Longtanhu Park, a suicidal excursion through streets without street lights, where bicycles and motor vehicles alike had only the dimmest of lamps, was greatly enjoyed by Andy, Henry, Conrad, Nick, Robbo and Jerry, brave souls following Jin Jun into the darkness. They probably gained great relief from it – as a surrogate for mountaineering danger.

Longtanhu Park is China's answer to Disney World. It seems to have been created as the sort of amenity that all civilized countries provide to keep the people happy. You walk along footpaths beside a curving lake, past three-foot-high coloured mushrooms from which saccharine-sweet Chinese music flows like narcotic vapour:

'They are your friends, you like being here, it is fun . . . we all like being here and having fun together.'

Huge ferris wheels rotated half empty, pin points of light against the darkness; empty roundabouts stood still on unkempt uncut grass, and Porky Pig, in English and Chinese, urged all those of a nervous disposition, with a tendency to cardiac arrest or suffering from any other serious disease, not to brave his whirling cups and saucers – which lay dormant like a cricket club tea on a wet Saturday afternoon. By contrast to the relics of the imperial past, this cheap imitation of the culture of the United States, a country whose history does not even begin to compare, seemed a puzzling waste of resources – as if such amenities were an essential qualification to becoming a fully fledged international capital city.

The roller coaster performed very much the same function as the cycle ride. Prevented from leaving the cars, either by choice or accident, by rubber-padded metal arms, we were cranked up to the top of a vertical slope several hundred feet high, to plunge downwards into a series of corkscrews and 360-degree turns.

Andy Aspinall sat beside me. Like most of the rest of the team, he had been on the roller coaster several times already while I had been wandering around taking photographs. Andy had played down the severity and nature of the ride – until I was strapped in and it was all too late. He was keen to see my face as I realized what was to come, and then the contortion of my features as the nightmare actually happened. It was the most wonderful ride; terrifying, unbelievable and horribly real.

Andy was not disappointed with my reactions. In all sorts of ways, we were testing each other out.

CHAPTER 4

Soldiers and Warriors

Our mountaineering equipment was still in Beijing, not rattling as it should have been across the Gobi Desert towards Urumqi. Flooding had blocked the railway lines west. We would have to pay an extra four and a half thousand dollars for air freighting before CIST would move anything from Beijing – and they would do nothing at all until our money was sitting in their bank account.

We had no choice but to pay.

After several days of worry, the money arrived from Britain and CIST was paid. However, our return air tickets, from Karachi to London, had not materialized – in spite of our having paid for them before we left home.

We imagined ourselves in November, in Pakistan at the end of our long adventure, haggard and gaunt, dressed in rags with scraggy beards and gagging for an alcoholic drink, being turned away from the departure lounge to wander the streets of Karachi having been declared Absent Without Leave by the Army back in the UK.

We invited the Military Attaché and his staff to our hotel for a small drinks party. Colonel Bill Clements, military and cool in a lightweight brown suit and carefully brushed steel-grey hair, said he would do what he could to obtain the missing tickets.

It was comforting to know that we had such a capable ally who could act on our behalf. As it was to turn out, his calm assurance (over the phone) was to be vital as we dealt with the seemingly intractable problem that was soon to beset us in the depths of

Chinese Turkestan, as we came up against the bureaucracy of Xinjiang Autonomous Province.

Beijing railway station was as clogged with humanity as Heathrow during a traffic controllers' strike. Huge, high-ceilinged waiting rooms hundreds of feet long were packed with people sitting on hard, long wooden benches. Some slept on newspapers amid dust, sticky pools of spilled soft drink or the gnawed bones and rice of discarded food containers. Others leaned blankly against dirty walls smoking cigarettes.

Uniformed servicemen slumped in patient postures, their high collared tunics loosened at the neck. Small children dozed or sat on the stone floor staring about them wide-eyed with wonder. A Mongolian family in traditional heavy embroidered jackets, fur-rimmed hats and heavy black boots, blocked part of the way through the huge hall, their wide, rosy-cheeked faces blank with sleep amid the bustle of passing feet.

The trains departed like aeroplanes. Their existence was registered on an electronic board, but the platform from which they would depart was revealed only when all was ready for passengers to board. The queue, through a second ticket barrier, was dense and painfully slow-moving, everyone clutching cardboard cartons bound with orange bailer twine. After some fast talking, Jin Jun side-stepped the queue through a side gate, and we joined the stream of hundreds of passengers jostling along an enclosed bridge and down steps onto Platform 9.

The train was miles long. Our carriage was number six, so we had to walk past thirty, twenty-nine, twenty-eight, twenty-seven ... each carriage about thirty metres long. As always, we were heavily laden, me with eight umbrellas, a heavy grip full of film and my camera bag, plus a stook of aluminium poles – for marking the route through the snow of the mountain.

Our train left at 1.30 P.M., on the dot, and turned out to be even better than the Guangzhou–Beijing express. I was becoming very impressed with Chinese Railways, especially as our evening meal in the dining car was quite superb.

* * *

Journeys on trains are a wonderful way to sink into the landscape of a country, of abandoning oneself to days of solid and continuous travel where thoughts can ramble out and through the constantly changing countryside. There is none of the usual impatience to arrive. The train becomes a microcosm, with its own routines, people and character, and yet it is also a bona fide part of the landscape – with a sense of belonging, a little of which rubs off on its passengers.

Thoughts, because they flash into the mind of the railway traveller at the same speed as the objects that prompt them spin past the window, are spontaneous and almost subliminal. There is no opportunity to revise or reconsider as the next fresh visual experience rolls by, as relentless as a factory conveyor belt.

For a time, the countryside was flat and agricultural, our train pushing through anonymous dusty towns and small villages with huge, ugly railway sidings. Gradually the flatness changed to hills with cultivated terraces and dry river beds with over-wide concrete bridges – an indication of frequent flooding. We clattered through steep rock gorges into grey limestone country.

Across the stony, dried-up river beds, stone-built villages perched on top of steep banks on Italian-looking hillsides. Beside the track, gravel-making plants covered houses and fields with grey dust. Blue-clad workers pulled heavy carts from crushing plants to rail-side dumps. Cement and limestone works were cut into hillsides and straw-hatted labourers shovelled gravel into railway wagons.

The hills were steep and eroded, grey stone mixed with red. Villages were linked across the stony river bed which we were following by concrete bridges, the line skirting the edge of the hills to the left. We vanished into occasional tunnels, which cut through the spurs of red-grey rock created by the meanderings of the river to emerge again above the dried-out river bed.

The elaborately terraced fields were deserted in the misty light of late afternoon; kale and corn grew in narrow, stone-walled enclosures that followed the contours of the hills with the perfection of hard manual labour. These well-worked lands climbed from the bottom of small valleys until the steepness of the slope and the lack of soil made cultivation impossible, giving way to rough pasture. There were no dwellings, just the odd stone hut for storing the tools. The farmers walked to their fields from dirt tracked villages, from rough stone huts where children watched as the train thundered past.

The sun dropped down behind the low hills, bathing the fields in an orange glow and painting the sky golden against the outline of the horizon, with the sky a very pale blue overhead. Our now dirty green coaches snaked round the bends, pulled briskly by a blue diesel locomotive.

At 7.36 P.M. we stopped at Yangquam, an industrial town where the head conductor held a parade. He lined up all the attendants, smart young girls and men in white tunics, blue military hats and blue Terylene bell-bottomed trousers. Each was inspected, orders for the evening were issued in ringing tones, then they were dismissed. We looked on with a professional interest. They made a rather sloppy turn to the right – without saluting.

The next morning we awoke to find a steam locomotive had taken over from the diesel. For those who had never travelled in a steam train, romance was tempered by reality. With the window open, the tablecloth became covered with small particles of soot, speckling the white lace of the cotton seat covers. Those keen to see the engine soon pulled tousled heads back into the carriage, eyes smarting from the grit. The locomotive whistled frequently, with a mellow, slightly echoing, haunting voice. Occasional clouds of water vapour enveloped the carriages. In the morning sunshine, we gazed at the green fields and domed yellow hay stacks through faint, fleeting rainbows.

The railway is the focal point of life in provincial China – as it is in many other parts of the world. People walked and cycled along the side of the track, waiting patiently at platforms and gathering at crossings, watching as our green carriages rolled past. The railway carried everything.

I imagined Britain at the turn of the century to have been roughly comparable with what we were seeing – old-fashioned heavy industries completely dependent upon the train. Sidings branched off into goods yards, to piles of coal, drainpipes, wooden sleepers and building blocks; or towards factories and power stations whose chimneys pumped smoke out over the surrounding countryside. Dusty, cavernous buildings, the darkness inside made more gloomy by single, naked bulbs whose curly filaments glowed ineffectually. From the security of trains, the poignant beauty of such ugliness can be savoured.

The factories were separated by long stretches of countryside. The agriculture was intensive, but seemed not to be mechanized, the same fertile fields of the People's Revolution. A boy pulled a single-share plough on a length of metal tubing through soft ground. Perhaps surprisingly, we had passed only a few grazing animals: some cows, no sheep and the occasional herd of white goats foraging through the vegetation beside the track. Around the villages, chickens and ducks pecked, white amid the green of lotus-leaf ponds and paddy fields.

We arrived at Xian (pronounced Shee'ann) after the thirty-six-hour journey, only one hour late, at 10.55 A.M. The local CIST rep was there, a bespectacled woman in her early twenties, a student of English with, like all tour guides, a series of memorized speeches, who introduced herself by telling us her Chinese name, adding:

'But you can call me Yellow Jade.'

We were more of a novelty to the inhabitants of Xian than we had been to the sophisticates of Beijing. A huge crowd gathered as I filmed a roadside fast food shop. With his staff of four, the owner, in white chef's hat, was taking very thin slices from a slab of beef with a razor-sharp cleaver. We became fascinated, watching as the slices were thrown into a sizzling wok with chopped vegetables (and an alarming number of green chilis), then placed to order inside a pitta bread envelope.

In spite of just having eaten lunch, we bought several of these delicious dishes. Our interest stimulated the taste buds of the audience, creating an overwhelming demand which exhausted both the patience and the raw materials of the proprietor, who became bad tempered with the now-hungry crowd.

Ian Roberts and Jerry Slack surrendered themselves to barbers beside the market. Six chairs in a gloomy concrete shop were busy with male customers being shaved and trimmed by male and female cutters, the ladies wearing white headcloths and coveralls. They both pretended not to be nervous under the grubby white sheets, whilst receiving seriously short haircuts.

Robbo decided to have a shave as well; curiosity was coupled with the sense of abandon that affects all travellers who succeed in obtaining a personal service when they have absolutely no means of verbal communication. There was much amusement from all concerned — from those of us not brave enough to follow suit, and from the staff and other clientèle.

That evening we gathered outside a large dark room at the hotel labelled 'Bar'. Inside a female member of the hotel staff slumped listlessly at one of the tables, western style supermarket muzak playing and red-bulbed lighting illuminating a hot, empty room. The bar was a long glass counter with dusty drinks bottles on grubby shelves. A five-foot high wall of crated canned beer stood by the door.

After much ineffectual consultation between hotel staff, we determined that there was no cold beer — only the warm stuff by the door. They would not sell any of this to us as the manager did not know how much to charge.

Appropriately, we were able to buy a bottle of Henry Morgan black rum. On the balcony outside the grim and useless room marked 'Bar', we consumed the rum, mixed with cold Coke. I got out my guitar and the party began.

There was rock'n'roll, dancing and singing and several renditions of 'Wild Thing' (that once popular ditty by the Troggs), Jerry and Nick wearing their woolly and fur hats in lieu of long hair. Jerry revealed himself as a closet rock star with an outstanding ability for Jaggeresque poses. As the rum was consumed, the metal guitar strings removed all feeling from my fingers and long-forgotten songs emerged from my internal reservoir.

Jerry Slack, a Royal Marine out of water with an Army expedition, was tough, wiry and self-contained, about five foot eight, with slightly receding brown hair, a large, toothy grin and throaty chuckle, and a number of scars to shoulder and face, the result of a bad fall.

He and his brother had learned to sail on their father's yacht. Whilst still at school and penniless, they had taught themselves off-shore navigation, by trial and error, on illicit voyages from Liverpool to the Scillies. Jerry had learned his mountaineering in the same fashion, going to the Alps, staying in mountain huts, and following experienced-looking people up the peaks. The potential wildness that led him to have a go at such difficult, dangerous sports in such an independent fashion was tempered with thoughtfulness, common sense, strength and inner confidence.

Jerry had trained as a jeweller in his father's Manchester business, making diamond rings, bracelets and brooches. After the bad fall, the medical profession had predicted that he would never regain the proper use of his shoulder. Partly to prove them wrong, and out of boredom, Jerry had exercised furiously, regaining full mobility and strength, passing the very strict medical board imposed on all candidates for the Royal Navy by the Admiralty, and finally joined the Royal Marines.

After his young officer's training he had been posted to an Army unit rather than a Marine Commando. At that time, the Royal Marines had more young officers than vacancies for troop com-manders (a Royal Marine platoon is called a troop). Jerry went to 59 Independent Commando Squadron Royal Engineers, where he learned about Bailey bridges, making roads, airfields and jetties, and about laying and clearing booby traps and minefields – ideal training for a young commando. He came to know Robbo and Nick, and heard about the vacancy on the expedition, meeting most of the team during the Eiger trip.

My first introduction to the team had taken place in the spring, on that short Alpine interlude. Henry's aim had been to get most of the team together and experience a little of the effects of high altitude (at 3,970 metres, the Eiger is high enough to cause problems for the unacclimatized).

Bob Wood had issued us with our mountaineering gear in a large hangar in Portsmouth, we had narrowly escaped a thirty-two-vehicle pile up on the M25, and managed to leave my bergen on Basle station platform. After that, things calmed down considerably.

Sadly in the Jungfrau, the weather had been misty. The risk of avalanche was too great to do more than camp in the snow in a couloir above the Eiger-Gletscher cable-car station. The café there was the scene of several jolly and sociable evenings as we got to know each other. Those absent were John Day, still in the Cameroons, and Conrad Ainsley, who had not yet joined the expedition.

In spite of the conditions, we were able to practise roping techniques and essentials like ice axe arrests (used to curtail a slide down the mountain, or halt a partner's fall down a crevasse). This week away from the stress of trying to get sponsorship and solve the many last-minute problems had been for me a much-needed rest.

At our balcony party, before we became too outrageous, Nick Moore introduced a 'friend', an English-speaking Chinese man who launched into a prepared speech about teaching us Chinese drinking games. He challenged Nellie to the 'paper, scissors and rock' guessing game, winning and getting Nellie to consume rum whilst he carefully nursed his own can of Coke.

He offered his cigarettes around. The amateur smokers of the team had drunk sufficient alcohol to succumb. Henry disapproved of smoking and only Jerry actually bought cigarettes, suffering a continual scout-masterly pressure from 'H' to give up. This pressure irritated Jerry sufficiently to consider not giving up for the mountaineering phase – as he had planned. Several others enjoyed the occasional cigarette.

I suggested our Chinese friend should have some rum – as Nellie was on the way to being got drunk by him in what seemed a rather dubious fashion. He left quite smartly, forgetting his cigarettes, which were smoked by the amateurs.

The music flagged whenever my left hand ached too much to continue playing. In the silence Jerry became restless, unable in these interludes to continue his Rolling Stones impersonations (the fur hat seemed to facilitate the transformation). Instead, he lectured us on the overwhelming importance of 'Getting *Down*' to the music, with great emphasis on the last word – coining an expedition catch phrase.

* * *

China is bursting with exciting archaeology, some vandalized but most completely untouched. Official policy seems to be eminently sensible; many wonderful sites are being left until there is the time and money to excavate properly. Vandalism can be official, when the labyrinthine bureaucracy fails to link building projects with archaeological sites. The English newspaper in Beijing reported the bulldozing of a uniquely complete Bronze Age village in Dalien city.

For us, as professional soldiers, the Terracotta Warriors were the archaeological highlight.

Despite hangovers from the previous night's entertainment, and the overdose of culture and visits from which the team (as a team) were suffering, the terracotta army had all of us deep in thought amid the jostling crowds of the huge hangar which has been built over the site.

Emperor Qin Shihuang, a man obsessed with finding some means of avoiding death, created the army in an astonishing attempt to retain the means to rule in the after-life. The site was discovered by accident in 1974 by peasants digging a well.

They discovered an underground vault 200 by sixty metres, shored up with timbers. One year later, two more vaults were found, an underground barracks for over 7,000 fully armed terracotta soldiers.

The third vault contained only sixty-eight soldiers, possibly the command post from which the other 7,000 would receive their orders. The first contained the balance of the soldiers (6,000) and has been partially excavated, covered over with a concrete roof.

One-third of Qin Shihuang's army (about a brigade in modern terminology) has been brushed clean of mud and dirt and replaced standing upright as the craftsmen left them. We saw them as a real army on parade and could identify with each figure; one looks quietly amused, another rather stupid, one is grumpy, another happy, all in different postures. The generals, with square cloth-covers over their central bun of hair, look authoritative and their officers keen and reliable. The horses are lively, and all stand patiently in their ranks awaiting the imperial call to arms.

An army of craftsmen used an assembly-line technique, putting the component parts of each soldier together at the end. Achieving the vibrancy of life in brown clay figures from which all traces of colour have long since gone was an astonishing feat, especially in such huge numbers.

The figures are hollow, constructed from strips of clay rolled out and fashioned, then joined together through holes which were filled in at the very end of the process. All 7,000 were originally painted, but somehow (a fire in the vault is one theory) the colours have gone and they stand as brown as the earth from which they seem to have grown.

In the crowded museum beside the roofed site, artefacts from the vault are on display. The most striking was a miniature bronze chariot with four horses and an enclosed, low-profile, leather armoured palanquin for getting the emperor from one place to another at speed. This vehicle was smashed but has been perfectly restored. The horses are just over a metre high and look absolutely alive, the graceful, spirited, sure-footed animals that carried the most powerful man in China swiftly across the field. From the observation slits he could observe the battle, making the decisions that would decide the outcome – and who would live, and who die.

That evening we went to the Hanquou Cultural Institute to see the Shaanxi Dance Company performing Tang Dynasty dances and music. They played copies of Tang instruments in dance, opera, music and song recreated from surviving documentation.

The stage was set as an emperor's court complete with coquettish courtesans dancing and making eyes at the audience – which appealed to me. My favourite was the Masked Warrior Dance, in which four red-costumed dervishes wearing heavy silver and brocade masks threw themselves about the stage to wild drum and cymbal music. The violence and noise of the dance drives the devil away, overpowering and subduing evil, expressing the universal wish for peace and well-being. As Jin Jun told me, this piece is very popular with modern Chinese people.

There was some traditional opera, which I found tonally incomprehensible (but I find any opera more serious than *Così fan tutte* hard to handle). There was also some really beautiful harp, woodwind and bowed music that sent me drifting away across endless lakes and pagoda'd paddy fields.

I was worrying about film.

I had bought about a third more than I thought I would need – and my estimation had been very generous. For the mountain I thought I would take as much as the camels could carry, based upon shooting four one-hundred-foot reels every day.

Jerry Slack was also thinking ahead, about getting injured:

'You can break a leg just like *that*,' he muttered, snapping his fingers.

'As soon as the thought comes into your mind you have to push it out again.'

I loved the Chinese Railways' steam trains and was very keen to film them.

We took the cameras out, firstly to the Bell Tower – which is a remnant of Xian's massive city wall, now used as a traffic island. We humped all the gear down an underpass below the road and along a subterranean pedestrian walkway. Yellow Jade was our interpreter and guide. She was fishing for compliments about her English:

'How long you think it take for me to speak English properly?'

'Not very long if you were able to speak to English people regularly.'

'I sometimes cannot understand many of them. As example, the one with the fair hair . . .'

'Andy.'

'And the one I think he is called Robbo? I find it hard to understand what they are saying.'

'Many English people do not speak clearly and slowly enough. Also they use words that are not in dictionaries. The best way to learn is to come to England – but I suppose you cannot do that?'

She shook her head. 'So,' she said, 'I understand you perfectly. I will speak with you.'

There was a sadness, combined with a tired acceptance that accompanied this conversation.

We talked of how intelligent young Chinese people are educated, go to college and take employment. Jobs are easy to obtain and so there is mobility for the well-educated, moving from one job to another.

Jin Jun was a good example of this mobility. He had been a town planner but after being promoted to a senior regional appointment, had become disillusioned with the way his inexperience and that of his peers led to mistakes. Wanting a change, he had polished up his English to become an interpreter, and was seeing China at the same time as his western charges.

China was changing, opening up to the outside world and, partly as a result, the structure of Chinese society was altering. The large extended family was fading away rapidly and the less stable and settled nuclear family taking its place. The once venerated old were now admonished to be silent, since ancient learning was deemed no longer applicable to the young, the front runners of the new society. This policy did not seem to apply to China's remarkably aged political rulers. The traditional, ferociously dominant Chinese mother-in-law, who in the former large extended families ruled new brides with a rod of iron, was now officially 'discouraged'.

As I talked with Yellow Jade, there seemed another element to her sadness and acceptance of her lot. She was in her middle twenties, unmarried and would, so she said, get married in due course – but only if the right person came along:

'I would prefer not to be married at all if I do not meet the right person, someone who is a really good friend.'

Men may marry at twenty, women at eighteen. Birth control is practised; the large extended family is now a rarity, and abortions are free. Illegitimate children are treated the same as legitimate ones. There is, however, strong official condemnation of extra-marital sex, and official disapproval of pre-marital sex.

The divorce rate in China is low, six per cent in 1986. Divorce is permitted by the agreement of both parties and the 'sub-district people's government and judicial organ', which keeps it discreetly out of the courts.

Yellow Jade's curiosity about the west and the desire to improve her English was accompanied by the hint of another curiosity. On the surface, amid all the official disapprovals, sex seems not to exist in China. Men and women seem to be less polarized than in the west, wearing the same clothes and doing the same jobs. In the west, by contrast, sex is all pervasive, selling everything from washing machines to pipe tobacco.

But Yellow Jade suffered from the great problem that besets all proper travellers. You know what you want, but you don't know the etiquette of getting it.

At the turnstile at the foot of the stairs up into the Bell Tower, entrance was denied. We were not permitted to bring in cameras.

I asked Yellow Jade for the reason: it was to prevent terrorists. I tried to question this – how three huge and obvious Europeans with a pile of heavy cine gear could be a threat to the state by filming from the centre of a traffic island in the middle of China.

She was simply not interested in discussion, so I gave up. I wanted to keep my powder dry for our trip to the railway station.

We reached the ticket barrier by pushing through the crowds of arriving passengers. A dumpy, flat-faced girl in railway uniform looked at us with curiosity. Yellow Jade once again became obsequious in the face of authority:

'We cannot go in. We are not catching a train.'

'Can't we buy platform tickets?'

'No.'

'Why don't you say that we are meeting your grandparents from Beijing and my aunt and uncle from Hong Kong.'

Yellow Yade looked puzzled:

'We need to show the ticket office a telegram from these people, saying which train they are arriving on, before we can buy a platform permit.'

'Why don't we buy tickets for the next station?'

All this western subterfuge was becoming too much; she marched forward to the barrier and spoke rapidly in Chinese. The dumpy girl waved us through.

'What did you say to her?'

Yellow Jade strode briskly along the concrete passageway.

'I told her that you were students of railway technology in Britain and wish to study Xian railway station.'

* * *

A bona fide British student of railway technology would have been ecstatic. About forty lines ran into the station and in the centre a huge muddy hole was being dug by over a hundred labourers. It was like a child's encyclopaedia drawing of the construction of the pyramids.

The hole was being dug in three tiers. Those on the bottom dug out and shovelled up with long-handled Cornish-style shovels onto the second tier – and so on until the earth could be placed into wheelbarrows.

The earth sides of the hole were roughly shored up with the odd piece of timber and the whole site was crawling with ragged labourers of both sexes. They barrowed the earth across the tracks to where two steam powered cranes, sighing deeply and hissing like railway engines, scooped it up into battered lorries, the steam from their efforts making our faces, arms and hands wet in the afternoon heat.

Work stopped for the locomotives as they clattered through, old, battered and dirty, pulling enormous passenger and coal trains, the crews smiling and waving at us as they passed.

When you looked closely at one person to see exactly what he or she was doing in this busy mass of work, it became clear that they were all taking it very steadily. It was hot and very humid, and whenever a train went past it was necessary to stop and acknowledge its presence. There was much leaning on shovels and wiping of brows.

Down in the bottom of the hole, three or four worked with an air of furiousness, then climbed carefully up the ladder to examine the results of their labours with severely critical looks, they too leaning on their shovels. There was no obvious foreman, and the job – whatever it was – would take weeks.

Full employment in China does not necessarily mean useful employment.

Robert Nelson was helping me to film at the railway station and was fascinated by the scene. Nellie was a quiet, self-sufficient person, a little under six feet tall, with fair hair and skin that was likely to be prone to sunburn at high altitudes. He had the broad shoulders, slender torso and legs of an athlete, and the slight awkwardness of youth that another couple of years' experience would remove. He had been brought up in the Orkneys, travelling to boarding school on the mainland, returning home only on high days and holidays.

He knew about the elements, animals and birds in the instinctive way of children reared in isolated places. His self-reliance, the product of both life in the Orkneys and the regime of going away to school, was very much tempered by a gentleness of humour, speech and temperament.

Nellie had started rock climbing on the crumbling cliffs of his island home, getting into the sport in a big way when he joined the army. He came top in one of the final exams at the Apprentices College, and when asked what he would like to receive – the usual request was for an expensive text book related to the subject – asked for a 'friend'.

As Nellie was not notably reclusive, this request had to be explained: a 'Climbers' Friend' is a complicated expanding chock with a loop which is placed by a lead climber into a gap in the rock, to catch him if he falls. The General at the prizegiving, handing over a highly engineered collection of aluminium cams and cog-wheels whose purpose seemed doubtful, wished the newly qualified Sapper Nelson the best of luck with whatever he intended doing with his strange prize.

Nellie was the latest of Henry's protégés; encouraged and trained by him, and a veteran of several Morgan expeditions. Andy Aspinall was also a recent 'graduate' of the Morgan school, having like Nellie come through the Army Apprentices College. Nellie was an excellent rock climber – a 'rock athlete' regarded by Henry as a future top Army mountaineer.

At just turned nineteen, on a severe expedition like this, Nellie had age as his Achilles heel. He was surrounded by people with much more experience – both on mountains and in life, and the pressures to come might prove too much for someone so young. However he seemed mature, calm and sensible, and had been on holiday-type climbing expeditions with people older than himself. He knew several of the others quite well and fitted in as a very active team member. I knew that Henry intended climbing with Nellie whenever he could, and that mountaineering welfare was very high on Henry's list of priorities – so Nellie was going to be well looked after.

I wondered, at this early stage before we entered the mountains, how Henry would order his personal aims for the expedition, for these were several. He wanted to climb the mountain safely. It would be pointless to decide to climb a big mountain without any risks to life, as avalanches and other acts of providence can kill even the most cautious. He wanted to bring on his protégés (Nellie and Andy) and get as many of the novices up the mountain as possible, training us as he went; and get me as close to the top as possible with cameras. Finally, he wanted to let everyone find their own level within the group so that it operated under its own steam with the minimum of guidance from the leader.

I saw several contradictions in these diverse aims, especially as there were individuals singled out from the rest to receive preferential treatment. Also, we had no sponsor and the fifty to sixty thousand pounds cost of the trip was spread among the ten of us, as percentages based upon Army pay: Henry's share being almost twice Nellie's. Success in making the first ascent of the mountain would make recovering that money very much easier. Would money play a part in the decision-making process on the mountain?

Another steam locomotive laboured cheerfully past with toothy grins from the fire plate and the sweet smell of damp coal smoke. Nellie was both impressed and quietly amused by the hubbub of human activity at the railway station. The various engineering projects that we were watching excited his professional interest. As an afterthought, in his quiet Orkney burr, he reckoned they were very like the sort of tasks you get in the Army, digging defensive trenches by hand when the mechanical digger has burst a hydraulic hose.

Everyone was politely interested in us and smiled readily if we smiled, grinned broadly and nodded if we said 'Good afternoon', and shook hands enthusiastically if we offered. Eventually a group of white-shirted officials arrived.

'This,' said Yellow Jade, 'is the station manager.'

I nodded very politely to him, as he and his delegation walked towards the camera.

'Does he speak English?'

'No. He says you cannot take any films here.'

Yellow Jade had again gone blank in the face of officialdom.

I abandoned my intention to introduce myself as the railway expert fascinated by the complexity and efficiency of China Railways. The great man wanted his platform cleared of the uncertainty and possible threat that we represented. Instead I waved imperiously at Jerry and Nellie, shouting at them to put the cine gear away as ostentatiously and quickly as they could, as if we had not yet begun to shoot. I walked up to them waving my arms, pretending to give orders, our filming in any case completed.

We left very quickly and encountered no difficulties.

That night we took a walk to the new Xian Hotel. The huge marble plaza was airconditioned, with uniformed bell-hops and all the trimmings of a big American hotel – only the fountains had no water. To get into the marble plaza we had to walk across twenty metres of churned up mud just inside the barbed wire perimeter fence where the contractors (wrong word, there is no such animal in China, but nevertheless they seem to have some of the same characteristics) had failed to finish off.

We went immediately upstairs to the disco – at last, a disco in China! It looked like the real thing, flashing lights underneath the dance floor, chromium tables and pretty waitresses with trays. However, the music was turned down to conversational level and was sickly-sweet and tame. Three official-looking gents in dark suits were fiddling ignorantly with the tone controls oblivious to both the clientèle and the occasional dreadful electronic noises they were creating.

We bailed out, to the bar downstairs. The waitresses there were also good looking, and efficient. A photographer was taking pictures of a prosperous group of Japanese tourists for the hotel catalogue.

'Sport' hotels in China are intended, not surprisingly, to house visiting sports teams – the category into which we had been put. A

Japanese boys' basketball team had checked in to our hotel. They might have been aged anything from six to thirteen; they were so precocious it was hard to be more accurate. They wore brand-new baseball hats, T shirts and all imaginable sporting accoutrements.

Their meal times were noisy and messy, even by our standards. Being short, they stood up throughout their meals in order to get at the dishes. It seemed to be a contest to see who could wedge the most boiled rice into the food sacs that they seemed to have inside each cheek.

Their Chief Coach remonstrated with them in Japanese for ten minutes before they went under starters orders for the eating – probably basketball pep talks. For emphasis, he would gesticulate, a lighted cigarette in hand, the smoke swirling over the food-covered table, his charges responding in unison to his imprecations with guttural high-pitched cries like demented seagulls.

A team of Chinese lady gymnasts booked in. Striding through the dining room they towered over everyone else, square shouldered and muscular of leg. Wholesome girls, except for their coach who looked like a weight lifter who had suddenly stopped training.

The hotel stood in the grounds of the Shaanxi Sport College. Yellow Jade told me that getting onto the course was relatively easy. A four-year degree was taught, sports plus academic subjects, after which most students became PE teachers. All Chinese school students take exams and those with the best results go on to university, the cream to Beijing.

Jerry Slack and I went for a run. The Sport College was depressing. As we trotted along the pot-holed roads and debris-strewn waste ground, the college seemed like a building site half-completed ten years ago then left to degenerate. The basketball courts were bare of grass except on the edges, where play rarely reached – and grass grew thick and long. The wire netting was curled up at the bottom with large holes.

We ran through mud and puddles into the athletics stadium, to do some two hundred-metre sprints. A handful of disconsolate males were hoofing a football around with little enthusiasm on a run-down pitch. The tin roof of the small grandstand was curling up with age.

A bright-eyed group of giggling girls were impressed with Jerry's 'V-shaped' Royal Marines torso. They were very friendly. I basked in this reflected adulation as they told me with much nudging and gleaming of eye that he was 'very powerful'. Sadly we were not able to capitalize on this opportunity for some interesting cultural exchanges; we just didn't know the local rules.

The college buildings were dirty and anonymous, brown and grey cracked concrete. The sports hall had two table tennis tables, both in use most of the time, one without a net. The weight training room, investigated by me in a futile effort to acquire a powerful torso, remained locked while we were there. Throughout the large and decrepit grounds only half-hearted basketball or football games seemed ever to be played.

Andy Aspinall, an Army physical training instructor and expert at most team games and gymnastic events, was quite depressed about it all. He made one comment, as we drove out of the place for the airport:

'Look there . . . soccer using a medicine ball. How novel.'

CHAPTER 5

Going West

When we left the UK, we had only hand baggage and our weight allowance for trains and aircraft. Since Hong Kong our luggage seemed to have been reproducing. At each travel terminal we had 'lightened' this expanding load, putting unnecessary stuff into freight to save excess charges – but somehow it never got less. In the near future, I feared that we were going to catch up with (or maybe it would catch up with us) an enormous, quivering load of organically growing, discarded hand luggage.

Reveille on Friday, 14 August was at 6.15; an early breakfast was booked for seven – which the hotel staff did not get up in time to provide – and we were off to the airport for the flight across the first part of the Gobi Desert, to Urumqi.

On the way, our minibus carving through the 'rush hour' bicycle traffic – and as usual narrowly avoiding killing hundreds of people – I reflected on the differences between mainland Chinese and their capitalist Hong Kong brethren.

A Hong Kong crowd has a strong sense of purpose, elbowing one another aside as they push on to where they want to be. On a mainland China street, only the cyclists seem imbued with purpose, staying alive, whereas the pavement crowds drift, and form relaxed groups chatting on street corners.

On the mainland, the approach to work seems also to be different. Everyone appears to have a job, but much of the work seemed to be filling in time rather than making anything happen.

Huge excavations in the middle of the road, which completely disrupted the existing chaos of traffic, were created by men with shovels, a plank across the top of the hole supporting a hand-wound wishing-well bringing up wicker baskets of earth. Such work would take weeks. The waste was tipped in piles by the side of the road, blocking the footpath and compounding the aggravation.

I had seen eight men crawling in a line across a Beijing Park pulling up grass. We saw no lawnmowers in the People's Republic, nor any sign of their having been used; such a specialized and truly useless machine was possibly regarded as a frivolity.

In East Street, Xian, I talked with an aircraft technician whose day started at eight o'clock. He took lunch from twelve to two-thirty and knocked off at five before cycling home from the airport. As he had been to work that day and I was talking to him at four-thirty, I came to the conclusion that although doubtless highly qualified – he spoke English well, which indicated a good education – he was not over-burdened.

As we reached the suburbs of Xian, the flood of bicycle traffic thinned to a steady stream. Our minibus drove down a long, prosperous looking tree-lined avenue. Large 1950s-style limousines, lace curtains screening grand occupants, cruised past towards the city centre. Very large and stately houses were set back from the road, hidden behind shrubs and large iron gates, the official residences of top government officials.

Xian airport looked just like old photographs of Croydon airport in the early days (when ladies were escorted to the nearest police station to use the loo), a large house surrounded by trees. We passed through two security checks, the first was the wrong one and we had to queue again. Large black and white TV screens showed the flights (a blackboard would have sufficed), and I was permitted to refuse to put my cameras through the 'Made in China, Film Safe' X-ray luggage scanning unit.

Outside, the pad was busy with Russian made TU 154 passenger jets, looking remarkably like VC10s, painted in the livery of CAAC, the Chinese internal airline. The terminal doors opened, the crowd elbowed through and raced across the tarmac towards the plane. It was every man for himself, and Ian Roberts, who had diarrhoea, looked green and brought up the rear. Officials then made us queue for twenty minutes by the rear steps while the first class passengers were ushered aboard at the front.

Take-off was bumpy. Heavily made-up hostesses with baby-doll faces wore smart western-style powder blue and white uniforms. As the seat-belt sign went off, they donned frilly blue aprons and handed out four-day-old newspapers, orange juice, cups of tea, warm beer and one huge packet of cream biscuits per passenger, twenty-four biscuits in each. Below, 28,000 feet beneath our silver wings, brown hills and flooded valleys crawled past, the water shimmering in the sun.

After a time we were given more tea and I started eating my twenty-four biscuits. It became apparent that they were not the result of benevolent logistics, but lunch.

The passenger cargo was ethnically varied, Han Chinese, Central Asians of more solid build and ourselves. We were all crammed into triple seats on either side of the aisle and seemed to have been abandoned by the hostesses.

The front of the aeroplane was occupied by the first class passengers. From behind a dirty orange curtain, smells of food wafted rearwards. I slowed up on my biscuits in anticipation. Chinese music wafted over the tannoy. I peered behind the curtain.

All six hostesses were crouching down on the floor in that most inelegant and unladylike squat that you see throughout China, smart uniform skirts hitched up around their thighs, legs wide apart, noses stuck into bowls with bread rolls on the side, chop sticks shovelling large quantities of the First Class passengers' lunch into their mouths. The painted doll who earlier had spent ten minutes primping in front of a mirror was using her personal spoon to get it down faster. She gave me a hostile, blank-faced stare and, without standing up, jerked the curtain back across the doorway.

I tried to imagine BA stewardesses crouched down on their ankles, bolting down the tournedos and asparagus tips from bowls between their legs, staring reproachfully at anyone who peered through into the galley to catch them at it. It was impossible.

I resumed eating biscuits and borrowed Nellie's personal stereo.

The Sex Pistols were bemoaning England's lack of future and the degeneration of the royal family into a tourist money spinner.

We were flying over a desert hemmed to the north by a high range of mountains with bright snow on the peaks. Long, deep valleys ran down from the rock spine of jagged peaks and alluvial fans flowed dry and dead into a brown desert plain. In three hours, at thirty thousand feet and flying at over four hundred miles an hour, we had travelled less than a quarter of the way across China.

We landed at Urumqi in the midday heat and played hockey on the shiny floor of the arrivals lounge with umbrellas and a masking tape ball.

The expedition's 'Liaison Officer' joined us at the airport; first impressions were not good as he spoke no English, had a paunch and a cigarette hung from his lower lip. He was supposed to interpret with the non-Chinese speakers in the west of Turkestan and offer expert, specialized local advice to help get us to the foot of the mountain. He wore a baseball hat and T shirt from a previous Karakoram mountaineering trip. Although the shirt was promising, he did not look as a high altitude mountaineer should.

A dual carriageway ran from the airport, cycle paths at either side, a central reservation with iron railings down the middle, lined with trees every twenty feet. The whole town appeared to be one massive building site, badly weathered structures that seemed to have been under construction for some time. Some were factories, some dwellings and others looked empty. All had façades that, at one time, must have looked good on the architect's drawing board.

An elegant, gleamingly new modern hotel entrance caught my eye. The rest of the building was dirty concrete and sporadic scaffolding, with cement and debris passing up and down in wicker baskets. The smart front entrance was deeply pot-holed and muddy, surrounded by piles of bricks and gravel.

I hoped that our destination, the 'Petroleum Hotel', would be a little closer to completion.

We entered the Petroleum Hotel through a garden, with basket-ball courts, a café and ornamental ponds. Some very peculiar yellow and orange fish leapt from the unfilled tiles of a dry fountain. Each was twelve feet in length. In the garden, where the shrubs were wild and long, two giraffes and a deer, brightly painted and very much larger than life, leered myopically at new arrivals with boss-eyed stares.

From the outside, the Petroleum Hotel looked as though the snows had just melted. Debris, like flotsam on a beach, was everywhere. In the yard outside the large, hot kitchens, a ragged boy was limply shovelling a huge pile of coal through a rough hole in the wall to keep the black fires burning. Inside, pale bulbs glowed ineffectually in the gloom as unmentionable dishes were prepared by Swelter-like cooks wearing blue overalls.

The windows of the residential part were double glazed, two complete metal-framed windows six inches apart, the corridors lined with ancient hot water radiators – all of which indicated that it would be ferociously cold in winter. Running water came on at 8 P.M. for two hours, and tomorrow from 9 A.M. to ten. (Water seemed to be a problem in Urumqi.) Our half of the hotel, for westerners, seemed smarter than the other side, in which Chinese and Asiatic folk sat in the semi-darkness of dim electric bulbs watching us curiously.

After lunch in a large upstairs dining room looking out over the poplar trees, we went to the Chinese Mountaineering Association (CMA) depot to inspect our equipment, which had already arrived by air.

The depot was a row of dusty lock-up garages surrounded by decrepit concrete buildings in a run-down courtyard. A gang of labourers worked ineffectually on some unfathomable task involving reinforced concrete frames in a hole in the courtyard floor. A woman cleared her throat and nose loudly and thoroughly, placed the result on her tongue and let it slide slowly off into the dust. A male worker followed suit. They peered curiously into our lock-up as we counted the boxes. Bob Wood was amazed to find them all there.

We were not very well: Robbo still had diarrhoea, Ann looked doubtful and was not really eating and I had been enduring a bad headache and sore throat for the past three days. The food was good and spicy, washed down with lots of weak but gloriously cold beer.

We took the beer outside into the golden evening and sat beside the orange and yellow fish, amid groups of old men drinking endless mugs of tea. They were chatting quietly, admiring the strutting infants of proud young parents on evening strolls, topping up their lidded porcelain tea mugs from large, flower-patterned hotel thermos flasks.

The whole of the People's Republic of China works to Beijing time regardless of longitude. As we travelled westwards, time was slipping, everything happening later in the day according to how far west we went. I could not imagine how this helped the administration — for it seemed too ridiculous to be an administrative expediency. Civil servants across China could not all work from nine in the morning to four in the afternoon in order to be able to phone one another during office hours. In the far west, they would be getting up at the equivalent of two in the morning and finishing work at lunchtime. Perhaps it was a way of imposing the rule of Beijing on the outlying fiefdoms. In Urumqi, the sun had already fallen well behind the centralized norm.

Dawn occurred the next morning at 8 o'clock Beijing time. We left the hotel at 9, crammed into a minibus and Range-Rover. The city streets were slowly waking, stunned inhabitants stumbling indifferently from bed to work place. After three-quarters of an hour of bumping over urban pot-holes, we fell in behind a convoy of battered lorries and filed slowly out of Urumqi in a wake of acrid exhaust smoke.

We entered a barren landscape of dry scrub, fat-tailed sheep and isolated factories with piles of coal and gravel. One by one, the lorries turned from the road taking more coal and gravel to these piles, the choking blue clouds of diesel fumes going with them.

All day we drove through mountains and desert, several oases of green trees, crops and running water, and up and through three ranges of dry brown hills with hairpin bends and landslips. Between the ranges there was stony, very hot desert, mountains with snow on the peaks and lakes of standing water. We drove for over nine hours and about five hundred kilometres, through an amazing variety of country. The first few hundred kilometres reminded me of the hills and heather of north-west Scotland, but very much hotter with closer cropped vegetation. These relatively lush foothills soon became the more extreme and singular desert terrain.

The frequent culverts under the road appeared incapable of taking the large amounts of flash-flood water that seemed to have frequently swept away the bumpy tarmacadam in great bites. In several places, the road was completely washed away, forcing us to take to the dusty desert.

Lunch, in an oasis village, our first break from sanitized civilization, was a testing experience – particularly as two of the group were already ill. We parked at a dusty crossroads beside market stalls selling melons, vegetables and strings of hacked meat gathering flies in the hot sun. Jin Jun plunged off into unsavoury back streets, to shacks with outside fires and huge brass woks, where the red of freshly chopped meat was speckled black with flies. Tables under awnings were occupied by Asiatic men chomping happily through piles of rough-cut home-made noodles.

Jin Jun spoke to a proprietress and ordered a stir-fried meal, with tea. This meal, for all the shock of the surroundings, was as digestively safe as could be managed, especially as Jin Jun had thoughtfully brought chop sticks from the last hotel.

The tea was vital and excellent, hot, sweet, from a battered blackened kettle placed onto the wooden table top. The food was first class: vegetables and finely sliced meat fried up very quickly in a red-hot steaming wok, flames licking around the edges, and long strings of thick, freshly chopped, boiled noodles – huge steaming portions on chipped plates, greasy with fat and soy sauce.

Despite lots of adverse comments, everyone tucked in and enjoyed it, except Robbo who tried to eat, but made himself ill again. We were transformed from spectators to players instantly, keeping fingers crossed that our digestive systems would be able to cope.

We drove on, through hot, dry mountains to village petrol stops that once were staging places in the northern loop of the Old Silk Road. Suddenly, where waters from the distant mountains flowed, there were running brooks and fields of grain harvested by hand with threshing floors of sun-baked mud and men winnowing, throwing the chaff up to the wind; and rice paddies being planted by hand prior to being filled with water.

This sudden fertility was in narrow strips, totally dependent upon water from the mountains. Changes in mountain water courses have destroyed whole towns, and others have been buried during ferocious sandstorms. These lost towns were ruthlessly plundered of extraordinarily well-preserved early documents, wall paintings, sculptures and silks, by nineteenth-century European explorers, invaluable artefacts which now grace Western museums.

We were now well beyond the old Chinese Imperial Highway and Jade Gate (at Anxi, north-west of Yunnan) and leaving Marco Polo's China, the land of the Seres (literally 'the Silks' – the medieval name for the Chinese), by the so-called Silk Road. Pushed west into a barbaric backwater by the Khan, the Silk Road was not originally intended to open China for trade with Europe. The Chinese have never felt a need for communication with the outside world – and do so only when it is to their advantage. In this case, the road was built so that the emperor could acquire fast Ferghana horses (an Iranian breed) to match those of the Hun raiders who were causing trouble from the north.

By the latter half of the twelfth century, the Silk Road was so well established and prosperous that it was said 'a young girl could walk right across Asia without being molested.' This may still be the case; certainly no-one attempted to molest us.

After brief passages through field and pasture we again entered the arid lands. Gangs of labourers, men and women exiled to keep the road open, lived in sun-baked mud huts behind boulder walls built to divert desert flood waters.

The size of the country was staggering. The road, as it had been for hundreds of years, was the artery along which all life flowed, and alongside which all life occurred. In the irrigated areas cattle and sheep were herded, shaded by the poplar trees in the road-side ditch along which waters flow. In the arid lands drivers tinkered disconsolately with the engines of their broken down old lorries. Battered buses were overloaded with old men in embroidered Turkish-looking skull caps, with women wearing shawls and brightly coloured red, violet and blue dresses. Lorries drove at us, their passengers standing up behind the cab enjoying the cool wind, waving whenever they saw that we were westerners.

We drove past military camps: rows and rows of green lorries parked in lines behind smart brick gates. I was forbidden to take cine film of them, or of any bridges.

The hotel at Korla, as seemed to be the norm, was under construction. Also, the bits that had been completed were being renovated. The patios and paths outside were littered with building materials, tools and debris. The corridor outside my room had three men hacking the wall back to the brickwork, having ripped out several door frames; a fourth man with board and shovel was working a cement mixer. Otherwise it looked like a normal hotel corridor; a scene from Fawlty Towers in which O'Reilly has been given *carte blanche*.

The finished parts needed attention: tiles had fallen from walls leaving irregular patches of rough concrete; blocked drains spread pools of stagnant water across tiled surfaces; badly laid carpets were frayed and ripped.

The room decor however was fine: a smart red velvet cover with black piping over a TV set which did not work, a telephone, the usual huge thermos flask, a yellow and white plastic reading lamp, a spittoon half filled with water and clean bedding with large towels for use as blankets. As in Urumqi, the windows were double skinned for the bitter winters. (Now it was very hot and dry – a most extreme climate.)

I still had my sore throat and headache. Also a problem with the Liaison Officer seemed to be brewing; he was ignoring us and had started a trial of strength with Jin Jun.

The LO (Mr Wang – but we called him the 'LO' throughout) was from the Chinese Mountaineering Association, an organization unpopular with western mountaineering groups because of overcharging and poor administration – to the extent that CIST (China International Sport Travel), for which Jin Jun worked, seemed to have become the façade for CMA operations. We knew about the CMA and were alarmed at their involvement with us, and were determined that we would back up Jin Jun if it became necessary.

* * *

We got up at dawn the next day, 8.15 Beijing time, and were on the road by 9.15, blasting along a flat, dry plain with snow-capped mountains to the north. Sometimes the plain was gravel-covered and dry, or with sparse green tussock grass and thorn brush. Floods had washed large sections of the tarmac away and we proceeded for miles in a huge dust cloud, bouncing and swerving along a rough track. Teams of men and women shovelled earth into the ruts and only once did we pass a road roller – surrounded by labourers with long handled shovels. We stopped at a small village for the drivers to have a break, then at another crossroads village for lunch – a roadside restaurant where the food looked lethal but was actually rather good. A huge fish was served to two men on the next table, from a fish farm in the middle of the desert. I was fascinated by the idea of desert fish. They invited me to join them, insisting on my being given a set of chop sticks and becoming their guest.

Outside a traffic jam had developed. Lorries, horses, donkeys and oxen – and carts pulled by horses, donkeys and oxen – with motorcycles, buses and bicycles, were a shouting, hooting, dusty confusion that took over half an hour to clear.

Everyone looked very Muslim – with few Han Chinese. I doubted whether much Mandarin would be spoken. The loud music from the café and bazaar stall radios sounded Arabic and I felt that there would be very little love lost between these two very different cultures.

On the road again, the heat had caused miniature whirlwinds to throw up small dust clouds which ran like a mad person to and fro across the ground, swirling and dodging irregularly. Pools of water stood stagnant, or left ruins of salts and cracked mud where flood waters had evaporated. The donkey carts tapped slowly past, old men nodding curiously, wives bundled in brightly coloured scarves and thick padded clothes, their wide-eyed children following our progress from the safety of mother's shoulder.

We continued to be the object of much good-natured interest. Everyone wanted their photo taken – indeed some potentially good shots were ruined by those intent on finding out what goes on inside a camera lens, staring fixedly up the tube from a few feet away.

Conrad's ebony physique also remained a great attraction. His star qualities increased as we went westwards, causing everyone to stop stock-still and gape, all their usual natural good manners forgotten.

As the amazing countryside rolled past, we drank warm Cola (a gift from the company) and listened to a mixture of tyre and engine noise plus loud but barely discernible pop music on the land cruiser's stereo. The driver and the LO had been enduring western music for the past few days – Queen, from the film *Highlander*, the Eurythmics and Dionne Warwick. I had requested silence as my choice of music and had pointed out that what we had been playing might not be to the Chinese taste. I was amused when the LO slipped his own cassette into the machine, an auto-reverse so that we heard each side several times.

Their first tape, the box labelled in Chinese, featured a flawless voice as light as a bird yet devoid of any character. Being unable to read the singer's name or any of the song titles, after prolonged exposure, my imagination took over. She was called Mimi Kitten-Flower and told stories of her amorous adventures amid the lotus blossoms and fountains of south-eastern China. She led her men on shamelessly.

Jin Jun later translated a song to me: a wholesome, smooth-voiced man singing of beautiful, large-eyed, eighteen-year-old girls. My imagination may not have been too far wrong.

Remote Chinese towns are generally closed to westerners until they have been 'modernized'. This process seemed to entail bulldozing the city centre, with its bazaar, winding streets and alleyways. A modernized town has wide roads with central reservations that soon become overgrown, modern clocktowers, spaces for statues of Chairman Mao, dusty parks and a sprawl of single-storey concrete buildings with metal rods like loose threads protruding from the roofs. As closed towns were built mostly of mud-bricked houses surrounded by mud-and-straw-walled gardens, the bulldozers made short work of the clearance.

Passing through an un-modernized town, beyond the line of poplar trees that marked the watercourse along which the town had developed, the road would plunge into medieval turmoil. Modernization did not extend to creating a ring road, but did at least speed up the through-flow.

In the closed (un-modernized) town of Kuqa, several lorries were parked outside our hotel, the drivers sitting in their cabs smoking and chatting, occasionally leaning on their hooters to make up for the unaccustomed peace of the lorry park. On the road, lorries swept past the tattered canopies of the donkey taxis, herds of sheep and pedestrians, blasting out greetings to their comrades in the lorry park. All this took place below my window. Each fraternal greeting was punctiliously answered by strident horn blasts, which made sleep sporadic and difficult.

We were staying on the first floor of a Turkestan transport café.

After hearing John Day's reasons for climbing mountains, I had described him in my diary as 'a cynical pessimist'. He had rejected adamantly the old chestnut 'because they are there', going on to expound what seemed to me a negative philosophy that I found depressing.

During expeditions John declared himself cold, tired, hungry, fed up and lonely. The misery for him seemed unrelenting, with very little enjoyment in the doing. His reason for going on expeditions was so that when he got back home, normal life felt wonderful.

Despite my dislike of John's negativism, there is an element of truth in what he said. Travelling is lonely, a continual passing-through, a transient spectatorship of life, with only rare participation. You reflect from your own isolation on what is going on around. You relate and compare it to yourself, to your own experience.

Unlike the solitary traveller, we however were travelling as a group, regarding the world at which we were looking as a curiosity, as visitors would look at animals in a zoo.

It is said that the more a person travels the less they know; travel can be the postponement of real life, putting off getting to grips with reality by wandering from one curiosity to the next. We were having to do this, but not by choice as we wanted very much to get on with the reality of climbing. Constructive educational travelling should achieve some result: seeing the process of living a little more clearly or perhaps learning what should be done with the years that are left. It would take the extreme of the mountain to give us such a perspective on ourselves.

In real life, most people adopt a particular lifestyle and stick with it, catching it like a bus and going at its pace. We only experience the reality of the world outside if our 'vehicle' breaks down or crashes, or if we transfer to another, better style. We had deliberately left our home lifestyles and were developing a substitute 'team' home life to help us face the challenges that lay ahead.

A solitary traveller has usually no sort of protective lifestyle to hide inside, and without the comfort of home life and its routines, is totally exposed. The only form of protection is to keep moving, to pass by anything unfortunate. It is a strange position, totally exposed to real life but unaffected by it, skipping quickly through.

We were skipping through Xinjiang Province, kept from the total exposure of the road by our team spirit. We were spectators champing at the bit to get on with the work of climbing our mountain.

This enormous and daunting task made our incredible journey across China seem a discomfort to be endured rather than the experience of a lifetime. The team were more 'doers' than 'see'ers', and for some, the frustration of inactivity was not outweighed by the fascinations of the journey. If John Day expected the whole expedition to be unrelenting misery, perhaps he was suffering under the pressure of this expectation. If so, I wondered why he came on expeditions. I also fervently hoped he was wrong.

The transport hotel at Kuqa had hot showers, in a separate block behind the hotel. A huge coal-fired furnace like a mine engine, gleaming brass pipes, valves and pressure gauges, made hot water for the decreed two hours each evening. The two men on the door were friendly as I strolled along the wooden duck-boards across the sun-baked mud backyard of the hotel, with towel, clean clothes and soap. One showed me into the darkness of the single-storeyed concrete building. The line of cubicles was unlit with white sheets across each for privacy.

They were all in use.

He waved me towards the ladies' shower house. I hesitated, so he went across to ask permission on my behalf. A gnarled weather-beaten woman in brown trousers and dirty white blouse emerged from the entrance, beaming a welcome. With many toothless smiles and encouraging pats on the back, she ushered me into the deserted ladies' half of the shower house. The copious hot water washed away the dust and weariness of the road and I emerged clean and refreshed.

After supper Jerry and I went off into the town to take photographs in the evening sunshine.

A line of eight farriers were packing up after a long day shoeing ponies. The last customer, eyes bulging with indignation, tongue protruding from its mouth, was trussed up, suspended under a hockey goal structure with all four hooves off the ground.

It was the end of a medieval market day: families gathering up their goods, setting off for home sitting on the rear platforms of small, two-wheeled carts. Fathers with weatherbeaten brown faces, embroidered hats and long whiskers, flicked donkeys and ponies homewards with long whips made of stick and cord. Mothers and children perched behind, wrapped in brightly coloured shawls, the children's eyes shining with life. Along the road donkeys and empty carts, diagonally parked, some in the charge of children, waited patiently for their owners. Before the golden sun fell beyond the trees, the last business of the day was done and shutters were placed before doors and windows, the night bringing stillness and sleep.

We had started late as the sun rose on an overcast grey sky. The temperature rose slowly with the sun. The rough edges of the road were thick with donkey carts. We stopped on an embankment overlooking a wide, flat space at the edge of a small village. There were hundreds of donkeys, some tethered together, others harnessed patiently to carts filled with huge loads of rough-hewn timber. The morning sun was hazy, shining through a mist that had risen up from the irrigated fields with the dawn. The noise and bustle of this donkey market — where men argued for bargains, women breast-fed babies and small boys watched over donkeys, goats and scrawny sheep – seemed to fade into silence as the centuries fell away.

Down the highway, more donkey carts were on their way, overtaking one another, causing lorries (and ourselves) to hoot and brake and the donkey drivers to flick their whips accurately into the left eye of their animal to make it swerve over to the edge of the road. Long tree-lined roads stretched off away from the road into the flatness to the villages from whence came the carts.

The greenery around Kuqa gave way to gravel desert with pale red and grey hills to the north and barren flatness to the south. Occasionally a shade of green appeared like organic down on the grey of the desert, and in the west the next river appeared as a line of green trees that stood out suddenly in the heat haze.

Lunch was taken in the echoing front room of a large hotel amid the remains of old meals: fish bones, vegetables and animal bones on the concrete floor. In the kitchen, over a coal fire a huge cauldron of water boiled briskly and a freshly slaughtered pig lay pink and bloody on the floor. The meal, with gallons of scalding tea, was very good.

We were driving towards the USSR border and the LO became even more sensitive about my filming anything vaguely military: towns, bridges or railway stations. Jin Jun was unwell and had been gobbling down all the medication he could obtain.

Our carefully calculated medical packs had to last another two months so medication was very valuable. I gave him half the throat lozenges that Ann had given me in Urumqi, and was irritated to see him go straight to Nick Moore (with Robbo, one of our two medically trained people) for more. In addition Jin Jun was swallowing lots of aspirin which he should have used for gargling to anaesthetize his sore throat.

At our next stop he went off to the local hospital.

After all this, we reckoned Jin Jun's original symptoms must have become swamped by those of a drug overdose.

At Aksu, in a splendid Arabic-looking hotel with two turrets at each side and a circular tower at the front, we encountered the Chinese People's Army drinking tea in the huge upstairs sitting room. Over fifty officers in animated discussion were taking part in an Officers' Study Day, remarkably and amusingly similar to the usual British Army version.

I could imagine the proceedings: a series of presentations on the Soviet threat, detailing the numbers of their tanks, artillery and their deployment options – which, as the border is only about 100 kilometres to the north-east of Aksu, would be into their area. The home-team reactions to Soviet border incursions would be discussed: getting forces quickly from huge barracks with their endless lines of vehicles that spread across the outskirts of many of the towns through which we had passed, and consideration of the logistics required to keep them supplied.

The presentations finished (given by thrusting staff officers keen to catch their superior's eye), the general himself would have delivered a masterly summing up and tea would have been brought in, the signal for lively informal discussion. At this point in the proceedings, we appeared, incongruous in brightly coloured shorts, baseball sun-hats and T shirts.

We gathered before supper in Bob's room to drink warm Chinese beer. We played word association: 'Word association, football, match, burning, dragon, China, Karakoram, avalanche, death.' The chorus, and the joke, was 'Karakoram, avalanche, death'. The reality of what was to come was very much on our minds, making us irritable, but was very rarely coming directly to the surface, as for some reason it did on this occasion.

The dining room was across a dusty square, where soldiers in green uniforms, peaked caps and incongruous cuban-heeled black shoes, stood chatting. The meals were becoming very similar; the cooked dishes oily, often with the tang of the coal fire over which they had been cooked. The fish was very bony and usually served in a greasy sauce. Tomatoes were sliced and served sprinkled with white sugar; there were green beans with chili, tomatoes, onions and sauce, meatloaf, chopped chicken and, as fillers, suet dumplings and sometimes rice or noodles. Fruit, mainly watermelon, was usually served at the end of each meal.

I drank gallons of tea with every meal to replace the perspiration lost in the dry heat of the desert. We took our own chop sticks to meals, particularly to the roadside restaurants, in the pious hope that somehow they would save us from digestive disaster. After a few days they must have become far more insanitary than the ones provided.

After breakfasting on yoghurt, hot milk, sweet bread and cakes, rice soup and plates of cucumber and tomatoes, I had a long chat with Ann about John Day.

I was very concerned about my relationship with John. We seemed to bring out the worst in each other, and because of several unfortunate sharp exchanges of words, I had decided to avoid him whenever possible in order to keep the peace. But we were going to have to live and work closely together for a fortnight as, with Conrad and Nick, we explored the unknowns of the Upper Shakesgam Valley. I was worried, baffled as to how to go about establishing good relations with him, and needed advice.

Chatting with Ann confirmed many of my deductions: that John was under pressure because the trip followed on from the long period he had spent in Africa cooped up with another small group of soldiers. He was naturally cynical, the extra tension accentuating both this cynicism and his bite. Unfortunately, as seems to be usual where personalities are concerned, there was no simple solution to my problem. Avoidance, Ann felt, was no solution to the problem; besides I might have to rely on John, one of the most experienced mountaineers in the team, for my survival in the mountains.

The ball, in the game of bouncing egos that seemed to be developing, was in my court. I would have to bite my lip as often as I could to keep the peace. The emotional chemistry was such that I knew there would be times when I would not be able to prevent myself biting back, but at least now I knew the situation. For John's part, I assumed that he found my behaviour equally unacceptable and aggravating and that probably he was biting his lip too.

I am a person who needs to be liked, who to an extent plays to the gallery and needs to be appreciated. Not being liked or appreciated makes it very hard for me to be committed and work hard. I am in this sense a typical Sagittarian, the archer, the centaur, a juggler, throwing a myriad beautifully coloured balls into the air, saying, 'Look at me, isn't this fun!' hoping to entertain and gain approval and applause.

Sagittarians and Dragons are remarkably similar: extrovert and likeable, which makes not being liked particularly upsetting. With the Dragon there is an extra depth, the inner strength and confidence that makes it the most popular Chinese birth sign.

In the face of the challenge of both the mountain and my job within the team, and up against an unfriendly John, whom the others respected and whose reactions to me I could not understand. I did not feel at all like a Dragon. My juggler's regalia was beginning to feel more like the costume of a clown.

We drove west for another eleven hours across flat desert with red and grey hills in the distance to the north. We lunched at a solitary halt with tumble weed rolling through the thick dust and single-storey mud-brick buildings at the foot of a crumbling cliff. In the afternoon, commuters to another Ugyar market filled the highway for some twenty miles with identical donkey carts, clopping towards us, their numbers swelling from unseen villages to the north.

For the last five hours of this long day we bumped slowly and painfully across hot, arid desert where the road was broken in several places. As we lurched from the road on frequent detours around where it had been washed away we were completely enveloped in a dust cloud, using the windscreen wipers and seeing very little. Lorries with huge trailers wallowed in the bumps and dips, appearing and disappearing into the hot, choking brown dust like cargo ships in heavy seas. Inside the vehicles we perspired freely, the dust catching in our throats and grating gently between our teeth.

The Taklimakan Desert, across which we were travelling, is broken only by oases centred on rivers flowing from the surrounding mountains. Lines of poplars break the horizon and on the outskirts of these thriving settlements, fields and crops appear, watered by a system of channels leading from the main river – over which solid concrete bridges carry the highway.

These oases were vital for the 'Silk Road' and have flourished for over two thousand years. The distances between each oasis and the severity of the desert in between must have made the journey of the camel caravans a very demanding way to earn a living – even without the danger from marauding bandits. On the outskirts of the villages, the vegetation faded to the tougher grasses and bushes of the desert, and herds of sheep were watched and watered by brown-faced men wearing dark blue or black suits, with matching peaked caps.

Over the crest of another hill we stopped by a small group of huts, a stream running beside the road and three large piles of rough-hewn coal in lumps several feet across. A small boy perched atop the biggest pile waved to us. A donkey cart stopped and the boy scrambled down, broke up a lump with a sledge hammer, which seemed impossibly large for him, and shovelled the bits onto the space behind the driver.

The mining tradition in this area goes back a long way. Marco Polo, writing carefully for a readership whose ignorance could easily have led them to discount much of what he had to relate – but who, ironically, were perfectly happy to be regaled with tales of sorcery and dreadful pagan practices – described coal, which was, at that time, unknown in Europe, as: 'large black stones which burn like logs. If you put them on a fire in the evening and make them catch well, I tell you that they will keep fire all night.'

The LO and driver carefully washed the desert dust from our land cruiser. They were very proud of it; as a new foreign vehicle it conferred much status onto them. We sliced open a water melon. A woman with a kind smile carefully picked up the skins and pips, making us feel very irresponsible at having littered the roadside. We arrived in Kashgar, the place where east once met west, where Peter Fleming was impressed by bodyguards wielding machine-gun and executioners' sword, and from where Henry's fiancée Catherine and her chaperone, Ann, would fly back to Beijing. From here, we would leave on the last and roughest part of our road journey. I was still not feeling too good after a sequence of bad nights with a headache and severe chest cough.

The notorious Chinese Mountaineering Association had now

taken over from CIST, but despite the floods our equipment had arrived by road, so we went immediately to the CMA depot to start checking and repacking.

Henry, who had helped to design the special high calorie rations we would eat on the mountain, laid them out in batches according to the various phases of the mountaineering. He was worried about how much the camels would be able to carry and, unknown to the rest of us, was lightening the load by adjusting what we would eat. (This only came to light several weeks later when, deep in the Karakorams, we discovered he had removed all the Rollos, leaving mostly boring boiled sweets as the main source of extra calories – to give 5,600 calories each per day.)

Rations were the biggest part of our supplies, about half the total weight. Henry was batching the rations for the different phases: for the walk-in, the exploration of the Upper Shakesgam Valley, the mountaineering and the walk-out at the end. Rations would be dumped in batches along our route.

He and Nellie beavered away in the hot sunshine lining up hundreds of packets of chocolate bars, dehydrated meats and rice, biscuits, dried milk, lavatory paper, salt, sugar, coffee, tea bags and the like. Each box was weighed then marked with batch and weight for the telling moment, in a few days, of the first loading onto doubtless protesting camels.

Robbo, Nick, Jerry and Andy patiently erected all the tents, checking guy ropes, zips and poles, repairing and replacing where necessary. Nick and Andy singed their eyebrows testing each stove; Conrad, our radio expert, carefully checked all the hand-held transceivers for communicating between the different camps. I weighed all the camera gear and film, trying to work out how much I would need for each phase.

As I had never done anything remotely similar, this calculation was not easy. I thought I could physically manage to shoot a maximum of ten one-hundred foot rolls of cine film a day. I reckoned therefore on an average of about five rolls per day for each of our forty days in the mountains, with some days when I never shot at all. Henry, concerned about the overall weight, needed to know exactly what all the film gear would weigh. In my uncertainty

I preferred to see what he could allow me. We arrived at a mutually acceptable figure, which was very heavy, one complete camel's load of filming gear in all.

I overestimated. At the end of the expedition I still had a lot of film unshot.

We started on our own equipment. Long-looped cords were tied onto all zips so they could be used wearing thick woollen mittens. We had two pairs of heavy gloves, woollen mittens and Gore-Tex outers, and would also wear light thermal inner gloves all the time, to prevent skin sticking to cold metal. The heavy gloves were tied together with cord and worn like Paddington Bear, inside the sleeve of the jacket, across the shoulder and down the other arm to hang down securely when not being worn. The loss of gloves on the mountain could prove a serious mistake.

At the hotel our rooms became impossibly jumbled with thermal underwear, thermometers, thermos flasks, ice axes and ice hammers, crampons, duvet jackets, quilted trousers, sleeping bags, bivvie bags, inflatable sleeping mats, cooking pots, lightweight walking boots and the heavy plastic outer climbing boots and the thickly insulated leather inner boots upon which we would depend above nineteen or twenty thousand feet . . . It was a nightmare of personal administration which made me feel a little ill.

I was just about coping with my photographic gear, but the sudden arrival of another deluge of vital equipment was too much. Everyone else set about adjusting their harnesses to fit, taping up loose straps, packing and repacking small items into handy pouches and loading bergens so that everything was exactly to hand and no void was left unfilled. I wandered from room to room, looking on and trying to keep calm.

When you have to carry everything on your back, a well-packed bergen is as important as properly fitting boots. Soldiers take this a stage further: it becomes just as important to look well organized, 'jacked up'. Appearing to be jacked up is a matter of personal pride and prestige.

A well-packed bergen becomes a high fashion accessory bestowing the respect of peers upon its wearer. Huge efforts go into being jacked up; I was wondering, as I surveyed with dismay my own pile of gear, whether the extra few moments saved when fumbling for the matches or one's penknife, were worth all this intense and preoccupied preparation.

There were two other dimensions to this: it was the first and vital stage of the mountaineering; everyone was pleased at last to be getting on with the job. Also there was a slightly worrying side to it: everyone was getting heavily involved with their own equipment, sorting themselves out and making sure that they had what they needed. There was much wandering around inspecting what others were doing, then rushing back to do the same thing if it seemed to be a good idea. There was a whiff of selfishness in the air.

Quartermaster Bob Wood came round from time to time to help. I confessed to being baffled as to what kit to pack for the walk-in and exploration of the Shakesgam Valley so Bob gave me his expert thoughts. Everyone else spent hours making sure that, come what may, they had what they needed carefully packed.

Bob Wood was a sergeant (aged twenty-eight) who taught mountaineering, hill walking, rock climbing and canoeing to young soldiers. Softly spoken, of wiry, slender build, with brown hair, he had the clean-cut good looks of an American fifties rock'n'roll star.

In his last job, with the Royal Engineers Commando Squadron, Bob had fought in the Falklands War, doing combat engineer tasks like clearing minefields and booby traps so that the infantry could attack the enemy positions. The engineering had been complex, arduous and always under appalling conditions, either from the weather or the enemy. Before the actual battles, while other units were awaiting their chance to fight, the Royal Engineers were working furiously to create usable jetties and fuel depots, and install water purifying plants as the Argentine Air Force pressed home their frighteningly successful bombing raids.

As the quartermaster, responsible for determining what was needed, purchasing it all and keeping tabs on it throughout the journey, Bob was ideal. He was careful, patient and thorough, and had researched for months in making up the equipment list to ensure that we would have the best.

In the group, Bob was quiet, thoughtful and slightly reserved, going along with everything that was mooted, asking questions, but mostly keeping any worries he might have to himself. On an Austrian train, during our sociable trip to the Eiger, he had in private expressed concern to me over the financial arrangements for the trip. He was to marry a beautiful, dark-eyed French girl on our return, and suddenly being told to take out a bank loan for five thousand pounds had made him doubtful about whether he should be coming with us.

I wondered whether, beneath his calmness, Bob was harbouring any other worries about what he had let himself in for, or about the organization of the expedition. He had been involved with the planning for over a year and the unexpected, last-minute shock over money had upset him. I wondered whether he had other worries and was keeping quiet out of loyalty to Henry.

During the few days we were in Kashgar, a South Korean climbing team arrived at the hotel after an unsuccessful attempt on the Kongur. The snow had been deep and the sun hot, preventing the formation of a supportive crust of ice over which they could walk at altitude. Wading through waist-deep snow had exhausted them and they had retreated with several bad cases of frost-bite (from wet feet). They were thin and fit-looking, very deeply tanned (a striking characteristic of high altitude mountaineering) and limping.

One climber was an attractive girl who told me she had walked for ten days back to the road:

'You know, like a race walker but with tiny steps, very fast because of the pain.'

The Kongur is quite close to the road so this must have been a protracted, slow and painful journey. Everyone was impressed with the girl:

'Seriously tanned,' said Andy Aspinall, '. . . and tasty.'

We were also a little subdued by our first contact with mountaineers fresh from big mountains, especially as the Koreans had been climbing only a few days' drive down the road. We had before us twice their drive and a ten-day, one-hundred-mile walk, before even catching a glimpse of our mountain. Our perception of the isolation and enormity of what we were attempting was swiftly changing; from a concept which presented practical problems which we had to solve, into a reality that we would soon have to face, a huge challenge without solution, which could only be endured.

The times for meals were getting still later. Breakfast in Xian had been at 7 A.M. In Urumqi breakfast was at 8.30, in Korla and Kuqa 9 and now, in Kashgar, at the absurd hour of 10. Dawn in Kashgar was at 9.30 and the hotel bar remained open until the sophisticated hour of 2 A.M. For those interested in their stomachs and late night drinking – rather than the distances travelled by Eratosthenes' camels and shadows cast down wells in Alexandria – the steady progression of meal times as you proceed across Central Asia provides unchallengeable proof that the earth is round, and that we were indeed travelling westwards.

By 0230 everyone had gone to bed, leaving only lone barking dogs to break the silent blackness, a sudden urban void without street lights.

I walked around Kashgar as dawn broke the next morning. A beautiful lake was wreathed in mist, an island linked to rich market gardens on the foreshore by an arched, bow-shaped willow-patterned bridge. On the island, partly shrouded by green trees, pagoda roofs were blue in the early morning, glinting orange as they were touched by the sun. Sleepy gardeners stretched and yawned and a father taught his young son to fish from the dark banks at the foot of the slopes leading up to the main road.

The town was coming to life on a truly golden morning. The clocktower and mosque in Id Kah Square were glowing with colour. Two dentists' surgeries, next door to each other, were opening up, beside a row of barbers' shops. There was also a street of hatters, making splendid Genghis Khan Cossack fur caps. (I bought one for my mother, who wears it on winter evenings as she returns from the swimming pool.)

In one dentist's surgery a young man was fitting gold teeth to rows of plaster casts of stump-toothed gums. A timid girl with a rich red dress and headscarf crept in and was waved unceremoniously into a chair to wait until the great man was ready to attend to her. I smiled and she tilted her head shyly sideways towards me, her smile glinting gold as she waited for more of the same. I hoped that the dentist was not pulling or altering teeth in order to fix gold ornaments in place of serviceable natural ones.

The dentist next door advertised with a splendid hanging craft sign of a head in profile, the face sectioned to reveal in glowing colour the nasal cavities, tongue, teeth and their nerve roots in the jaw bone, the eyeball and its muscles, and the optic nerve. Three girls in white headscarves and white coats ate breakfast from large porcelain bowls, ripping up unleavened bread and dunking the strips into their tea. One sat eating in the wooden dentist's chair, a pedal-powered, articulated string-driven drill by her left elbow. Another was reading a lurid-looking magazine and the third was melting amalgam in a metal crucible using a gas torch.

That evening Robbo lost a filling from one of the teeth on his lower jaw. With great glee Nick Moore thrust him into a chair and summoned the rest of us. He had spent a day with an Army dentist at Chelsea Barracks, and had filled teeth – although he much regretted that no hapless soldier had presented with teeth so bad that they required pulling.

The tooth removal process had only been described to him: you have to push the tooth back into the socket before you pull, and beginners are recommended to lie their patients down so that, with boot-prints on the dental bib, good purchase for a strong pull can be obtained. Nick's keenness was alarming.

Nick's DIY dentist kit had mirrors, scrapers, prodders and clamps; he looked reassuringly competent as he mixed the cement and cleared the cavity for a temporary filling. Robbo was exceptionally stoic.

Nick's dentistry work lasted Robbo for the rest of the trip, through minus forty degree temperatures, alternated with hot cups of coffee, hundreds of packets of Army biscuits and stews made from gravelly glacier water.

CHAPTER 6

The Shakedown

As the sun rose on Friday, 21 August we were bowling along roads that were sometimes good, then, where flooding had swept the surface away, suddenly very bad. The desert was at work, predatory snouts of sand dunes beside the road steadily engulfing hard-won irrigated agricultural land.

Mountains appeared ahead in the mist, some with snowy tops.

After five hours, we arrived at the Mountain Centre hotel in Yechung: echoing tiled floors, dim, bare light bulbs and huge sacks of vegetables piled under the stairs beside the foyer. Curious locals sat around eyeing us blankly. They had seen western climbers before and were interested not in us as people, but in what fresh curiosities we might have brought with us.

One of the waitresses was dark-haired with a lovely coy smile and waist-length black hair coiled underneath a headscarf. After several attempts at communication we established that her name was something like 'Taramarka'.

The food was fine, except for very black, sliced cold meat with doubtful looking, transparent fat. Andy Aspinall, helping himself to a large portion, commented that as we consumed the pile of black meat we'd probably find the rat's head placed carefully in the middle as the ultimate delicacy.

After supper we walked around Yechung. It was another 'closed town' where westerners were not usually permitted. Opposite the hotel, from a new open-air theatre of tiles and concrete, distorted pop music blared out and a crowd was queueing for some sort of show. Vendors on the entrance steps were selling dried nuts and various trinkets. Robbo, just recovered from illness caused by dates bought from a street vendor in Xian, shook his head good naturedly when urged to give these offerings a try.

Robbo, Ian Roberts, a corporal in 59 Commando Squadron Royal Engineers, was just a touch under six feet tall and powerfully built. As the assistant quartermaster, he had come over to Hong Kong a month before the rest of us, to receive and pack the freight. He had also to find and purchase a long list of essentials himself, then pack and despatch the lot onto a train to Beijing. When we arrived in Hong Kong he had been tired out, and very glad to see us.

Robbo was from North Wales, brought up amongst the peaks and rock faces of Snowdonia. As a youth he had been a bit of a fighter, taking on and beating local hard cases who fancied themselves in a brawl. The Royal Engineers had redirected his aggression constructively, building bridges, roads, airfields and the many other things that combat engineers do, first as a paratrooper in 9 Parachute Squadron, and then as a commando in 59 Squadron. The challenges of climbing and mountaineering were just part of Robbo's wide-ranging interests in physical outdoor pursuits.

With shy smile, gentle manner and quiet self-effacement, Robbo spoke softly and carefully, pronouncing and emphasizing his words distinctly. He was patient and diplomatic, yet never shrank from making his point of view known.

As well as helping Bob Wood with the equipment, Robbo was one of the lead climbers. I had the strong and certain feeling that he was one of those truly hard men whose inner strength would always emerge when needed.

Yechung formed a large grid with very wide tarmac streets and all-purpose ditches running to either side; poplar trees were planted every fifteen feet and there was a footpath on the outside. Thousands of people were out in the warmth of the evening, walking, squatting by the roadside or on bicycles or carts. The occasional lorry blasted through the crowds, horn sounding, speed never altering for one second. A cyclist's wobble or a donkey driver's moment of inattention would be fatal.

As we walked, we acquired a crowd of small boys who poked my camera equipment and made remarks that amused them all greatly. The crowd grew until a policeman in a shiny, army-style uniform gave us and our entourage a hard stare before shooing the boys away. For a few minutes we were left to walk on our own.

The bazaar at the centre of town was divided into different sections according to trade and produce. It was now deep twilight and the shops were closing or shut. The fast-food sector was in full swing; bare dim light bulbs illuminated kebab stalls, bread stands, fearsome butchers and dark, bustling restaurants where the food was cooked out front, flames licking under sizzling woks and delicious nan bread coming piping fresh from the sides of mud ovens.

The poorest vendors were cheerful, ragged women squatting in the dirt with a dozen tiny birds lying on metal trays, carefully dressed and cooked, the grease shining green in the lamplight. Their customers squatted beside the lamps grinning at us as they pulled the tiny birds apart and ate.

It had grown very dark indeed. There were no street lights and the traffic had not abated. Cyclists rang their bells continuously and rode swiftly, black shapes dodging across the intersections, weaving through the pedestrians. Strings of bells draped around horse-bus ponies' necks warned of their brisk approach. The only dim lights were those of the relentless lorries, speeding through with horns blasting.

The darkness gave us a degree of anonymity. Our entourage dwindled to one small boy, bare-footed in an over-sized dark blue hand-me-down suit and huge matching cap, who watched our every move through saucer eyes.

Back at the hotel the electricity was off. The corridors and the entrance partially blocked with piles of cabbages, onions, peppers and a huge sack of garlic, echoed with the continual shouting of locals who seemed to use the place as a club. A TV set in the corridor outside our room had been blasting away, the volume turned up to the maximum for apparently stone-deaf viewers who sat peering only a few feet from the screen. Mercifully the set was now silent, a blank screen in the candlelight. We fumbled in the darkness and went to bed, thankful for the peace and in need of rest.

An hour later, the electricity came back on, and with it the lights, stimulating more shouting in the corridors, bringing back the roar of the television set with a vengeance. At 1 A.M. the door crashed open and the room light snapped on as the others arrived, having stayed on in Kashgar to see the girls off on the plane, then been shown to our room by uncomprehending hotel staff.

Henry entered looking rather tired. Had I a copy of the English translation of our contract with the Chinese? There was some sort of problem over the route we were to take and Henry needed to refer to the agreement.

Several days earlier, there had been a disagreement with the LO over who would do the route planning and navigation. Henry had said firmly that he would do it all himself, so that there could be no argument about how we would climb the mountain. We were in a difficult position as we had only a large-scale map (1:250,000) which was not very accurate. The surveyed part ended at the Chinese-Pakistan border and the rest seemed to be based upon photographs and guesswork.

The LO, however, had a 1:100,000 Chinese government map of the area, but refused to show it to us, for security reasons, he said. We could not therefore judge the accuracy of our map.

After a visit from the LO doing his liaising, the local military commander was said to be concerned about the route we were proposing to take, particularly over our going into the Upper Shakesgam Valley.

Our immediate supposition was that the surly LO, now in his home territory, living with his wife and children in a flat on the second floor of the hotel, had stirred up the military in order to get his own way with us. He was not our favourite person as he seemed to be making life difficult rather than easing the way for us. Our worrying, at the edge of civilization and poised on the brink of the great adventure, had an element of paranoia.

An example of the LO's unhelpfulness was his refusal to use a

Coleman's Peak stove in the mountains. This may sound trivial, showing how tense we were about having to rely upon him, but in mountaineering terms it was important. We were contracted to provide him with a cooker and, rather than use the ordinary pump-up Coleman, he wanted one of our precious and very expensive MSRs. We only had four of these MSRs, very lightweight, easy to manage rapid cookers for use at high altitude. The LO was remaining at the foot of the mountain, at base camp. His rejection of the Coleman seemed churlish. Perhaps he expected us to 'lend' him all sorts of equipment which we, being rich westerners, would not require him to return.

Because we could not speak directly to the LO, our suspicions were piling up, and were not helped by his making no attempt to establish any sort of relationship with us, while we in turn were making little or no effort to get to know him. The longer we stayed in Yechung, the more our suspicions of the LO grew.

Henry had mooted the idea of taking a couple of sheep along as fresh meat on the hoof, for nourishment and also to add interest for those in the team used only to tinned or supermarket food. Two sheep were already tied in the back of a pickup truck outside, price 150 Yuan each. Conversation with locals in the hotel established that the proper price, even for westerners, who are always charged double in China, was 100 Yuan – about £20 as opposed to £30. This rip-off fuelled our suspicions; profiteering was not supposed to exist in China and we objected strongly. Two years earlier, the hotel manager told me, sheep were 10 Yuan each to expeditions. For a controlled economy, this was very healthy inflation! (The ever topical BBC World Service news announced the next night that inflation in China averaged five to six per cent per annum, with Guanghou suffering 100 per cent in the last year – Canton's high rate was blamed on poor harvests, poor management and the special economic zone's transition to an open market economy.)

When the LO told us that the poor, bleating, over-priced sheep were already bought and that the seller would not take them back, the feeling that we were being lined up for a last minute shakedown grew strong.

* * *

The next morning the news was worse; Jin Jun and the LO, laughing with embarrassment as they returned from a long night of parleying with the military authorities, informed us that we were only going to be allowed to attempt to climb the Crown from the south and that we had to pay more money to film the Upper Shakesgam Valley, despite having already paid a hefty filming fee.

The final insult was that the Crown had been double booked. A team of Japanese mountaineers had been there since May attempting the southern route. They would come out as we went in. If the Japanese succeeded in making the first ascent of the mountain we could only follow in their footsteps. By restricting us to the southern route (for 'military reasons'), the CMA would be able to charge a future expedition 'first ascent' fees for a different route.

Morale was very low indeed. I was feeling ill – having had a disturbed night, being woken by John's wrist alarm (that failed to awaken him) and with a chest cough well established in my lungs.

At first we blamed the LO for our situation, especially when we discovered that he received a percentage of whatever we paid. We discussed simply going to the mountains, ignoring the military orders.

Jin Jun, in a difficult position and very concerned and worried, assured us that despite its being potentially disastrous for both himself and the LO if word ever filtered back to the authorities, they had both seriously considered this option. This admission placed the LO in a better light – although Jin Jun was a masterly diplomat and could easily have been trying to please us. We would have to rely very greatly upon the LO so I hoped our suspicions were without foundation.

To ignore the military authorities, climbing the mountain from the north and exploring the Upper Shakesgam without permission would be very risky and stupid. It would also be as dishonourable for us as the present impasse was for the Chinese. It was not really a viable option.

Henry phoned Beijing to seek the wise council of Colonel Clements, the Defence Attaché. It was Saturday, so a message was left for his return on Monday morning. The military authorites forbade us to leave Yechung, so we were stuck.

To occupy the time, each specialist in the team gave a lecture – me on the basics of photography, John on mountain navigation and use of the altimeter and Nick opened his medical pack and talked us through the contents.

Nick Moore, about five feet ten and stockily built, was the third novice mountaineer in the team (apart from Conrad Ainsley and myself). He had been on a ski-mountaineering trip to the Alps so the environment was not completely new to him, but climbing was, and he was desperately keen to learn and do well at it. It was hard to place Nick's age exactly as his round and slightly ruddy face and receding hairline made him look twenty, going on thirty-five. However, his clearness of eye and power of body soon dispelled any initial estimate that he might be older than his actual twenty-two years.

Nick was also from 59 Squadron, he and Robbo sharing his house in Plymouth. His sport was the triathlon: a race of consecutive endurance events, long-distance swimming, cycling and running, demanding the highest possible standards, of application in training, of fitness, stamina and endurance. Nick was clearly going to be a very useful man on the mountain, irrespective of his novice status.

Nick took both his sport and his work very seriously. He seemed to be measuring himself against some yardstick, like a novice monk seeking enlightenment. Each day he would carefully stretch his body with slow, yoga-like movements. He spoke in a slow, careful manner, addressing his questions to those he thought to be the best mountaineers, filing the answers away inside his head.

Nick softened his seriousness with a deadpan sense of humour, a behavioural trait that gave him several options. He could use the deadpan humour to sound people out, changing a joke into a serious question or comment if joking turned out to be inappropriate; or he could mock, which he did rather well in a completely detached fashion that, like a suit of armour, protected him from any barbs that might be flighted back in his direction.

For most of the winter and spring of 1987, both Nick and Robbo had worked in the casualty departments of hospitals learning to sew and dress wounds, attending operations and practising first aid. In his impromptu lecture, Nick's first point was that Eric Shipton in 1937, the last westerner to venture into the area of the Crown, took no medical kit of any sort with him – despite a three-month trip. Shipton was a hero to us all; adventurous, yet wise and prudent, and what was good enough for him was good enough for us.

In spite of the illogical reassurance that this gave, I thought our medical packs very small, which made me think about how much on our own we would be. There was simply no space for more medical kit, so our capacity to cope with a disaster was very limited.

Henry had decided not to take a doctor for two reasons: because no-one with suitable qualifications had come forward, and because he reckoned that Nick and Robbo's first aid would be as good or better than that of any doctor – who in the usual course of events relies upon hospital equipment and the first aid of casualty nurses and ambulance men.

Nick talked us through stitching up wounds, bandaging and giving injections. All his injecting fluids seemed to be for the bottom, and he gave us full warning of what might be to come: we would have to bend forward, bracing against a rock with our toes pointing inwards. This manoeuvre makes it impossible to clench your buttock muscles, and is one of countless, timelessly devious ploys of the medical profession.

After the obligatory 'this won't hurt a bit', or 'you may feel a little prick', Doctor draws a cross on the buttock he has selected and delivers the needle directly into the quivering flesh of the top outer quarter, right up to the hilt.

Nick finished by describing the various appendectomies he had watched in hospital:

'During the second one, the surgeon couldn't find it, rummaging around for ages. If you think Robbo or I are going to whip yours out on the mountain then think again – because we ain't!'

Throughout Saturday afternoon (22 August), negotiations with the military continued as we sat miserably whiling the time away. The Xinjiang authorities were insisting on being paid an additional £3,000 for filming the Upper Shakesgam Valley, while the contract for which we had already paid specified that we might photograph, video or otherwise film in any way throughout the trip.

The authorities objected to our attempting the northern route onto the mountain; we planned to take the camels as close as possible, dump the gear at the northern foot and climb up the long gullies and glaciers onto the upper ridges and then on to the summit.

The southern route looked precipitously steep all the way up, and the valley leading to the foot of the southern approach was blocked by the massive Skamri Glacier. Before even starting on the southern route, we would have to carry all our food and equipment fifteen miles or more from the camel dump.

To our knowledge, no-one had ever been within ten miles of the Crown, so we knew nothing at all about routes. To be restricted to one approach was deeply disappointing.

I tried to see the problem from the Chinese military point of view. The Lower Shakesgam Valley, along which we would have to trek and camp in order to attempt the northern route, seemed to be a possible link from an inhabited valley on the West Pakistan side of the border. Footpaths were drawn on my map, crossing the border and running east-south-east down the Lower Shakesgam Valley, although no habitations were marked.

Could a paranoid military commander see some possible danger in our going to that area? I wondered if our being British Army soldiers had any bearing on the problem; the days of the Great Game were long finished but maybe some residual mistrust remained. Perhaps our filming was regarded as covert surveying of this sensitive border region of the Chinese People's Republic?

Surprisingly, perhaps, I discounted this last reason. Throughout the trip so far there had been no interest from any Chinese people in our being British Army soldiers. After seeing the way the Chinese People's Army is completely integrated into their society, wearing uniform all the time, well regarded and comparatively well paid, it seemed to me that for them, being a soldier was a perfectly normal part of citizenship. They would assume that all British people might just as well be soldiers (sailors or airmen) as have any other occupation. It followed that they would see no particular extra threat to border security from having ten members of the British Army lurking there for two months.

Our situation seemed to be simple. We were being taken to the cleaners by the local authorities for our last drop of foreign exchange in a cynical and completely disinterested fashion. The LO was probably obliged to do this to every expedition, most of whom, having come this far, simply paid up and got on with the mountaineering.

The next day, after an evening drink, a few beers and glasses of ferocious rice spirit offered in peace by the LO (we returned the hospitality with a large tumbler full of Black Label whisky which he and his friends tried, then rejected with obvious distaste), the negotiations continued. Mr Loo of CIST in Beijing supported the local authorities, insisting that we pay the extra money.

The only thing that kept us from total bitterness at seeing our great adventure corrupted in this way was Jin Jun, who was absolutely furious and disgusted with his own superiors. As a young progressive Chinese, he saw in what was being done to us a corruption and ignorance that was keeping his country moored in the economic backwaters of the world. He had recently taken a Swedish party to Tibet (the other autonomous region of the People's Republic), where he had encountered similar problems.

Jin Jun advised us to refuse to pay the extra money and stick it out in Yechung, adding that unless the head of CIST in Beijing, who seemed to have identified this problem some time ago, sorted it out satisfactorily in an honest and honourable fashion, he would resign his post at the end of the trip. With his experience as a town planner he was confident of getting a good job easily.

Among the bureaucrats with whom we were dealing there seemed to be no understanding of the power of contract, nor of the way we felt outraged at being cheated. They were bureaucratically inefficient as well as greedy. CIST in Beijing regarded it all as a problem to be solved, and saw that the simplest and easiest solution would be for us to pay the money and get on with our journey. Beijing bureaucrats seemed to be used to people doing what they were told without argument. They also seemed to regard us as wealthy.

We decided to gamble that our stout refusal to pay would perplex and embarrass the Chinese. We could not afford any more expenditure, the extra air freight charge (that no western travel company would have dared pass on to a European tour organizer) had put us even more deeply in debt – the total was now well over £50,000. We also felt that we owed it to future expeditions not simply to cave in under pressure, in what we saw as a poker game.

We were also debating giving up and going home.

I sat on my bed gazing out of cracked and dirty windows at the huge chimney of the hotel compound furnace house. Our problems were not part of the struggle between communism and capitalism, but a try-on to see whether we could be persuaded to part with more of our seeming abundance of foreign exchange. John Day called it 'rape', at the end of the line when we were too far into the trip to quit.

Maybe CIST had made a mistake when they originally priced the trip, maybe they had overlooked the filming charge and the military considerations ... we were too far from home for such magnanimity.

Henry spoke to Colonel Clements on the phone; he said we should accept the route change, as getting the Chinese Ministry of Defence to react would take far too long. He would contact CIST, then the Ministry of Foreign Affairs, and finally, if still nothing had changed, get HE the Ambassador involved.

The young girls who served the food and cleaned our rooms were becoming more interesting every day we spent in Yechung. Dark-haired, rosy cheeked with small, firm bottoms and twinkling smiles, they were very attractive, and much international sign language and good natured lust was communicated. That unfortunately was as far as it went; we had no idea of the moral climate here nor how to initiate closer relations; the Chinese were said to be very moral, with no sex before or outside marriage. I teasingly suggested to the others that the girls were probably dying to get to know us, but that as neither side knew how to go about it, nothing could happen.

Henry was under great pressure at this time and doing extremely well. His expedition looked like failing at the first hurdle through no fault of his; morale was at rock bottom and Catherine was on the plane back to Hong Kong, having left several sealed letters for him to open on given dates in the future. Although he kept it to himself, he obviously missed her badly. He had now to make the transition from a rather jolly holiday to some very serious mountaineering.

We whiled away the time wandering through Yechung town centre and into the narrow winding streets of the market. We were in another age. Surrounded by blank mud walls, the old market was crammed with people, shops, street vendors, donkey carts, lines of barbers' chairs under huge square canvas umbrellas – massaging scalps, shaving heads and tending long white nicotine-yellow whiskers; butchers without fridges, selling mutton from a single freshly killed carcass, tail fleece still attached, or horse meat with the complete tail hanging from the split haunches, and lesser vendors squatting on the ground trying to sell the grey and dusty entrails.

Beside the barbers, rows of tailors sat behind sewing machines, blacksmiths further down hammered horse and donkey shoes, leather workers made tack for donkey carts and live, scrawny pigeons were sold from large circular cages. By day the cooked food section was more obviously insanitary, littered with the remains of previous meals under the tables of restaurants, black and unsavoury, with fires and woks at the front and dark, greasy tables in the darkness to the rear.

I lay listening to the Yechung dawn chorus of lorry horns, barking dogs, shouting, loud and thorough clearing of throats and nasal cavities, and the deliberate and comprehensive spitting that follows.

Had we reached the end of the road? It was depressing to think that it might all end in such a negative way.

Henry came in after breakfast. I was reading *Lord of the Rings*; Frodo had just arrived in Rivendell. Henry had a huge grin, but was speaking quietly and calmly. We had to lock spare travelling kit in a store at the back of the hotel, leaving only our mountaineering gear.

The problems had been sorted out. We were leaving Yechung at noon.

CIST had agreed to pay the local authorities a filming fee from the lump sum they had taken from us. It was very much less than we had been asked to pay, only £1,800. For our part, we agreed to limit ourselves to the southern route up the mountain, which did have certain mountaineering advantages, and served to reduce the time we would have to spend on reconnaissance. As a face-saving proviso for the Chinese there would be a reckoning of supplementary charges to be paid when we returned from the mountains and before we left China.

Jin Jun told us that an Italian expedition had encountered similar problems and had left the country owing a lot of money, which was still outstanding. He advised us to do the same.

Perhaps in a country where saving face was all important this was what we were expected to do.

CHAPTER 7

Into the Mountains

We left the stagnation and ill-feeling of Yechung, driving south, at first on tarmac roads through arid desert, then on dirt, entering the hot brown mud foothills of the K'un Lun Mountains. Very finely granulated dust in hot, dense clouds penetrated the vehicles, crunched in our teeth and made it difficult to see ahead. The road steepened and grew worse, winding upwards into very serious hill climbs.

Our truck developed fuel problems, power fading and the engine cutting out on the steep gradients. The road became precipitous, the bends built out and upwards from the sheer cliff forming 'U'-shaped bridges of loose boulders which looked anything but secure as we viewed them anxiously from below. It was not exactly a busy road. That day, seven lorries and numerous donkeys came from the other direction and we pulled over to the inside bends to let them past.

Hairpins with precipitous falls wound slowly up to the first pass, of 3,470 metres. We looked down upon small farmsteads, fields of green hay and grain, with animals grazing. The houses were low, square mud buildings partly dug into the ground. Far below, the valley bottom with its unseen river was dry and rocky.

Henry, John and Robbo, enthused at being in mountains at last, ran down a narrow footpath to the distant valley bottom while we took the long, tortuously winding road route, enduring the fumes of two very slow lorries, neither of which would let us pass, despite our driver's hooting. The LO abused them roundly as we eventually got past, and Nellie called the last lorry driver 'a dipstick'.

We were now travelling through proper rock country, serious mountains of 15,000 feet and more at either side, and less of the depressing, brown, heavily eroded mud slopes. Huge banks of dangerous looking brown conglomerate (a mud and rock cement), containing large round boulders held up only by the crumbling earth, overhung the road at various places. Work parties, anonymous male and female figures in dusty green tunics, repaired the road and telegraph wires.

The road followed the river's edge, passing the occasional small settlement. The river was full with glacial meltwater, flowing hard and fast with rapids. When the valley narrowed the river thundered along one powerful course, and when the valley widened, the river split into several different channels across the width of the rocky floor.

A group of twenty camels were drinking in the shallows and eating grass by the side of the road. Incongruous but beautiful and naturally dignified, they had immediately recognizable affinity with this harsh terrain. In the sunshine, their coats were several different shades of brown, the longer hair of their heads and necks shining. Their handlers were simple, serious looking men with deeply tanned faces, some with grey whiskers, others with clean-shaven open faces and Middle Eastern features.

We stopped and the LO asked them in Chinese if they were from Maza Dala, thinking that as we were already two days late for the rendezvous with our camels, these might be them. They were not.

After seven hours' spring-jolting driving, we arrived at a grey, bleak Chinese Army camp surrounded by huge brown mountains hazy in the evening, the air pleasantly cool after the heat of the plain. I was still feeling rough; bad tempered with a sore throat, fuzzy head and a chest cough that was producing unpleasant-tasting phlegm.

Supper was served in the barracks dining hall, a huge round-roofed concrete building with benches and rather grubby tables, an urn for hot water and a doorway leading through into a dark and dubious kitchen. The chef was at least fifty, a venerable looking soldier wearing an officer's green jacket – four pockets not two – who presided over supper rather than served it. Jin Jun told me that he had been the cook here for more than thirty years.

I was astonished. Thirty years was more than a 'life' sentence in prison. Outside the grim walls of the camp, the small village of Quei had little to recommend it: a dozen or so houses beside the river, goats with the odd sheep roaming along the road and two grimy tea houses. The usual tour of duty in Quei lasted three years, its soldiers manning even more remote border posts and returning to it as their company base – home for around 100 men.

In the British Army we regard Hohne or Fallingbostel ('Effing Bee'), in the depths of West Germany's Lüneburger Heide, as deadly remote postings at which the statutory two years deadens the mind and chills the soul. In comparison Quei was a quite ludicrously isolated place.

However the cook here would have a very firm grip on the local scene. He would control the food – and after so many years, the transport that brought it all in. Particularly in winter with deep snow blocking the roads, such control would lend him an omnipotence which would spread to other matters. Perhaps he had remained in Quei for thirty years, not out of duty, penance or because of a broken heart, but because he had become the boss.

Jin Jun had heard of this cook from a Chinese television documentary; the programme called him 'Grass of the K'un Lun Mountains' as he had been there for so long. The army had wanted to retire him with a medal to some plum posting inside China. I asked Jin Jun for an example of a plum posting and he suggested Yechung.

The cook refused to leave. He was unmarried. He was the big fish in the small pond, the cock ruling the roost. 'Grass of the K'un Lun Mountains', like soldiers the world over, had once been a rolling stone but became so overgrown that he had disappeared into the hillside.

His food was nothing to write to Egon Ronay about either.

After supper the loudspeakers started, very loud and terribly distorted fairground barrel-organ music played by a military brass band. We offered to play basketball with the bored-looking soldiers. Their boredom vanished. They became competitive and insisted on having their own team rather than playing with mixed sides as we had offered. Most of the expedition, feeling off-colour from the higher altitude, were not interested.

In the ensuing match Andy Aspinall came into his own. Athletic with fair hair and Saxon good looks, by reputation the team joker, Andy was five foot eleven with the V-shaped torso of a gymnast, and legs that were by contrast a bit spindly — about which he accepted teasing with amused good nature.

Andy was noisy, the life and soul of the party and the irrepressible maker of loud comments from within the group which could easily be insulting to others outside it. This rude but very often amusing persona was a façade behind which an uncertain, rather shy individual took cover.

I very much liked Andy. Underneath the laddish front he was a truly strong and capable man. However, somehow he had become unsure of himself. I wondered if maybe he wished he was a different sort of person. A lack of regard for yourself makes it very hard to be confident enough to love and respect others. (I understood this because I have suffered the same problem myself.)

Andy thought of himself as a shallow person, with nothing much to offer other people. Others seemed to him to be far more able, intelligent and imbued with character. Surviving a war helped me get over a similar hangup, and I was certain that getting up a very big and dangerous mountain would do the same for Andy. He had not realized that everyone suffers terrible crises of confidence and that the most fearless on the outside are often the most uncertain underneath.

Andy's noisy front only operated in the company of people he knew and in surroundings that he understood. It was fuelled by a strong desire to be one of the lads so as not to be thought weak. Unfortunately the act had become too good. The 'lads' were faced with someone much more laddish than they would ever be, with a smart sports car and a string of attractive girlfriends. The real, very capable and likeable Andrew Aspinall had still to discover his own set of values.

An Army physical training instructor, Andy knew everything there was to know about playing and organizing games. On the pot-holed basketball court in Quei his carelessness, the shallow pose, his thoughtless, acid banter evaporated. He ran the game, in spite of the lack of communication between the two sides, as sporting, easy-going fun, telling us exactly how to counter our opponents' moves and play effectively without wasting effort. He also kept it friendly, allowing our hosts to win by a slender margin.

The game very soon became hard work; we were at 3,300 metres and could really feel it: dry throat, headache, strained chest – my current symptoms much exacerbated, I was probably stupid to have played, but I could not have missed such an interesting event. We played until dark and were all very tired.

Henry, who did not play, measured his pulse. He had been sitting on the steps by the basketball court watching the game and writing his diary. His normal resting rate was forty-seven and now it had risen to seventy-five, the effect of the altitude.

We shared concrete-floored rooms in the broken-windowed, echoing barrack block. The ablutions were very basic and smelled but the bedding was warm and free of insect life. The lights did not work so we settled down to an early night – which was soon broken by a distorted TV set at full volume and the loud, tuneless and interminable playing of an electronic organ. I had seen one of these in Xian; it was a basic imitation of the battery powered keyboards we have in the west, but very crude, with no rhythm section, different voices or accompaniment, just the blaring of two octaves of inaccurate single notes.

Breakfast was scheduled for 9 A.M., before dawn, early so that the military camp could get on with its work. However, 'Grass of the K'un Lun' did not produce food until just after 10, by which time we and the soldiers were hanging around hopefully in the cold of the dark dining hall tapping our chop sticks on the sticky table tops.

My chest cough was even worse so Nick started me off on a course of antibiotics – large blue and white pills called Magnapen. I was worried about going to still higher altitudes with a worsening chest infection.

* * *

Feeling ill was not a problem. I was quite used to that, thanks to the ME, which, although it no longer reduced me to complete exhaustion, made me feel moderately-to-badly hung-over each morning. I was used to being very tired, and to ignoring it. It made me irritable at times, especially if my tiredness coincided with someone wanting to present me with a complicated problem. I was used also to forcing myself to work regardless of how I felt, which was hard but no longer a worry as I knew that there was nothing physically wrong with me. The Queen Elizabeth Military Hospital at Woolwich had made sure of that. If I overdid things, worked too hard or did more than a very modest amount of running, I became depressed, followed usually by a bad sore throat and several days of flu symptoms.

The first ten months of the ME had been the worst. I am convinced that the whole thing was related to a build-up of stress which had precipitated an otherwise modest virus into a physical collapse, which was followed closely by mental problems. The source of the stress, for me, had been the Falklands War.

During the fighting, there were several different levels of stress, which often had to be endured at the same time. The circumstances raised everyone's base level of tension to a constant high. When I received orders for our next operation, this level of tension rose considerably. Danger superimposed itself onto this base level, stimulating fear, excitement, relief, intensified worry and anxiety, sadness and exhilaration.

The anxiety of going into action grew to a crescendo during helicopter insertions. A helicopter accident in which sixteen SAS men had been killed early in the campaign had shaken my faith in these aircraft. Being inserted by helicopter at night — flying over enemy positions and landing behind enemy lines — was dangerous, and as passengers we had no control over events. We sat strapped into the back watching dark hillsides and the occasional frightened sheep flash past twenty feet below, while the pilot flew into total blackness, relying upon the green image from his night vision goggles. In the back, we were an inactive and highly stressed cargo.

Life on board ship could be equally stressful: lying under stout wooden tables examining the weave of wardroom carpets as Oerlikons pumped shells up at incoming Argentine fighter-bombers.

The most frightening time of all for me was a half-minute period in HMS *Avenger* – one of the in-shore gunships. Three Argentinian jets, a Super Etendard fighter bomber and two Sky Hawk fighters, were detected by radar. A single sweep of the Etendard's radar was picked up by *Avenger*, which then picked up the launch of an Exocet sea-skimming missile. *Avenger*'s computers predicted its course – ten feet above the waves straight for our ship.

The twenty-three seconds that we endured between the tannoy announcement of the radar-observed launch and the predicted impact of the missile were, for me, the most impotent and frightening moments of the war. *Avenger* shot down a Sky Hawk, and a neighbouring ship the Exocet missile. The more dangerous things, sea insertions in rubber assault craft, gun battles, the long periods in observation positions behind the Argentinian lines, were not nearly so stressful as we felt more in control of our destiny.

Throughout the fighting, we lived life day by day, and sometimes minute by minute when it all seemed particularly fragile. Gun battles, being shot at and firing back, were surprisingly stimulating, lifting everyone from the misery, cold and gnawing fear into a hyped up, adrenalized high which faded hours later into the stabbing realization of what might so easily have happened. The sense of relief that followed moments of danger washed away much of the stress, and was in its way therapeutic.

There was also a reassurance in the knowledge that our fears and worries were real and natural. No-one could seriously accuse us of being wimps.

On returning from the Falklands, I had been struck quite hard by the reimposition of the stresses and worries of normal life. The return to real life, which had grown in our expectations to something so wonderful that we were bound to be disappointed, was surprisingly difficult.

From being a relatively carefree young captain, I had matured into someone who understood the harsh realities of life, and the elemental truth that disasters are not things that happen only to other people. During the war I learned how to worry properly.

The joy and euphoria of being safely back home was quickly dampened by the worries of real, modern life. By comparison with the things we had worried about in the Falklands, these were trivial. But there were so many of them, and they were relentless, unrelieved by those incredible moments of great relief and joy of life that characterize combat. Everyday modern life was boring, exhausting, complicated and frighteningly stressful.

The physical reactions of worry are the same whether you have stepped off the kerb in front of a taxi or are listening to the singing of 155mm howitzer shell splinters as they ricochet off rocks with which you are trying to merge. My body had learned to react to fear, but could no longer differentiate between trivia and real, physical danger.

One of the characteristics of growing up is learning to worry. During the war I had grown up. Unfortunately the war had turbocharged my nervous system, and I now no longer needed the extra adrenalin in order to survive.

My medical war-related problem emerged slowly, months after coming back. Like an overwound clock spring, stress had built up inside each of us over the three and a half months we had been away. At the end, I felt perfectly normal; very glad to be back and astonished at the welcome – but unaffected, as if I had been on an exercise and not on a real operation. Underneath, below the level of self-awareness, a spring was wound tight, reducing my natural resilience.

It took seven months for the pressures of real life to combine with the pressures that had built up during the Falklands operation (Op Corporate). In what seems to me to be a logical natural reaction to over-abuse, my body threw in the towel, succumbed to some virus (probably glandular fever), then refused to get better.

Unlike a broken leg, there is no timescale for such a disease, nor is there any prescribed treatment. Also, in those days, ME was not well known by the medical profession, so a sufferer, once all the dire possibilities suggested by the symptoms had been eliminated, was dubbed a malingerer, a hypochondriac or in need of psychiatric help. I wanted desperately to be better, the worst frame of mind for an ME sufferer as the only cure is to lie back and let the body sort itself out.

I never appeared to have physical symptoms. I only felt them. Even when severely sore my throat looked perfectly normal and I never had a high temperature. The tiredness and illness seem to be something to be endured. There is no point in worrying, as I had done to the point of bad depression in the early months of the illness. Eventually, so the doctors tell me, the ghost-like symptoms may fade away.

But now, six years after becoming ill, I am never completely free of them.

I had been hoping that the expedition, four months of clean and simple living in a straightforward physical environment, well away from modern life, might complete the 'cure' of my ME. My self confidence had been restored by four weeks' hard physical activity at RAF Headley Court – which had convinced me that there was nothing seriously wrong with me. The expedition, I believed, would help to smooth away those tensions that remained, the deep-rooted stresses that might be the cause of my continued symptoms. But so far, this did not seem to be happening and my hopes for a cure seemed rather forlorn.

My worry now, in Quei, was that I actually had real symptoms, a real chest infection that had to be cured before we started walking at altitude. I did not know whether my body's immune system had been affected by the ME. I also had to separate the ME symptoms from the real ones, so as not to confuse Nick Moore.

Our journey continued south along a steepening valley, the rough road running beside a glacial river. Orange-necked birds flew across our path. Several marmots watched us from a grassy plot before scampering off into their burrow. Henry wanted to press on, saying there were certain to be many more marmots when we got into the mountains proper.

Marmots are elusive, and very characteristic of the Karakoram, so I was keen to film these, knowing that I had to take shots when they appeared. I insisted on stopping to take photographs, well beyond the family group, who were playing in a small grassy hollow, so as not to frighten them. Irritatingly, our second vehicle stopped too, right in front of the animals. Everyone clambered out noisily, clutching their cameras. The marmots dived away down their burrows, and we never saw any of these little animals again.

The road, a narrow, pot-holed track, continued along beside the river. Hump-backed cattle, with long, shaggy, black and brown hair and long curved horns, grazed by the water's edge. We overtook the occasional large, battered lorry as it ground noisily and steadily along this track, the main route into the west of Tibet.

We began to climb up to the first of two more passes, the first around 3,500 metres and the second 4,900, the height that our base camp on the Crown would be. At the second pass, the air was clear and cool, and the sun warm. I felt light-headed carrying the camera up a steep slope from the road to a small spur. Below, through a spectacular mountain desert, the road wound downwards as far as the eye could see.

The huge, overbearing, brown mountains, the very highest softened by snow, were oppressive. Debris had flown down from their eroded sides, sometimes cutting the road. Some of the slopes were nothing but debris and finely puckered brown mud, and some were sheer rock.

Towards the bottom of the second pass, on impulse, Conrad decided to leap from the back of the truck while it was still moving, to take a picture. The grumpy LO was driving – badly – going downhill in neutral, at times with the engine turned off. He stopped the truck and I leapt out to see if Conrad was all right. He had picked himself up and had bounded down the hill to the next hairpin bend, where he was waving up from below.

I knew that a show of speaking to 'Rad was necessary because the LO was furious about his leaping out. I rushed back to tell Henry, in the next vehicle, what had happened, including my thoughts on the LO's free-wheeling. It seemed, however, from Henry's lack of response, that he thought I was over-reacting.

At the next stop, the LO, Jin Jun and Henry had a conversation and no-one looked too happy. I approached Henry after I had shot some film and said I hoped I hadn't caused any trouble. He told me rather sharply to leave things like that to him in the future rather than jump in with both feet:

'If you feel strongly about something, tell me then leave it. I prefer to do things in my own way. If you see that after a few days I haven't done anything then mention it to me again. By leaping in like that you have forced me to do something now.

'I would in fact have waited and then talked to everyone about taking risks in the mountains, about the inevitability of having to take risks but ensuring that the gain is worth it. I could have used 'Rad's performance as an example of bad judgement.'

The LO was particularly fed up. He was adamant that he hadn't been driving with the engine turned off, although he did admit to driving down in neutral.

Henry was probably trying to keep things sweet with the LO for the moment, so that a serious argument and the risk of falling out could be saved for more important mountaineering matters later. I wanted us all to get that far, rather than be killed plunging over a cliff because Chinese drivers, with limited driving experience, don't understand how to use engines and gearboxes when going down very steep hills.

We had lunch at the army post at Maza, a desolate spot by the river where the road emerges from the mountains into the wide, flat valley of the Yarkand River. A handful of soldiers were hanging around the battered barracks, some wearing their own black 'Mao'-type suits rather than green uniform. Lunch was an hour late, and we were all very hungry, except Nick who had helped himself to the mountain rations, having been put off local food by his bout of illness in Yechung. When lunch appeared, with lots of rice and noodles, it turned out to be very good.

We loaded half our gear into a four-ton army truck and, with five people aboard to unload at the other end, set off down the very bumpy track towards Maza Dala and the rendezvous with the camels. The road was too bad for passenger vehicles and the last bridge had been washed away by flooding. If the truck was not able to get through, the camels were going to have to come back up-river to collect us.

Five of us remained at Maza, settling on rough mattresses in a dusty barrack room to while away the afternoon, listening to the wind whistling through cracked window panes. In the sunshine it was warm, in the shadow, so cold that your skin goose-pimpled.

All the vehicles driving through these mountains seemed to carry food if they had spare capacity. Our trucks had carried four large sacks of vegetables which a group of locals took off to the nearby village. When the four-tonner returned from the camel rendezvous, a group of tough, sunburned men in ragged woollen suits leaped from the tailboard, having taken a lift.

The twenty-five-kilometre drive along the Yarkand River to Maza Dala took just over an hour of hair-raising driving and bone shaking bumps, past some astonishingly beautiful scenery. Two of our camel drivers had come along for the ride, sometimes sitting, sometimes standing to absorb the bumps.

The ramps up onto two of the stone bridges across smaller branches of the river were washed away by recent flooding, the bridges themselves standing isolated and intact like teeth amid a sea of boulders. We had to drive through the water. Scree had flowed down from the mountains across the road. The lorry was forced to negotiate thirty- to forty-degree slopes which ended abruptly in a drop down into the seething river, skirting the crumbling edges of holes where the road itself had broken away into the river twelve feet below.

It was late in the afternoon when we left the army camp at Maza. The sun was in the west throwing beautiful light at the eastern slopes: many shades of brown, some almost white, others golden and chocolate with the grey of the scree flowing like river deltas down the mud and rock surfaces. Beyond the immediate mountains, 6,000-metre peaks peered over the tops, jagged razor backs softened by the snow, set against a perfectly blue sky.

The air here at 4,000 metres was very dry; we could feel our lips and noses hardening in the touch of the hot sun. Andy stood in the rear of the truck wearing a baseball hat, totally reflective glacier glasses and his new white silk scarf (from Kashgar) streaming out behind him, a legionnaire riding shotgun through enemy territory.

On the bends, overhanging conglomerate had collapsed, leaving huge rocks on the track. The driver stood on his brakes, throwing us one over another in the back, before edging past or driving up over the boulders, the suspension achieving some peculiar angles. These conglomerate cliffs had been undercut by the river leaving large boulders set into the dried mud which were often overhead as we crept past.

Eventually we came to a steep rise. The road curled anti-clockwise downwards, cut into a steep cliff created by a wide meander of the river far below. A stone bridge stood at the bottom of the cliff and on the far side of the river camels grazed happily on the green grass beside our orange bell tent and Jin Jun and the LO's green tent. Our equipment, unloaded from the lorry, was in lines outside a tumbledown building where twenty or so donkeys stood tethered. The bridge was still in sunshine and our camp site was in shadow. Huge brown hills and scree slopes loomed overhead.

We had arrived at Maza Dala, the building being the village marked on our map. This was the end of the road.

The sun slowly sank, throwing deeper, more polarized light back from the rocks: browns, greys, bleached-out whites and even yellows. We ate a very contented supper of Army 'compo' rations: minced beef, mashed potatoes (referred to as 'pomme') and peas followed by dehydrated apple flakes and tea. It was fresh, clean and peaceful and we were all pleased to be under our own canvas at last.

There had been much discussion about how cold it would be at night and so what to sleep in; Henry felt that by keeping our mountain sleeping bags clean we should preserve their thermal properties, not using them until we needed to, instead sleeping in our Gore-Tex bivvie bags with just a cotton liner. After sorting out my kit I decided to take Henry's advice and, swallowing my Magnapen pills and two aspirins, crawled into the bell tent and tried to get to sleep, to the sound of Feargal Sharkey, played by Henry on his tape machine.

A few hours later, I was woken by the smell and sound of terrible farts. My head ached and sleep was impossible. I twisted and turned, trying to regain that elusive sleep position. I analysed what was wrong; my mouth was very dry and I was dying for a pee. I had a dehydration headache, and there was no alternative but to get up. I scampered naked out onto the chilly meadow, had a pee and ferreted around in my day sack for a water bottle, which I drained. I was shivering when I regained my bivvie bag, the others shifting as I wriggled noisily back into position, beside Henry, against the canvas of the tent wall.

After another hour I was definitely chilly. I had a stuff bag handy containing a polar underwear suit, so as quietly as I could I slipped the top on. One hour later my legs were cold. The temperature outside had dropped from a warm evening to five degrees centigrade and I was wedged up against the tent canvas. I unzipped again and put the trousers on. At 7.30 Beijing time Henry's alarm went off beside my head. At around 8 everyone stirred and two people got up to boil water for breakfast, which was due at 9 so that we could leave at 10.30. After my broken night, I didn't want to get up so was last out, packing my gear away and slipping out into the chilly darkness where everyone else was standing chatting around the hissing stoves.

John and two others had decided to sleep outside, using their sleeping bags. Theirs had been the right decision. They arose later, when the rolled oats were ready.

I spent the next hour sorting out my cameras, carefully cleaning the lenses and fitting filters. As we would now always be higher than 8,000 feet and in a thinner atmosphere through which more UV penetrated, ultra-violet filters were essential to prevent the extra UV affecting the film, making the blues too hard and strong.

In spite of Henry's instructions there were no signs of life from the camel drivers across the river. By 10 they were still feeding their animals.

The loading took ages; the drivers strolled about lifting packages, making piles of assorted boxes, arguing, then catching their camels, gathering them together into patient groups of four, where they lay on their haunches in companionable, self-generated mires of dung and urine.

Bob stood by anxiously with a clip-board trying to keep tabs on where all the equipment was going. Although it had all been carefully weighed, we could not be certain that they would actually load it all. Bob was also anxious to ensure that nothing would be surreptitiously dumped en route, and intended walking at the rear to check that this did not happen. As each group of four camels was loaded they moved off towards the bridge, tied together by short halters. When all were loaded, there were no packages, boxes or bundles left on the ground, so we set off, across the broken stone bridge, over where the flood waters had breached the parapet, onto the water meadow and along the right-hand side of the valley, going south along the first of many bends in the Yarkand River.

With Andy, 'Rad and Jerry as my 'cine crew', I hurried ahead to film the occasion, the three of us heavily laden with tripod, lenses, film and cine and still cameras. The camels sauntered around the corner into the shadow of the mountains, the rest of the team following steadily, wearing shorts and small, very light packs, some wielding umbrellas and looking peculiarly English.

As the cavalcade wound towards us we saw that Jin Jun and the LO were astride small donkeys, their feet dragging along the ground, hitting the poor beasts to keep them going. The LO was chain-smoking cigarettes, ending for us any idea that he might be a mountaineer.

After 400 metres the caravan stopped. The LO had cross-threaded a seal on a petrol container and the precious fluid was running down one of the camel's hind legs onto the road. The LO was prevented from helping with this problem, since he still had a cigarette glued to his lower lip. The added misfortune of a burning camel would not be a pleasant sight. The caravan progressed across another stone bridge and on, up the river valley.

As we walked the sun came over the mountains and the temperature in sunlight rose into the forties (centigrade). We were passing through a severely eroded environment, past impossibly narrow gorges that opened out into wide flood plains with streams of water flowing in different courses across a smooth, boulder-strewn valley floor. The path was often buried by huge boulder falls from the steep slopes above, or cut away by the river on the outside of a meander so that we had to climb up onto one of the higher terraces to get through. The river itself was a powerful brown flood of glacial meltwater thundering eastwards.

The heights of the vertical river terraces were staggering, as was the sheer scale of the relief. Above all this rock and rubble, beyond the jagged brown ridges, brilliant white snow-capped peaks, over 6,000 metres high, glinted in the morning sun.

Camels move at a leisurely pace, a long, relaxed stride with gentle footfall over the most difficult and treacherous ground. Their legs are marvellously articulated, the lower part flexing under the load and the power being applied to the rear legs at the knee by huge haunch muscles. The front legs by contrast seem oddly short. Their barrel chests, slim waists and heavily muscled rear thighs give camels a profile similar to that of a greyhound. The feet, padded and tough, spread out over the area of a large dinner plate as the weight comes onto that leg.

All but one of the drivers rode little donkeys, trotting in front of the lead camel of each four. The lead camels were always male, controlled by a halter attached to a sharpened wooden peg or nail punched through the septum of his nose. When the donkeys were not being ridden by the drivers, they would nestle up close to their lead camel in an obviously close relationship.

The fact that Jin Jun and the LO were riding donkeys further fuelled anti-LO feelings. Donkeys manage to look very down-trodden, with their soft, doleful eyes and long, pretty eyelashes.

We stopped away from the harsh noonday sun in the shade of a rock cliff to eat our snack lunches. When the two of them rode up the LO stopped and remained on his animal's back, grinning and nodding at us. Unknown to him, his donkey started having an enormous and seemingly endless erection. He leaped off and sat down with us, by which time the black member was almost touching the ground.

Jin Jun came round the corner, stabbing his donkey in the neck and beating it with a stick, his chic blue baseball hat at a jaunty angle. We remarked that the LO's donkey seemed pleased to see him. Happily Jin Jun did not seem to understand. We assumed that the LO's donkey's reaction was stimulated by having stopped and in expectation of the weight of his passenger leaving his back.

'In the unfairness of creation,' I noted in my diary, 'I feel that I understand how the humble donkey is able to bear so much abuse and such heavy loads. Behind a mask of patient toil, he mocks lesser creatures with an extravagance that makes one wonder how he is able to remain conscious and on his feet.'

Our actual conversation at the time was a little more basic; we felt even more sorry for donkeys if, in addition to everything else, they were condemned to endure massive, debilitating erections every time the loads were removed from their backs, and in conditions where it was most unlikely that they could ever be satisfied.

'Whoever heard of a one-hoofed shuffle?' asked A. Aspinall.

The best that could happen would be to tread on it.

I began to get watery, gritty eyes and a headache like the prelude to snow blindness – which is caused by the higher levels of ultra-violet radiation at altitude. Bob Wood, having examined my glacier glasses, lent me his stronger spare pair (which I used for the rest of the trip). My problem was aggravated by constantly squinting through camera lenses without any glasses at all in the extraordinarily bright light.

Our first camp was on a grassy strip at the base of several hundred feet of red sandstone river terrace, at the junction of the Surukwat and the Yarkand rivers. From the top of a deep rock gorge, the river curved round, expanding into a very wide sand and boulder-strewn valley. A small, neat stone bridge over the narrowest part of the deeply eroded gorge carried the path around to the left and down, along the foot of a castellated terrace. Its turrets of fine red conglomerate were the creation of water erosion, and there were piles of collapsed stone and mud at the foot. The tents were already up, their orange and green shapes surrounded by boxes and plastic drums, the twenty-four camels grazing amongst the thorn bushes beside shining pools of clear, shallow water.

We washed, ate and felt content that at last we were on our way. For me this contentment alternated between the excitement and satisfaction of the moment and worrying about the implications of being so far into the wilderness; for example, about how many days – or rather weeks – we were from a hospital.

* * *

The food and equipment were loaded onto twenty camels, with two more for the LO and Jin Jun's gear, and four for the drivers' and camel fodder. A very colourfully painted chest of drawers (swirls, scrolls and Van Gogh flowers) had been spirited into one of the loads, and was now carefully unpacked beside the rest of our gear. Perhaps it was the cameleers' mobile office – their accounts and receipts?

The mystery was resolved when children's heads appeared over the top of the river terrace. On our map there were no human habitations along our route. However on the LO's there was a dot marked 'Illick', from which, presumably, the small delegation arrived pushing a wheelbarrow.

The camel drivers had been amusing themselves by the recreational riding of their beasts, and the arrival of the two men and swarm of chattering children from Illick became a social event. The colourful chest, doubtless ordered months earlier, was loaded onto the wheelbarrow and pushed away up the steep path towards the unseen, unmarked village.

Parts of this day's route, especially the incongruously well-engineered bridge across the gorge beside our camp, looked as though it might have been a vehicle track. Jin Jun confirmed this, saying that the last vehicle came through in 1982 or 1983 on an expedition to K2. Since then, apart from the Japanese expedition currently trying to climb the Crown ('our' mountain), it seemed the locals had the place to themselves. We were in a very marginal outpost of humanity, where cheerful, hardy people clung onto a basic survival as goat and sheep herders.

According to Jin Jun, the Japanese expedition on the Crown had entered the area in May before the spring melt of winter snow made the rivers uncrossable – and were an all-woman team! Imagination ran riot for several days. How would they react to ten males after three months on a glacier?

Sadly, or perhaps fortunately, this was one of Jin Jun's quiet little jokes.

On Thursday, 27 August the film crew left camp early to get ahead to film the caravan approaching and passing. We climbed up several hundred feet onto the river terrace, filmed, then moved along the terrace rather than going down to the valley floor. The terrace rose higher and in the blazing sunshine the temperature went suddenly up into the forties. We were in a hot, dry, thorn bush desert, with sharp rocks and very dry air. A group of wild camels with large nicotine-yellow teeth took exception to our presence and chased us away.

Ahead was a sheer drop of over eight hundred feet down to the valley floor, with no footpath down. We had the choice of pushing on in the hope of finding a mountain ravine that would give us a route down, or retracing our steps and losing several hours of hard walking – and another confrontation with the wild camels.

We pushed on.

The terrace went up even higher. I was reflecting (without relish) on the number of days lost by Eric Shipton through this sort of difficulty during his exploration of the area further south. Nick spotted a donkey track. As donkeys were now high in our estimation, we followed it.

From the edge of the terrace, the valley spread out at either side, the mud walls, like ancient fortifications, were breached by huge silt deltas that flowed down the mountain slopes onto the valley bottom. This terracing, and the very deeply incised meanders, indicated at least two or more lowerings of the overall profile of the north-flowing river that had created the valley. These changes could be likened to twice pulling out a huge bath plug further downstream, allowing the upstream water to flow very much faster and cut directly downwards.

A lowering of sea level could have achieved this, but a more likely cause would have been tectonic rises in the mountains themselves. The Karakoram are very young, the highest mountains in the world and still growing as the slow collision of the Central Asian and Indian plates push them upwards – above even the rest of the Himalaya.

As we threaded our insignificant way along the top of one of these massive orogenetic relics, following the vital donkey path, I was grateful for this faint but comfortingly familiar trace of animal life amid a terrifyingly implacable alien world of rock and water.

Donkeys do know best and the path wound down a deep, water-cut gully all the way to the valley floor.

Our caravan had vanished; even as tiny dots last seen creeping along the bottom of the massive conglomerate cliffs they were by now completely lost into the overpowering scale of the terrain. We had miles yet to go, over boulders and up steep scree barriers that had slipped down from the valley sides. We had to cross the river several times, and it was fast, cold and heavy with sandy-grey glacial silt.

I was very tired, my head aching, legs feeling dull. I felt in a dream. Andy offered to carry my camera bag and I felt better, if only because of his sympathy. The orange of the bell tents appeared suddenly around a huge buttress, the camels and our gear amid the thorn bushes.

So far, we had marched just over nine miles each day, with temperatures of nine degrees in the shade and over forty in the sunshine. When the wind blew it was like the cold breath of winter; the cold, very dry air whipping the heat of the sun's rays away in any slight breeze. With this very dry atmosphere and a high wind chill factor, we needed lots of water.

On this second day's march I had drunk three litres of orange squash and water purifying tablets mixed with salt, a rather horrid-tasting drink but it provided both salt and glucose. We were all tired, and wandered about the camp site drinking lots of fluid before enjoying supper: beef granules, dehydrated peas and pomme, apricot and apple flakes and a large brew of tea.

The approach march was our vital acclimatization for the mountain. We were now about 4,000 metres above sea level and therefore candidates for altitude sickness. We had to walk steadily carrying light loads, gaining height slowly, sleeping each night a little higher than previous nights. If we rushed the process by going too high too soon or carrying loads, our bodies would not adapt so quickly to the altitude and we ran the risk of altitude sickness. We were all fit, which was vital, but very aware that younger climbers often suffer more from altitude sickness than older climbers — a phenomenon related purely to age and not to previous high altitude experience.

At high altitude there is less oxygen which makes exercise very much harder. During acclimatization the body produces more red blood corpuscles which allow oxygen to be taken up faster, but this vital adjustment takes time. The blood becomes thicker, which at higher altitudes causes problems like thrombosis. Amongst other effects, altitude causes the body to retain water rather than excrete it through sweat and urine, the face, hands, feet and limbs swelling up.

Altitude sickness can be mild, a headache and tiredness – or it can be fatal. Splitting headaches can lead to unconsciousness and death within hours, or severe pneumonia can develop with terrifying rapidity. These symptoms are caused by the build-up of fluids in the cerebral and spinal cavities or in the lungs, and are called cerebral and pulmonary oedemas. They both start mildly with headaches and sickness, progressing overnight through the full gamut of symptoms. They can turn a man zipped up inside his sleeping bag at night with a headache into a corpse by morning.

Drugs can alleviate the symptoms of altitude sickness and make acclimatization less painful. Once altitude sickness has started there are no cures – other than losing altitude rapidly. Back in England, we had decided to use drugs only to get a sick man off the mountain. Drugs could mask the milder symptoms of the early stages until it was too late. They could not prevent the relentless build-up of body fluids that kills so many high altitude mountaineers, to which Julie Tullis succumbed on K2 in 1986, on her way down from the summit.

I went through my equipment yet again, sorting out what I would take for our exploration of the Shakesgam Valley. This needed to be as light as possible because for at least three days we would have to carry everything on our backs. The camels, having dropped our equipment at the foot of the Skamri Glacier, would be returning together to their village eight days' walk to the north. We would have to walk without camels for at least three days, from the foot of the Aghil Pass round to the Crown Base Camp. I was therefore ruthless with my equipment, taking only what I thought absolutely essential.

I was concerned about the condition of my film stocks. I had carefully wrapped their plastic bins in wet hessian sacks before leaving every morning, to find in the evening the bins standing uncovered in the sunshine, warm to the touch. Film is very sensitive to heat, although not to cold provided care is taken not to crack celluloid made brittle by really extreme cold. The colours are liable to fade or be altered by heat.

The others were not interested in my problems. I suppose in such an environment, keeping film cool seemed rather a ridiculous thing to be worried about. As we were again leaving early the next morning to film the caravan's approach, I asked Henry to supervise the loading of the film, to have it placed underneath other items, away from the baking effect of direct noon sunlight.

I passed a comfortable night in the open, amid grazing camels making windy camel noises, and the clearest, brightest stars overhead. The rocks gave off the day's heat, until around 2 A.M. when the chill set in.

The third day started with a wet river crossing and a long tramp up a boulder-strewn valley to a narrow gorge where the river had sliced through a severe rock fall. The route was across the river, up the steep slope and onto a narrow goat track along the side of the ravine. Bob had taken a wooden staff to help cross the river. Facing upstream and edging sideways into the torrent, you placed the staff in front and leaned heavily, gaining a third leg and much extra stability.

Andy, Bob and Jerry had crossed the river first. It was about thirty metres wide, flowing fast and cold with three rocky outcrops as a break en route. Jerry crossed safely to the other side and lobbed Bob's staff back to me; he threw so negligently that it fell into the river and was rushed away, back north from whence we had come. I was furious and the noise of the river washed away much of my bad language.

I asked Jerry to throw over his umbrella and crossed leaning instead upon the two curved handles of a brace of black gamps. In my diary:

'No Englishman should ever travel without at least one umbrella.'

The path along the deep gorge was crumbling and only inches wide. The camels were patient and sure-footed, handling the climb with some screaming and a little shouting. I filmed as they vanished away up into the rocks. The walls of the gorge were sheer, of conglomerate, rock and eroded sand. Our filming party emerged into another wide terraced valley with two valleys running off and no sign of the camels. It was very hot. We chose the valley that went in the correct direction and continued walking, hoping to see the camels in front of us.

An old man with weather-beaten face, black jacket and faded cap, appeared behind us, walking steadily, spinning rough yarn from black sheep's wool. He stopped and we entertained each other as best we could; we by demonstrating our self-erecting umbrella and he offering me a roll-up cigarette made from a strip of yellowed newspaper, filled with some dried leaves from his pocket which smelled like grass cuttings but could have been anything.

We stopped by a lake and lay around in the sunshine, sheltering underneath our umbrellas, arms and legs carefully covered to avoid sunburn.

Nick and Robbo were carrying the tripod and had made life difficult for me by wandering off ahead rather than keeping together so that we could film. They were bored with the constant stopping necessary for filming, and tired. They wanted to get to the next camp as soon as possible. I was tired myself and just as keen to finish for the day.

By pushing on, Nick and Robbo were putting me under pressure not to film. If I wanted to film something I had to call them back and they returned only reluctantly. As it was my job to film, this lack of cooperation seemed to me selfish, and was very wearing. I was tired, and at times, especially when suffering the headaches and phantom sore throats of my ME, more irritable than anyone else. This made me difficult when organizing shoots.

I have since discovered that most, if not all, film directors can be difficult. Being director, camera and light man, producer, sound man, etc, and at the same time carrying a third of the filming equipment on my back made for a difficult situation that was certainly not improving my temper.

Each step along these rocky footpaths brought incredible scenes into view. The frustration of not being able to film them all, and not having the time to think shots through because of the need to push on, was intense. I needed to slow down, to think about the next scene and look about me reflectively. I could not do this because my crew kept vanishing over the horizon.

We stopped by the lake to film. While I worked out camera angles, light readings, apertures and lenses, and filmed, everyone else slumped on rocks and rested. When I had finished, they were bored and ready to go. I needed a rest. Nick and Robbo wanted, yet again, to forge on ahead. I was irritated to the extent of having a few heart-felt words with them. I think that Robbo understood how I felt, but that Nick did not.

We were due to camp at around 4,300 metres, well below the top of the Aghil Pass. As we walked up from the lake, the camels and the orange tents of camp failed to materialize. Nellie, who was walking in our group, which had dwindled to six, had become sick; vomiting, with a splitting headache and dizziness, having to rest frequently in the shade.

We had been told that the camp would be just beyond the second set of sheep pens. After continuing well past this point, we stopped opposite another set of stone sheep pens and a flat-roofed dwelling. Our friend, the man spinning yarn from earlier in the day, appeared from the buildings with two women and several children, bringing them out to meet us. They were transhumance shepherds, grazing sheep and goats as far up the mountain as they could in the summer, moving back down to the valley in the harsh winter.

The women had wide, capable faces, dark hair and gold fillings. The children were grubby, a little shy and hilariously amused, especially when they discovered British Army boiled sweets. They wore thick padded clothes: the women and girls with long warm skirts and red ochre coloured shawls, father and the boys dark woollen caps, trousers and jackets.

Henry went on ahead to find the camp, returning over an hour later saying he had been to the very top of the pass, finding no-one. We had no faith in the LO's ability to remember the route. We thought the caravan could have taken a wrong turn down at the lake.

Nellie was quite ill and I was concerned for him. His symptoms could be mild or even medium altitude sickness – which could easily get worse. Also, it was late in the afternoon, 5 P.M. HMT, and already there were shadows on the western side of the valley. (Rather than persist with meaningless Beijing time, we invented Hunglee Morgan Time, in which we got up at 7 A.M. and went to bed around 8 P.M.)

Henry returned from his reconnaissance. We then had an involved discussion about what we should do, while Nellie lolled about trying to drink salty water, looking pale and ill. Henry argued that we should split into two parties, one to go and bring the others back up onto the proper route and the remainder to remain here with whatever warm clothing we had until the others arrived later. This splitting of the party was downright dangerous and I argued strongly against it.

After keeping this discussion going for some ten minutes, Henry said he had been joking and that the others were just minutes further up the pass, much higher than had been intended, but only over the next couple of rises. He said he had enjoyed listening to our arguments about what we thought should be done.

This odd little incident could only be a throw-back to the years Henry had spent teaching junior soldiers the basics of map reading, climbing and hill walking. Also, from stories the others told about previous expeditions, he was a tease. This was his teacher/leader/scoutmaster persona, setting us a little problem when we were tired to see how we would react.

Unfortunately we had a sick man on our hands; the situation was real and I didn't feel the need for a tutorial.

The discussion turned to Nellie. Henry believed him to be suffering more from youth and immaturity than from the effects of altitude. I felt that in the absence of anyone in the team who had actually experienced altitude sickness we should do exactly as we had been taught and take Nellie back down to sleep at a lower altitude for the night. He could recover and catch up the next day. Nick Moore, the trained medic, felt the same way; we had discussed it while Henry was away up the pass looking for the campsite.

When it came to the argument, in the face of Henry's determination not to be slowed down by Nellie, Nick would not speak, withdrawing from the conversation. I felt I had disagreed with Henry over too many other things already, and that there was a danger of his disregarding my views completely. So having said my piece about getting Nellie to a lower altitude, I shut up.

We all continued up the pass, proceeding with painful slowness up the hill. A donkey was led down from the camp, Nellie suffering the indignity of riding the last six hundred metres in the shade of a garish '7 UP' umbrella.

When I made it to camp, in the wake of the donkey, I felt dreadful. But after soup, numerous hot, sweet brews and supper, I felt better than for some time. I talked with Nellie, who lay quietly in his sleeping bag. He felt bad, no energy or willpower, with a splitting sick headache. He was continuing to force down a salt, sugar and water mixture to counter dehydration. With his fair skin and complexion, walking in the harsh sun all day, he could easily be suffering from a touch of sunstroke as well as the effects of the altitude. Henry had unrolled his sleeping bag by Nellie's side, to personally ensure that he would be all right during the night.

This, our fourth camp, was beautiful; a rocky slope between two 6,000-metre peaks with a stream running along the bottom. The sun was going down over the mountains, the last golden rays touching the massive peaks to the north that rose up over the saddle of the Aghil Pass. The camels were leaguered up together in their groups of four, facing inwards against the cold, their feed in the middle.

The drivers bought a young goat from the shepherd, carried it bleating down to the edge of the clear brook and cut its throat on the shining green grass. The sunset seemed to last for ever. Even after darkness had fallen, the snow tops to the south-east remained touched with gold, a strange and wonderful glow.

That night, Friday, 28 August, was terrible. I had a splitting headache, a very dry mouth and was sweating heavily inside my sleeping bag. Something was rummaging around in our rations. Thinking an animal was raiding the store, I zapped it with the concentrated beam of my headtorch. Andy's white face gleamed as he stumbled around in the dark, my torch beam having destroyed his night vision.

'Cheers,' said he.

I got up wearing only my shorts for a drink of water and pee as both thirst and bladder pressure were unbearable. The mugs had been put away and took me some time to find. The temperature was well below zero. Once I had drunk deeply, several mugs-full from the jerrycan, I was hopping from foot to foot, shivering and muttering, my teeth chattering with cold. Leaping through the darkness back to my warm bag I stubbed my toe and went head over heels in round, dry goat droppings.

Andy chuckled from the warmth of his bag.

The next morning I still felt dreadful but forced down rolled oats and brews of tea and coffee, then packed slowly and thoroughly for the ten-day exploration of the Shakesgam Valley.

The film crew again set off in front of the camels. The head of the pass was over an hour's walk with a lovely calm lake set in green moss and grass just before the final rim. We walked up through gravelly pasture-like peat bog, over several false crests, past the lake to the real head of the pass, which was a narrow cleft thirty metres wide, a dead camel lying just over the other side. We ate lunch a few metres down-wind.

Our barometric altimeters read 4,900 metres and the Chinese map 4,776 metres. I felt very tired, plus the usual headache and dizziness. The filming was hard work and I was rather sorry for myself.

We went briskly down the southern side of the Aghil Pass, steeply down through huge boulder runs and a narrow gorge. At the bottom, the pass suddenly opened out and we saw the valley for the first time.

The scale of the Shakesgam Valley was impossible to determine. I looked at its broad, completely flat floor, estimating it to be 300 metres wide. When the camels crossed to the far side later in the day, they became dots at the base of huge cliffs, showing the valley to be actually over a kilometre wide. The unexplored south-eastern upper part of the valley swept towards us and past the entrance to the Aghil Pass, turning in a long curve west and then south-west out of sight to our right. Six-thousand-metre peaks towered above the steep rock cliffs of the valley side.

To the south-east (to our left), the mysterious Upper Shakesgam Valley vanished into a bowl of legendary mountains, all snow-capped with swirling white streaks of cloud against a deep and glorious blue. Far, far away at the end of the valley, the Gasherbrums, the Staghars and the Aghil Mountains stood before us, with K2 (actually called Mount Godwin Austin) to the right, tantalizingly just out of our view.

We gazed in silence at a valley scoured flat by vast amounts of debris and water, the main drainage channel for an unbelievably large catchment area. The four of us (John Day, Nick Moore, Conrad Ainsley and I) were going to walk up this valley until we discovered the reason for the catastrophic floods that had created the flat, swept valley and destroyed villages, killing thousands of people in the inhabited region to the north and north-east.

We hoped to be able to discover whether remote sensing devices could be placed along the valley to warn of rising water levels and measure the usual fluctuations of the river so that impending floods might be predicted and defensive measures taken.

The scale of the terrain confused us all; Henry became quite irritated with me as he pointed out what he imagined to be different coloured muds on the valley floor. He wondered what geomor-phological process had caused this. I could not understand his question at all as I saw (on a much larger scale) several different water channels flowing amongst boulders, the water darker than the lighter grey of the stone. The lighter alluvial material had been sliced off at the base of the cliffs by the main water flow. Henry's 'muds' were in fact the water and boulders seen from a long way off.

The scale and flatness of the valley floor were disturbing as well as misleading. Whatever caused the catastrophic floods that had gouged out this extraordinary channel lay just out of our sight. Once on the valley floor, the steep alluvial cliffs at either side would make it impossible for us to get out if flood waters did come down. Floods had occurred every three years or so, and it seemed that a flood was now one year overdue.

We were looking at a very powerful environment: of brutal,

swiftly changing weather and the potential energy of countless billions of tons of ice, rock and water, like a super-charged battery from which unimaginably destructive forces could be unleashed at any moment. It was awesomely beautiful, and the sweep, curve and breadth of the valley, its flat floor and apparently small rivulets of water trickling in the sunshine so far below seemed ominous – as well as wildly exciting.

Above: Seven of the team crossing the Shakesgam River on the backs of camels, en route to make their first reconnaissance of the Crown. This photograph was taken from the foot of the Aghil Pass, looking south-east up the Shakesgam Valley.

Below: Andy Aspinall, Bob Wood and Conrad Ainsley drinking tea on the Hong Kong to Beijing express.

Above: Cleaning express trains at Beijing railway station – one of many labour-intensive jobs in the Chinese People's Republic.

Left: A Chinese tourist smokes a reflective pipe beside the water garden of a temple outside Xian. The site of former capitals of China, the area around Xian has much astonishing archaeology, attracting tourists from all over China.

Below: A venerable Muslim outside the mosque in Kashgar, Chinese Turkestan's principal Islamic city. The far west of China is ethnically Middle Eastern, governed (like Tibet before the troubles) one step removed from Beijing – as Xinjiang Autonomous Region.

Above: A Kashgar blacksmith's small son learning his trade early.

Below: Kashgar Lake in the early morning.

Above: A baker stirs up the coals in the bottom of his bread oven – in the bazaar of the usually forbidden 'closed' town of Yechung.

Left: Carpet merchants in the Kashgar bazaar.

Below: A barber and long-suffering patient in the Kashgar bazaar.

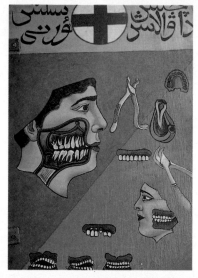

Above: An anxious patient awaits her turn at a Kashgar dentist.

Far left: Our 'dentist' Nick Moore fills one of Ian Roberts' teeth in Kashgar – just before we enter the mountains.

Left: A Kashgar dentist's alarmingly explicit sign.

Below: A Yechung bazaar 'fast food' stall – poor vendors selling tiny cooked birds to equally poor customers.

A Kashgar butcher eats his lunch, with a freshly butchered sheep on the hook beside him. Without refrigeration, only one animal at a time can be killed, and a sub-class of very poor street vendors can often be seen trying to sell dusty, over-ripe entrails.

Left: The fast-flowing Yarkand River, which our path into the Karakorams followed.

Below left: A tiny, isolated village on the road through the K'un Lun Mountains, on our route to Maza Dala.

Right: Our route to the mountain: up the Yarkand River valley and its massive river terraces, overshadowed by daunting Karakoram peaks.

Below: Filming on a river terrace above the Yarkand River, one and a half day's march south from Maza Dala.

Inset: The only grass for hundreds of miles: striking camp at Durbin Jangal, the beautiful oasis where Victorian explorer Sir Francis Edward Younghusband was said to have lost his spectacles.

Main picture: Taken just downstream of where the snout of the Urdok Glacier enters the Shakesgam River, the last rays of the evening sun illuminate K2 – seen (very unusually) from the east.

Right: Loading the camels.

Below: John Day taking notes for our survey of the Upper Shakesgam Valley while Nick Moore rearranges his kit, the Aghil Mountains behind.

Right: Massive nunatooks thrown up by the Gasherbrum Glacier's flow into the Urdok Glacier at the head of the glaciated part of the Shakesgam Valley, seen from the lateral moraine to the north.

K2 (Mount Godwin Austen) seen from
just below where the Urdok Glacier
enters the Shakesgam River.

Above: Packing up the Crown Base Camp: (left to right) John Day (rear), Conrad Ainsley, Henry Morgan and Robert Nelson (Nellie).

Left: Jerry Slack carrying a load on the Skamri Glacier from the Crown Base Camp to Camp One.

Below: The summit of the Crown seen from Camp Two.

Main picture: The view from Camp Two at 22,000 feet southeast into Pakistan, with K2 looming over everything else.

Inset left: Henry Morgan and Robert Nelson belayed onto 'Nellie's Ledge', a resting place two hours below Camp Two.

Inset right: Andy Aspinall, Jerry Slack and Bob Wood carrying loads from Nellie's Ledge to Camp Two – with Conrad Ainsley closest to camera. The summit of the Crown is to the right.

Below: Group photograph taken at the Crown Base Camp just before walking out – the Crown in the background. (Left to right) sitting: Nick Moore, Ian Roberts (Robbo), John Day, Robert Nelson (Nellie), Bob Wood. Standing: Andy Aspinall, Henry Morgan, Conrad Ainsley, Jerry Slack, and author.

Above: Conrad Ainsley and author cooking a feast on our last day at the Crown Base Camp.

Below: One day's march from the southern entrance to the Aghil Pass, in the Lower Shakesgam Valley. Wang, the Liaison Officer, and Jin Jun ride the camels during the walk-out.

Above: The author and the summit of the Crown – taken from Camp Two.

Right: Winter arrives early, making the rough, unmade road through the K'un Lun Mountains and back to civilization treacherous with ice.

Below: A Chinese soldier opens the barrier to allow us to proceed to the head of the Kunjerab Pass and thus leave China.

Above: Turkestan mosque in a small village to the west of Kashgar, on our route to the Kunjerab Pass.

Above: Ferocious polo on the ancient practice ground in the centre of Gilgit.

Left: An elaborately decorated lorry in Gilgit.

CHAPTER 8

Dragons, and the Valley of the Shadow

A place known to exist, but which no-one has ever visited, becomes the subject of legends. Ancient cartographers stated – confidently, as none could contradict them – that in such places 'be Dragons'.

In 1937 Eric Shipton and friends marched from Pakistan into the south of our region of the Karakoram and mapped it for the first time, Shipton calling his excellent book *The Blank on the Map*. Legends suggested ancient trade and cultural contact over the impenetrable Karakoram watershed, between the Balti to the south and the Turkis to the north. Shipton drove himself, his friends and reluctant porters up treacherous valleys, searching for elusive, long-forgotten high passes, concluding that many of these legendary routes could not have existed.

Eric Shipton did, however, find evidence of another legend. With great reluctance he described tracking footprints in the snow for several miles, of a bipedal animal which stopped to drink from a small pool, of the tracks leading onto and across a bare scree slope, never to reappear. His sherpa porters told him afterwards that without any doubt the tracks had been made by a yeti, the smaller, five-foot-ten-inch maneater, rather than the larger, shaggier and more benevolent herbivore.

Shipton was a serious explorer, a geographer and scientist. The last thing he wanted was to be part of the 'Abominable Snowman' controversy. His careful revelation of what he saw is therefore doubly valuable as the sober recollections of an honest man.

The yeti legend flourishes throughout the high mountains of the

Himalaya, on both sides of the watershed, with a remarkable consensus of description between peoples separated by impassable ranges, very great distances and language. Animals and birds somehow manage to survive even where we were going (although I cannot understand how they get through the savage winters): rabbits, ibex and huge black ravens – who watch ominously from a safe distance, throwing shadows of doubt across a mountaineer's soul. Why should a larger and more intelligent creature not also survive there?

Satellite photography has removed all the blanks from the map of the world, but has left plenty of uncertainty and a lot of inaccuracy. Dragons could still hide themselves away under rocks, so until humans have been to all these last remaining unexplored places, who is to say that dragons do not exist? Mystery is stimulating, nourishment to the human soul. To that extent we need dragons.

The Chinese say that dragons keep the world going round. Perhaps, once the last secret places have been inspected, when explorers are able to say, with dreadful finality, that there are no more dragons, it will stop spinning. (Without the spark of human interest, maybe we will destroy it anyway – with under-arm deodorants and furniture spray.)

For me, entering the citadel of the unknown was deeply exciting. It was an unashamedly Rider Haggard thrill, the stuff of old-fashioned boys' comic-books. The great explorers had often, literally, nothing to sustain them but this emotion. In our totally-informed, modern world, we are closeted by the media. It was wonderful to be free of it all, and to be one of the privileged few who can really be called 'explorers'.

The camels threaded their way down the pass and onto the top of the massive river terrace, plodding half a mile south-east to a place where the alluvium cliff, breached by a stream, allowed us to scramble down onto the valley floor. We waited on the river's edge while the camels crossed, dumped their loads, then returned to carry the team across the raging torrents.

John, Conrad, Nick and I said farewell to the others, shaking hands and waving them off. We would not see them for at least two weeks. Clutching each other's waists, they lurched two-up on the camels' backs into the deep, fast channels of the Shakesgam River. In four days they would reach K2 base camp, then walk a further day to the tip of the Skamri Glacier where the equipment would be dumped. The twenty-four camels would return to the Aghil Pass, and over, back to their villages, to wait until we had finished on the mountain.

In less than two weeks, we hoped to have explored the Upper Shakesgam valley and be back at the Pass. Our two camels would rendezvous and walk out with the others. We would be left with a five-day load to carry to the foot of the Skamri Glacier, where we hoped the others would have set up base camp.

The camels dwindled into a line of small black dots beneath the curtained face of the far terrace. Our next camp site was a beautiful green knoll on the northern side of the valley, with grass and bushes. It seemed most unlikely: there was a white bell tent pitched on green grass, of the sort used by jousting knights in Hollywood medieval spectaculars. Discarded ration tins painted military green with Chinese writing were strewn about the sand, indicating that the Chinese army had been here, probably some time ago as the tent was beginning to rot. We unloaded the camels and settled into this unexpectedly luxurious accommodation.

Our intrepid exploration of the Upper Shakesgam started badly. Having had a wash in a pool where the sun had taken the edge off the usually glacier-cold river water, I was gazing reflectively across boulders and water to where the twenty-four camels had disappeared. I noticed our camel driver running across the gravel banks in the centre of the river waving a stick.

Trotting irresponsibly ahead of him, looking round then trotting further on, were our camels, free of their loads and very fleet of foot. All were soon on the far side, dots moving around the curve and then out of sight. I hoped the camels would stop when they regained the company of their brethren. We were stuck without them.

There was nothing to be done except cook supper and go to sleep. We were now on a full ration every day rather than the eight rations for ten to which so far we had been limited. It was a good feed.

The next morning (Sunday, 30 August) the camels and driver had not returned. After the five days' march from Maza, and a night down at just less than 4,000 metres, I was feeling much better. The backs of my hands, constantly exposed to the sun, were red, rather sore and slightly puffy – possibly a touch of high altitude fluid retention – and my lips were beginning to crack in spite of liberal use of lip salve and barrier cream; but my lightweight walking boots, like ankle-length running shoes, strongly recommended by Henry, seemed to be standing up to the terrain. I had slept well, even managing to avoid taking an involuntary sauna in my high altitude sleeping bag by sleeping naked and keeping the zip undone.

At 11.12, firmly tied together and not looking the slightest bit chastened, the camels were brought back. We loaded quickly and set off, walking up-wind of the animals.

All morning the river had been rising. Just after midday we were blocked by the outside of a meander flowing hard against the conglomerate cliff. With much hissing and tapping of forelegs with sticks, the second camel was made to kneel and I clambered up to perch on top of the load. With the driver on top of the lead camel, we set off into the water.

The driver seemed to understand the river; we lurched into the network of cold, very fast streams, he choosing the crossing points with great care and whacking the lead camel with his stick if he attempted to turn away. In the centre of the channels, which were between thirty and two hundred metres wide, the water surged well above the camels' knees (waist height for us), pushing them downstream, making them scream with fear and reluctance. They stumbled in underwater pot-holes, then climbed out up the banks with laboured heaves and lurches.

The crossing, to the inside of the meander, took three-quarters of an hour. Wearing only Union Jack-patterned shorts (the flag must be shown when exploring unknown parts), I found sitting on a plastic drum soon became uncomfortable. While the unloaded camels returned to pick up 'Rad, Nick and John, I had lunch and a snooze, carefully covered up from the fierce overhead sun.

We reloaded the camels, then walked along the boulder-strewn valley floor until late afternoon. But when we attempted a second river crossing, the camels noisily refused to leave the bank as the water, late in the day, was too fast and deep. We could go no further, so found a sandy indentation in the valley wall that would do as a dry and reasonably sheltered camp site.

Nick cooked supper, boiling water to pour over the dehydrated meat granules and spooning the resulting sludge into metal mugs. He volunteered for this duty as a mind-occupying task. Unfortunately his efforts were not very successful; the water from the fast-flowing river was grossly silted, the plastic water bag looked as though it was filled with cement, which made the stew and pomme disgustingly crunchy.

Nick, who had spent most of the day walking with the camels while the rest of us picked another route away from their flatulence, told us our driver's name was 'Issac'.

Of indeterminate age, twenty-four to thirty-eight, Issac spoke no English or Chinese and was quiet with a lovely smile and an enthusiastic nod when he understood and agreed. He wore a green Chinese army peaked cap, a dark brown suit and worn plimsolls. His shirt was thick and embroidered and he smelled of wood smoke. Issac was worried about the river; if I understood his sign language correctly, he was uncertain about how far we would be able to travel the next day.

Issac was carefully adjusting the saddle of his second camel, ripping bits of cloth to cushion the cord tied around the front of the first hump. The primitive saddle, two sticks parallel to the camel's spine running either side of the humps and lashed together with strong cord, looked most uncomfortable. A thick straw mat hung down on either side, and the loads, lashed onto the sticks, hung down onto the matting. The loads counterbalanced each other and were lashed together over the top, the total weight spread along either side of the animal's spine. Cross straps kept the two sticks together and they dug into the front of each hump – which looked painful.

The humps themselves were squashed by the loads without apparently causing pain or coming to any harm. The large male camel's first hump was completely floppy, hanging down to one side like an old fur garment. Both their coats were brown with thick, darker fur on the humps, lower neck and upper front legs, like fashionably clipped poodles. Their tails were short and stumpy, shiny and hairless, waving from side to side as the camels walked along. The heads and necks were thick and strong with large incisors in the lower jaw, yellow and worn from their interminable chewing.

Camels' legs are remarkable. On getting down to be loaded or to rest at night, they fold up until the animals are lying on their bellies, two metres of leg tucked away underneath. When they rise incredible double-jointed articulation can be seen with even the feet and ankles folding back on themselves. The camels scream and complain at having to go down onto their knees, especially onto stony ground, but once down seem content to stay there – provided there are no additions to their loads.

The phrase describing the camel as an animal designed by committee gives more credit to committees than they deserve. It is purpose-built: powerful head, shoulders, neck and forelegs with barrel chest curving sharply upward to a slender waist and the thigh muscles of a greyhound. The legs are long and thin with large, soft feet that are beautifully adapted to all sorts of terrain; the size of a dinner plate, with two toes surrounded by soft pads, the feet are placed carefully onto the ground and spread out as the weight goes onto the leg in two careful stages, to prevent slipping; the ankle then bends forward to allow the leg to be swung economically into the next easy stride.

Riding a heavily laden camel is not easy as its shorter front legs tend to make you slip forward and the motion is jerky and uncomfortable. The 'ship of the desert' analogy is fair, for a small vessel in choppy seas.

Already I was alternating between deep interest in our Great Adventure and counting the days before we started walking back out again. I thought that most were feeling like this; it was an endurance course, better afterwards to look back on, with the odd moment of enjoyment.

I was worried about Issac. The LO and Jin Jun had told us that he was self-sufficient, that we had to provide neither food nor shelter for him. Today he had eaten nothing so we gave him biscuits and sweets, and a share of our supper which pleased him greatly. We could not continue to do this, however, as we had only enough victuals for ourselves.

Issac was also woefully ill-equipped for the weather and terrain; mist had rolled in from the east bringing dank, cold, wet weather. Luckily we had brought a small tent for our stores so he was able to sleep in the dry, wrapped in his thick embroidered quilts. I asked him to show me his food; small loaves of hard bread which he indicated he would dunk in water from the river: 'No problem,' he mimed, 'I'll be back with the others in ten days or so.'

Unfortunately, if he got wet, with holes in his plimsolls, no socks and no waterproof, his low (or no) calorie diet would cause him to suffer from exposure very swiftly. We decided to give him brews whenever we made them, plus all the boiled sweets and food we could spare. Ironically it transpired that he was saving the boiled sweets for his children rather than boosting his calorie count. He was very friendly, rushing off to refill water bottles or wash out cooking pots, doing jobs whenever he could identify them.

I felt sorry for him and annoyed with the CMA for not thinking about the welfare of their drivers. But the reality was that if they had thought of the drivers, the CMA would have made us provide for them at exorbitant cost to us, and profit for themselves.

We comforted ourselves by saying that Issac expected very little, if anything at all, that his standards of comfort were different from ours and that he accepted the rigours of this hard environment. We had missed the point; people who live in extreme conditions share what they have with one another. Issac would have been expecting that we would do the same – indeed he would not understand that we could do otherwise.

After supper, Issac untied the camel-food sack. His animals were on their feet in an instant, the male urinating and crapping with anticipation, probably in a natural reaction to imminent food, his digestive system being designed to retain natural waste and wring the last joule of nourishment from it. Issac measured out straw and grain onto a canvas sheet, made the beasts kneel side by side and placed the sack before them, carefully turning up the edges so they formed a trough.

They ate carefully, thoroughly and in a civilized fashion. Issac watched closely, adjusting their harnesses and saddles, until all the food was gone – which took about forty minutes. He removed the sack and made them kneel in line, the male in front, wrapping a thick cord around the male's front legs – bent double – and the saddle, hobbling them to prevent a second and potentially disastrous repeat of the previous night's bid for freedom.

In the cloudy cold that now prevailed, there was nothing else to do but go to bed, in sleeping bags inside waterproof bivvie bags. My eyes were very sore, I had a headache and a slight but constantly bleeding nose, probably from the dry atmosphere of the past week. The sun dropped behind unnamed mountains to the west and I settled down to endure a disturbed night of unpleasant dreams.

The next day (Monday, 31 August) was cold and bleak. The river was running high, and after half an hour's careful investigation and noisy refusals by the lead camel, Issac – with Nick on the second camel – got across. The lead camel was hesitant and reluctant, losing his footing several times. Issac indicated that he didn't want to risk coming back for the three of us, but that if we climbed up onto the terrace and walked along past the meander, he would cross back at a less dangerous place and pick us up. This proved to be quite exciting.

John, 'Rad and I had to scramble across a steeply angled scree slope that ended with a twenty-foot drop into the fast-flowing river. John found a little cove with shallow water and a sand beach. We scrambled across the scree and down a steep gully towards the beach. The gully passed under a large dried-mud arch and was filled with loose, round boulders that rolled down freely whenever we disturbed them.

Issac couldn't get the camels into the beach so we had to climb back out. This took over an hour, the loose, dry mud and stones giving no firm holds, requiring much use of knees, elbows and chins.

Our situation was becoming serious. The waters were rising rapidly as the glaciers melted, and our kit, food and transport were the other side of a raging torrent. Issac managed to get across to a point below one of the cliffs, and it was up to us to climb down to him. The rock was very loose, we had no ropes and could not see where we were placing our feet. Eventually we all got down and onto the camels, who were standing in the fast- flowing water. I perched behind Issac, John and 'Rad on the second camel. The patient beasts waded back through the torrent to the other side of the meandering channels where we reloaded the equipment and continued up the valley.

A village, Marpo La, was firmly marked on our map, but as we approached there was no evidence of anything remotely human to be seen on the ground. The cold, dank weather and worry about being trapped by the waters was getting us down. We might have been walking past the site of the lost civilization reputed by legend to exist somewhere in the mysterious depths of the unexplored valley – but we did not care. No-one even commented on the matter as we stumbled past.

The day continued cold and miserable; I was becoming increasingly tired, having to rush off behind rocks as my bowels were playing up. We tramped on past the base of a glacier and 'Marpo La', seeing nothing but alluvium and with no interest in anything except getting as far up the valley as possible. At a rest stop we fantasized briefly about an old man dressed in white inviting us up into a citadel carved from the living rock to meet his four nubile (and rapacious) daughters. The wonders of Marpo La (no monks with the secret of eternal youth here) probably existed only in the mapmaker's imagination.

We camped that night amid large boulders and gravel in the dry course of a water flow that looked like a massive municipal rubbish tip. The valley ahead was completely blocked by a huge black wall of glacial debris hundreds of feet high, with the bright, white nunataks – ice ridges and splinters pushed up as the ice sheered under massive internal pressures – of the Gasherbrum Glacier protruding like sharpened teeth over the top. A stream too powerful for us to cross with the camels ran from the west through our camping ground from a deeply eroded gully, gouged away as if by open cast mining. The boulders and silt were as white and grey as the cold, grim skies overhead.

Our food was again very silted; we attempted to cook rice which remained hard despite the use of much valuable fuel, and was grey with grit. Even with our waterproofs and thermal clothing, the damp cold was getting into our bones, and supper provided no relief from the misery.

Issac was feeling it particularly badly, squatting in the rain rubbing his hands together. The tent was up but Nick was inside writing up his diary, which prevented Issac from laying out his quilts and getting warm. I mentioned Issac's plight to Nick, receiving a disdainful glance and the comment that Issac would just have to wait. That night, crawling into our sleeping bags at 6 P.M. in order to get warm, I comforted myself by reading about altitude sickness causing sleeplessness. Insomnia was denying me the oblivion and escape from reality of a good night's sleep. The book was a comforting acknowledgement of my plight.

The next fifteen hours were exhausting; fitful sleep broken when nightmares brought me back to grim, lonely reality – to worry: about the safety of what we were doing, whether I would come out of it in one piece, the dangerous location of our camp in the centre of a floodwater channel, the cold, wet weather continuing endlessly . . . all sorts of gremlins and idiocies, completely out of proportion, and consequently particularly depressing.

The noisy drops of rain hit my bivvie bag a few inches above my head. It was like trying to sleep while stiff cellophane was crackled beside your ear. The zip leaked, dripping cold water onto my neck which the down of my sleeping bag soaked up like blotting paper.

My anxiety turned into a physical reaction that affected my stomach. Pressure seemed to build up. My digestive system was not working terribly well anyway, causing flatulence of such frequency and smell that I was forced, even with the freezing rain pouring down outside, to open the bivvie bag for fresh air. In a faint light, storm clouds were gathering down valley and working their way up towards us like an express train.

The worry, and the corresponding physical reaction of my guts seemed to combine, forcing a rapid exit from my warm but unpleasantly smelly bivvie bag into the cold wet night. I made it to the rocks with seconds to spare, to find I had used up all my loo paper on an earlier foray.

Back in the warm, damp darkness of the bag, I found myself

calculating the number of days left to endure, listing the dangers to come, and generally regretting ever having become involved with this expedition.

I felt isolated from the others in the team, and in particular from John Day, whose apparent suspicions, jealousy and hostility might be spreading to the others. His was a powerful personality and I was worried that his attitude towards me could become a darkness in the minds of the others about which I could do nothing.

The isolation was becoming a psychological problem for me. There was no alternative but to struggle on, doing the filming work that might, if I could do it well enough, help the expedition overdraft. In my depression, the behaviour of some of the others seemed terribly unfair: that they could not see how much of a gamble the trip was for me; that they wanted to climb in the Karakoram to fulfil their life ambitions as mountaineers but that such a thing was neither here nor there to me as I could be just as terrified in North Wales.

The dragons seemed to have deserted me and the shadow of the valley was on my soul. It was one of the blackest of nights.

The next day, the first of September, was a little pentecostal. It started for me at 6 A.M. with stars twinkling above and a rushing wind. The weight of depression seemed to have lifted a little. The rushing wind, heralding a welcome change in the weather, seemed also to have a touch of comfort, of an answer to the prayers of the previous night.

I fervently hoped the clouds would clear. At 7 it was cold with a clear sky, my bivvie bag stiff with ice. At 8.15 the sun touched the tops of the peaks to the west, driving away the remaining bands of mist that clung to the sides of the Aghil Mountains. We started slowly and reluctantly to get up. I felt sick and stumbled about putting on every item of clothing I had brought. Issac wandered disconsolately, toes protruding from the ends of his ripped-up plimsolls, watching his camels carefully and wrapping his torn corduroy coat around his shoulders.

John started making the breakfast porridge, pumping the petrol stove and decanting clear water from the top of the water bag in which the thick, grey silt had settled to the bottom during the night. Nick, who had been doing the cooking up to now, was 'organizing' his kit; he often did this, methodically putting his boots into a special bag and laying out gloves, shirts, camera, etc in orderly lines on top of his sleeping mat. John asked how much water to put with the porridge,

'Three mugs full.'

I took over the stirring of the mixture, to be told by Nick that the porridge would be useless without having been soaked overnight. This would have been impossible as the silt took all night to settle out.

'Gritty porridge would be utterly disgusting,' I replied.

Conrad asked me if the brew was thickening up.

'Hard to tell.'

'I told you,' grumbled Nick, 'it'll never be any good not having been soaked all night.' He stomped off in the direction of the river.

'That,' said John emphatically, 'is a bloody unhelpful thing to say. It really gets up my nose.'

As the cook, I decided to stop wasting fuel on the watery porridge when what we really needed was a hot brew of tea. Poor Issac was crouched beside me warming his hands by the stove. I made him a pint of tea with a full sachet of sugar, about three heaped teaspoons. He grinned and delved into his tucker sack for a small iron-hard loaf to dunk.

'Chai, chai,' he said.

He took up some drinks sachets and amazed me by reading the English printing:

'Soogar . . . two five gums . . . innerstand cohfay.'

To the south-west, mountains had appeared from the mists of yesterday prompting me to wonder whether the very prominent peak, half-obscured by a nearby hill, could be K2.

'Not a chance, that's just some insignificant pimple on a ridge,' said John.

I started looking at the map. Nick came over and agreed with John's verdict.

'I find it very difficult to relate these huge peaks to each other because they are all jammed into a relatively small area – or they are so huge that you can't judge how far away they are,' I said. 'I can't see what else it could be, apart from K2.'

'No,' said Nick with authority, 'it must be Skyang Kangri.'

I peered at the map again.

'Skyang Kangri is 24,750 feet, not a pimple. If you could see it from here, then K2, at 28,250 feet, would tower over it to the left of that gully.'

There was much sucking of teeth and recognition of mountain ranges previously read about in mountaineering magazines: the Gasherbrums, the Staghar Group over the top of the black wall of the glacial moraine, and the Aghils to the east.

'Anyway, it doesn't look like K2,' came the definitive comment — from Nick again. As none of us had ever seen K2 from this direction, the north-east, I wondered how recognizable it would be.

'You are the mountaineer,' I said, 'which is why I asked you in the first place.'

(Three weeks later, Henry told me that Nick was a novice, like 'Rad and myself. I was surprised at this, as I had gained the impression that he was quite experienced. Perhaps, in Nick's keenness to become a mountaineer, he wanted to distance himself from 'Rad and me, to be considered with the others for a chance at the summit of the Crown. Without hindsight, all I knew at the time was the tension that both he and John were creating.)

John came over and consulted the map.

'I think in fact you are right, Hugh,' said he. 'That is probably K2.'

Even at a time of gloom and unhappiness, my shutter finger itched to photograph this great peak from a new direction.

A huge, black raven had investigated us thoroughly the night before and now returned, keeping a respectable distance but making forays into the panful of silty, abandoned rice. Around us, twelve- and fifteen-foot boulders sat dumped in the middle of the rock fields, some smoothed by water, others jagged from freezing and sudden thawing in the hot sun. Smooth banks of fine sand lay in piles above the jagged rocks, some mixed with brown soil.

Throughout the confusion and devastation of this no-man's-land, small tough plants with fine green stems and leaves somehow flourished, delicate orange and yellow flowers that were quickly spotted by the camels and eaten.

This was not a place for the living.

The day's activities started with an argument between John and me over what we should do. Henry had told me that we were both 'in charge' of this part of the expedition, John to lead on the surveying side and me to do the photography. John had thought out a reconnaissance plan based upon moving camp to the other side of the river. Without knowing what lay at the other side of the huge black wall of lateral moraine, and therefore how far we and the camels would be able to walk, moving camp immediately seemed to me premature and a waste of time and effort. John, however, was absolutely set on carrying out his plan.

In what ensued, John must have assumed that he was in charge and that I was being awkward or trying to usurp his authority. But I was not going to be dictated to without a proper discussion, especially when we were talking to a great extent about how I would do my job. The vagueness of Henry's command structure, with each of us finding our own level in the expedition, was not going to work for John and me.

I understood by now that John did not like opposition or discussion, especially when it came from me; nor did he like personal criticism, which my questioning of his ideas seemed to imply. I was accused of being awkward and producing a 'conflicting plan', namely to wait and see what Issac wanted to do with his camels and plan around that. Issac was entitled to rest them for two days, so we had to ensure our plan allowed for that to happen.

This argument was surprisingly bitter; it was made very clear to me that my opinions, as a novice mountaineer perhaps, were not very highly regarded by John, who was the expert. It seemed, nevertheless, that I won the argument, although it did end badly:

'OK,' said John, 'I'll give you this one – even though I don't agree with you.'

He made it sound as though he were doing me a favour, with the strong implication that next time I was to shut up.

'I don't want you to give me anything. We are not talking about winning and losing,' I replied. I was sick of having to struggle so much to have my 'non-mountaineer' common sense taken into account.

'You decide what to do.' I said, turning away. 'I spent all last night worrying. I don't want any more worries. You decide.'

As it turned out, Issac led the camels back off down the valley, making a change of camp site impossible that day. We filmed and surveyed the western side of the valley and the main gully leading up to the Skyang Lungpa glacier. Issac did not like being so far up the Shakesgam valley. He was worried about the river – and was not on his own as I shared similar fears. He had vanished from sight down the valley. Had he not left his tucker sack, knife pouch and ropes at the camp site, we would have suspected him of abandoning us.

We were camping at 15,000 feet (4,500 metres), and I woke several times on the second night with the crazy, breathless dreams of Cheyne-Stokes breathing – when carbon dioxide builds up in the body during sleep because of shallow, sea-level breathing. You then dream very realistically of drowning or of being suffocated, waking in a panic, gasping like a four-hundred-metre hurdler. Mercifully I did not suffer the stomach cramps and diarrhoea of the previous night.

I awoke at 7 to a clear, very cold day, threw stones at 'Rad's bivvie bag and we tramped off with the camera to film the sunrise on K2 from the top of a large drumlin. After two hours we returned weak and tired to rolled oats and a brew.

After packing up the camp, we set off towards the black wall of moraine. Issac pushed off on his own to graze the camels. John, Conrad, Nick and I continued to the east side of the valley and climbed to the top of the moraine.

From below, the moraine looked like a yacht marina – the nunataks like sails. From the top of the moraine, the nunataks protruded like shiny white teeth from the dirty debris-covered glacier and green, ominously dripping lakes. The whole glacier seemed wildly incongruous, like some huge arctic amusement park.

The glacier was alive with constant noise, as boulders and stones rolled and slithered down from the top of the ice flow. Each had split from the underlying rock, emerging after hundreds of years of upward progress through the ice as it moved slowly from mountain to valley snout. Below our feet, the moraine was under pressure from the constant movement of the glacier, wide cracks slowly opening, dislodging boulders and making deep breaches in the earth rampart of this enormous natural wall.

The Gasherbrum Glacier runs from its own valley out into the Shakesgam Valley, and would have buried itself into the base of the Aghil Mountains opposite had not the Shakesgam river cut a narrow channel fifty metres wide across its snout.

We had thought the huge black wall, about four kilometres long and over eighty metres high, must be the terminal moraine. The glaciers and accumulated floodwaters (which we presumed to be the cause of the catastrophic flooding) were behind. On climbing to the ramparts of the moraine, it seemed to be a lateral moraine: a wall created along the side of the glacier by the debris being exuded from its downstream side.

In the centre of the glacier a huge conical pile of debris towered over the nunataks – pushed-up ridges of fractured ice – higher than the moraine. In the distance the Gasherbrum and Changharlung Glaciers flowed down like filthy, frozen torrents, their movement too slow for us to perceive. The massive, slow-motion collision produced this strange mountain of rubble.

Without reference objects to give a scale to what we were looking at, distances and heights were impossible to judge. These two glaciers contained the ice created from the drainage of the eastern side of K2, Skyang Kangri, the Broad Group, Boltoro Muztagh, the north and east of the Gasherbrums and the west of the Staghars – a massive area of the highest mountains in the world.

Behind our black rampart, the lateral moraine wall, ominous dripping pools contained billions of gallons of water and endless ice. The mud and boulder walls had been breached in several places, probably by meltwater. From the huge size of the breaches, it seemed that they would have been the source of the catastrophic floods.

And in the distance, beyond a long bend in the river, there was a second wall of black moraine. More incongruous white sails of ice beckoned, nunataks of the massive Urdok Glacier.

* * *

Moving from our previous camp, and seeing the mountains to the north-east from a different perspective, solved the argument about K2. From the river at the bottom of the black moraine wall we could see up the Skyang Lungpa Glacier gully. The impressive mountain I had spent several hours photographing was plainly not K2 but an unnamed 20,000-footer. The weather had cleared and behind this usurper there was a ridge, the centre obscured by cloud. The real K2 was in the centre of the ridge, not visible, lurking in its own envelope of bad weather – as do all really big mountains.

The discovery of the real K2 ('Not now, K2', in the style of Peter Sellers, became a catch phrase) was the start of a row with Nick Moore, who had listened to the argument with John earlier and had decided that I was wasting time.

'Rad and I were filming while he and John ate lunch. While we packed up they pushed on to the moraine. We were tired, having been up for two hours filming early in the morning, and wanted our lunch too. Nick came back to tell us to hurry up, saying that I'd wasted a whole day taking 'happy snaps' of the wrong mountain and that John was unhappy at the slowness of my progress.

Apart from asking John whether he blamed me for the mistake over K2 – and as he had been even more wildly wrong than me, it was as well that he demurred from this – I bit my lip, although I was furious. Once we were together on the eastern tip of the moraine and John was busy sorting out his survey notes prior to my doing the panorama photos, I had a go at Nick:

'You and I have got to have some sort of understanding if we are to avoid getting right up each other's nostrils. All the photography is important and I am the poor sod that has to do every single bit of it. *We* did not waste a day filming the wrong mountain – just 'Rad and I this morning while you were still in your bivvie bag.

'No professional camera crew wanted to come on this trip because they didn't think they would be able to integrate with us. You are making me feel an outsider, a boil on the backside of the expedition. While you scoffed your lunch and wrote up your diary, 'Rad and I were working. And then you have the neck to tell me I'm working too slowly. You have made me absolutely furious and I'm not going to lose any more sleep bottling it up.'

I'm not sure what Nick's reaction to this was, but it certainly made me feel a lot better.

The survey of the moraine took the rest of the day, stumbling over the dried mud and loose boulders to the far end, at the valley side. We had intended to camp there, up from the valley floor and to the side, safely away from the river. However, there was no water and the camels were unable to cross the loose boulders that had flowed down from the breaches in the moraine. We walked the four kilometres back along the length of the moraine to the Shakesgam river, camping to the east on soft sand and pebbles. The water was icy, making bathing before supper a brisk and agonizing business.

After many rehydrating brews, curry, peas and pomme – rice with silt having been struck off the menu – we stood about talking until it grew dark, then lay in our bags discussing the glaciers.

I reckoned that the Gasherbrum Glacier and the Changharlung that feeds into it had created the extraordinary moraine, which was possibly a combination of terminal moraine from the Changharlung and lateral moraine from the Gasherbrum. The Gasherbrum Glacier was in the ascendancy at the moment and the moraine appeared to channel it across the Shakesgam Valley into the cliffs of the Aghil Mountains, where at the snout the river had eroded a gap of between fifty and one hundred metres.

The next morning the early sun touched the mountain tops with gold. However, the summit of the mountain we now knew to be K2 remained irritatingly cloaked in a small and very local cloud. Hoping that it would be blown away, I crawled from the warmth of my bag and set up cameras.

Issac had spent the previous day collecting purple roots and dry vegetation. He built a fire as I worked with cameras and tripod, squatting warming his hands in the smoke, then hanging around the cooking place hoping for a cup of 'chai'. He had annoyed Conrad the night before by watching him pack away the cooking gear, then asking for tea after he had finished. This morning 'Rad ignored him, feeding us porridge, then tea and coffee.

Issac wandered off foraging with the camels again as it was

another 'official' rest day. By this stage he probably preferred their company to ours.

We regarded him as a half-wit, ill-prepared for this environment and incapable of doing what he had been told. With hindsight, I can see that Issac was never far from doing the right thing, although none of us would have given him any credit for it at the time. Despite the language barrier, and the imposition of our values on someone who had no clue as to what those values might be, he did well, keen to act as was required if only he could identify what that was.

We were intolerant and very narrow-minded, but perhaps there was an element of necessity in this for us. We were behaving badly, not only towards Issac, but also towards one another. Perhaps this was in order to keep ourselves going, as some sort of defence mechanism against the alien environment through which we were travelling. Perhaps we were creating tensions and difficulties amongst ourselves to avoid having to think about the reality of our situation.

Although unhappy, we were far from becoming ineffective. Despite the ill temper, we were keeping to schedule, completing the tasks we had set ourselves across very difficult terrain.

It was the camels that stopped us from going further. They were defeated by the boulders at the foot of the moraine wall, so further exploration had to be done on foot. We wanted to cross the snout of the Gasherbrum Glacier and walk on to the Urdok Glacier. South-east of the Urdok, the valley narrowed from being several kilometres wide to less than one thousand metres, becoming the more usual river-cut 'V' shape in cross-section rather than very wide glaciated 'U'-shaped cross-section of the main Shakesgam valley below the moraines.

We left camp at 9. As we walked through a gap in the moraine and along the edge of the glacier, the sun had not yet touched the ice, and the rubble over which we were walking was firmly frozen together. Even so, there was the constant sound of running water as ice melted, and the ominous rattle and deep plop as rocks became dislodged and rolled down ice slopes into the deep gorges of glacier lakes and ponds. After some steep climbs and sharp scrambles, we emerged at river level on a small pebble beach. We could see along the valley, past the Changharlung Glacier to a dry valley, and the second moraine with the ice teeth of the Urdok Glacier.

After lunch (Army 'Biscuits Brown', chicken paste – known as 'dog breath paste', half a tin of luncheon meat and half a Mars Bar) we set off for the second moraine. We laid bets as to how long it would take to reach the top. The guesses ranged from thirty minutes to three hours. The distance was impossible to assess.

After an hour, and another hard climb, we gazed across the tops of the Urdok nunataks, dirty and covered with rubble. This glacier had only deep black crevasses rather than fresh white ice. The dry valley up which we had walked from the river seemed to be the gap between the two moraines rather than an abandoned watercourse. The walls of debris were clearly identifiable as lateral moraines, like the first wall, breached massively in several places by meltwater and ice.

From the Urdok moraine we could see up the last part of the Upper Shakesgam Valley, to where the Staghar Glacier comes in. A narrower 'V'-shaped valley turned around a corner beyond the Staghar, rising and finishing at the foot of the Kyagar Glacier.

This 'V'-shaped valley profile made it clear that no massive flood waters had swept down the upper end of the valley. The box-shaped profile of the valley below the glaciers indicated glacier and extreme flood water action. We had found the source of the flooding.

As we returned to camp in late afternoon, the Gasherbrum Glacier was melting in the heat. Ice and debris were loose, slipping on the smooth, wet ice beneath. We scrambled up and down deep slopes, skirted deep ponds of blue water, and walked warily underneath black, shiny ice walls and white ice pillars. We watched constantly for the fall of loose boulders perched precariously above where we were walking. I was tired out again, fed up with the constant pressure of filming.

After another bad night, I awoke to mist, below zero temperatures and falling snow. We loaded up quickly and were soon walking beside the camels, pushing hard back down the valley to rendezvous with the other twenty-four, three days' march away. The sun came out and soon the bone-chilling cold was replaced by the grill-like heat of the unfiltered sun.

One hard day of flat-out walking, helped by a slight downhill gradient and the fact that we were leaving this desolate valley, covered ground that had taken us two and a half days on the way in. After one river crossing on the camels, we reached our camping ground, a beautiful oasis area with green grass, flowers, a running brook, sheltering cliffs and little birds. I believe this to have been Durbin Jangal, where Francis Younghusband lost his spectacles. I cannot, however, be certain, as we did not find them.

I had left the cameras on the camels, feeling tired out and totally fed up with filming. With a light pack on my back for the first time, I sought out John and engaged him in conversation – an effort to establish some sort of normal communication. I had attempted the same with Nick Moore on the way up the valley but without, it seemed, too much success.

John and I talked animatedly about books, the trip, the others on it, attitudes towards the Army, what we were going to do when we got home, etc. We reached the campsite around 4 P.M., cooked supper and talked with Issac about where we would go next. It took some time. He wanted only to get to the foot of the Aghil Pass and wait for the others, and we wanted to get as far round the valley towards the Crown as time would allow.

After washing in the warm, clean stream, drinking coffee free from crunchy silt and feeling soft, fresh grass underfoot for the first time in weeks, I was sitting cross-legged beside the stone windbreak, boiling water. My mind was relaxed, running blankly without control through disjointed thoughts.

After the pain of anxiety, blankness is happiness, the Buddhist idea of making oneself an empty vessel into which the power of life can flow. From being filled to capacity with conflicting emotions that nullify and exhaust, tired emptiness is a strong base from which to rebuild.

I thought of home, so far away as to be another world – as the water in the tiny stream ran busily past. The waterfall ran noisily down into the moss and grass; little birds hopped carelessly on the pebble foreshore, investigating the stream with long black beaks, standing clear of the water on stilt-legs. The water surface was smooth and glistening, textured by the rounded pebbles and brown sand of the watercourse, transparent diagonal lines occasionally intersected by an aerodynamic interruption from a twig, insect or irregularity at the water's edge.

The sun slipped behind the mountains and it grew cold. High above, the last snow-peaked mountains were capped by the lowering sun, which was now well below our horizon. Golden rays like theatre spotlights picked out a mountain to the north-west in rich chocolate brown. At either side of our oasis, sandy conglomerate terraces, deeply eroded into huge fantasy vaults and towers, stood like the walls of an ancient city waiting for a trumpet blast, to slump downwards and be washed away by the river.

The next day (Saturday, 5 September), we waited for the sun to reach the valley bottom to give me good light for filming. I asked John and Nick to put the tent up for a second time, as they had taken it down too fast for me to film. I then filmed the loading of the camels, Issac posing outrageously. Consequently we left the oasis late and were delayed by three river crossings which, as the river was running very fast and deep, were particularly difficult.

The female camel was not at all happy and refused to lie down to be loaded, spraying disgusting green, regurgitated fodder at us when we came too close or attempted to clamber aboard. We passed the medieval-tent oasis on the other side of the river; then Issac made one crossing too many, which delayed our crossing the line of the Aghil Pass, and our entry to the Lower Shakesgam Valley.

Henry's cache was supposed to be at the next oasis. We had run out of food and needed to find it. We searched each group of bushes carefully, eventually finding the plastic drums, hidden from the sun and prying eyes under brush-wood and stones. We started organizing ourselves for Issac's departure with the rest of the caravan, rearranging our kit for the load-carry.

Everything was put into piles, then swapped around until each of us had around eighty pounds. We hoped that there would not be too many wet river crossings. Without the camels they would be very cold, and dangerous.

Our sense of conquest at getting to the glaciers of the Upper Shakesgam Valley was slightly dulled by the thought that Chinese Army surveyors could have travelled up the valley from the tent at the oasis. I have since read of Julie Tullis's and Kurt Diemberger's foray up the Urdok Glacier, during which they appeared not to have reached or gone beyond the first of the moraine walls. We had noted ways in which remote sensing devices could warn of increases in water levels, and thereby help to prevent the devastation and loss of life caused by the flooding. The value of the photographic survey could only be ascertained when the pictures, as ground proof, were compared with satellite imagery back in the UK. The exploration was over and we had to get on with the second part of our task, rejoining the others and climbing the mountain.

As we walked round the corner and into the Shakesgam Valley proper, I felt relieved that we were leaving this remote and hostile place. Being so close to the awesome and threatening power of the glaciers, like standing beside a fully-primed car bomb, was to live under a black shadow. Although a breaching of the glacier lakes through the lateral moraine would have swept us into oblivion wherever we were in the Shakesgam Valley, somewhat illogically, we felt better as we got away from those black walls of rubble.

CHAPTER 9

The March to the Mountain

The afternoon sun was hot, the cobble of rounded boulders on the flat valley floor shimmering southwards into the oblivion of a heat haze. A nameless 5,710-metre mountain rose uncompromisingly above its shivering lower slopes.

Something was emerging from the haze, moving slowly towards us, taking shape and substance until we could identify a camel and driver, plodding steadily, rhythmically and purposefully. As they drew nearer, the one animal became several, with other drivers leading other strings, each of four beasts in the footsteps of the first. The caravan, which at first we assumed to be ours, had more animals than our twenty-four, and sidling along the edge of the cliff were a dozen walkers, wearing faded clothes, moving carefully through the loose rocks.

As they drew closer, moving steadily, survivors from the void, we understood who they were. The Japanese expedition were walking out from their attempt on the Crown.

As the caravan came closer we recognized our camels, the drivers and beasts that had carried in our equipment. The perfidious CMA had charged us for empty camels returning to their home pastures, then used them to bring out the Japanese, who would certainly have paid for load-carrying camels at the end of their attempt on the mountain.

As they moved into the thick clumps of undergrowth beside the stream, we were frightened to ask the big question:

'Had they climbed the mountain?'

Over the next quarter of an hour, the caravan straggled into the campsite and started unloading. We made contact with the Japanese leader and introduced ourselves. They had more camels than our twenty-six because, very sensibly, they had decided to keep half a dozen camels at their base camp for use in an emergency during the three months they had spent on the mountain. We could not have afforded such a sensible precaution. If anything went wrong, we were going to have to wait four weeks until the camels returned for us.

On their way in, the Japanese had used sixty camels to carry all their equipment, plus bringing fresh mutton on the hoof. The dead camels we had seen on the way across the Aghil Pass had been from their caravan.

All this indicated no shortage of money, an impression confirmed by further investigation. Their leader, a distinguished-looking, middle-aged mountaineering enthusiast, owned a pharmaceutical company and was paying the bills. They had several non-climbing team members: a cine cameraman, a stills photographer, an author and various others who remained at base camp. The mountaineering was left to dedicated climbers, younger men who seemed to be college students of some sort. They asked us:

'Who are your climbers?' And were surprised to hear that we were all climbers.

Even on their way out, they had piles of equipment. The hire charge for one camel was £500. They had one animal carrying nothing but folded-down cardboard cartons for repacking their equipment on reaching the road-head. There were aluminium ladders, huge cooking sets, tents galore . . . more gear coming out than we were taking in.

Their leader had travelled to the mountain two years earlier on a reconnaissance which had cost him as much as our very modest trip in total. They were siege mountaineers, money no object and equipment galore – but had they climbed it?

The Japanese climbers were lean and looked fit, with deeply tanned faces, cracked lips and burnt, peeling noses. They had attempted to climb the mountain by the south-east route, and had been defeated at 7,070 metres by a 150-metre ice wall. They said they were not disappointed by their failure to conquer the Crown and wished us good luck in our attempt. In politeness, perhaps, they seemed to think that we would be able to do it.

We were trying to assess their calibre, in order to evaluate our chances of succeeding where they had failed. John reckoned they were 'psyched out by us' because one of them had said to him, 'You are all so strong.' It was true that we were all taller than them. With the exception of Henry, who is deceptively slender, we were also more strongly built, especially Robbo, who resembles the deadly sort of weight-lifter who also runs a fast 400 metres.

And, contrary to Jin Jun's information, there were no women!

We thought Henry might have sent a note along with the camel drivers. After a little hassle, one of the drivers produced a grubby couple of exercise-book sheets from his pocket:

1. We have set up base camp in an area one kilometre short of and on the 'South Bank' of the Skamri Glacier.

2. Our route is to follow the Japanese route, the SE Ridge on which they failed – at 7,070 metres. Our chances are good.

3. When you leave the camels' RV, SW of the Aghil Pass, turn off, stay on the South Bank of the Upper Shakesgam Valley. You can have a dry walk with two detours from the valley floor. We have marked these detours with cairns.

Your first night's camp after the camel RV is a choice as the 'set one' is on the North Bank in an oasis opposite your short cut to our base camp over a col, the final one before the two-valley merger. This route starts with a discernible traversing rise West *about* two miles from the valley merger. Start at the main gully not at our cairns.

The LO and Jin Jun are at K2 base camp, Singhal Tangel, about one mile South of the K2 North glacier meltwater river on the South Bank of our valley.

Speak to the LO (and Jin Jun), collect our radio from them (as arranged), and prepare yourself for a wet crossing of the Sarpo Laggo glacier meltwater river as you head the final few kilometres to our base camp.

4. We may well have all moved to Advanced Base Camp (ABC) before you arrive. We will leave you some rations, cooker and fuel. Try to use a fire to cook your meals, not the cooker, so we can preserve fuel (we lost approx one-third of our fuel on the walk-in).

5. The walk to ABC is a 'bitch' over loose undulating crap. A route description will be left at the base camp with the timings of our 'evening call' – radio check.

6. Stay at base camp for twenty-four hours plus, sort out your admin and rest for you will all face several load carries to ABC, a mindles [sic], murdous [sic] and ball acking [sic] task. Two days of food will be left in a separate box specially marked for your thirty-six-hour stay.

7. Our stores dump is a couple of kilometres beyond base camp. Film, kit, etc is there. When you come through carry film kit as Hugh requires and subject to any spare capacity.

8. *Hugh* Ref film kit. We do not want any equipment carried beyond Base Camp dump, or higher than necessary. I estimate an average of six BC to ABC carries per person. Some people will do the tedious carry more than others. You will need to programme a share of carries into your filming plan. Six to ABC and some higher. I realize that you will require film gear early and so we will help you with that and then later, during non-filming days, you can carry the exped kit.

Please consider and comment if necessary.

Have a good rest at BC.

Henry

By 8.30 that night it was still light and warm. We were in an east-west running valley where the sun came over the mountains earlier and went down later. It was a tremendous improvement on the dank misery of the north-south running Upper Shakesgam Valley.

I had become suddenly aware of the mountaineering challenge, which lifted me from my unhealthy preoccupation with the photography. It was very clear from Henry's note that getting up the mountain would entail an enormous amount of hard labour. I hoped that there would be some climbing as well, but that it wouldn't be so technical that I became too frightened to be able to do it.

It was clear also from Henry's note that I would have to do the same number of load carries as everyone else, fitting in the filming around these. As I now realized, it was like doing two jobs at once, and was going to be very difficult.

However, after abandoning cine photography for the two days' walk back down the Upper Shakesgam, I felt much better. Yomping along mindlessly like everyone else was so much easier. Henry had set his priorities. Getting the loads up the mountain was the important thing. I decided, therefore, to try not to worry, and to film whenever possible.

Reunited with the other drivers, and doubtless having told the tale of our time together, Issac became a pain. He had asked for Nick's colourful umbrella, which Nick had denied him in no uncertain terms. The umbrella had disappeared. John had lent Issac his spare glacier glasses and now needed them for the mountain. They too had disappeared into Issac's cloth bundle. He hung around watching where we were caching our gear, trying to cadge kit.

John insisted on the umbrella and glacier glasses being returned. We had noticed that Issac's camel lashings were becoming very frayed. When the missing items were returned, John handed over one of our climbing ropes as a gift. Disappointingly, with no indication of thanks, Issac took the gift and wandered off to eat freshly baked 'nan' bread with his fellow drivers.

Night came slowly, a warm velvet sunset fading into mild blackness with a deep indigo sky behind the jagged mountains where the last of the light still lingered. 'Chinese' music sounded in the darkness. I slipped through the bushes with my sound recorder to investigate.

A thirty-camel caravan was moving steadily through from the Aghil Pass, each animal wearing neck bells which jingled and resonated rhythmically in time with their leisurely gait. Chinese Army officers in long greatcoats walked in the rear, chatting animatedly to one another. The file of men and animals creaked past our camp site to the far end of the oasis.

After a beautiful clear night with stars twinkling brightly against the jagged ridges of the mountains towering over our heads, sleeping on top of my bivvie bag to avoid its damp, over-warm claustrophobia, I awoke early as the dawn was lightening the skies beyond the Aghil Pass. But Sunday, 6 September felt like a Monday; we were back to work with a vengeance. After camouflaging the plastic drums in the cache with heavy rocks and brushwood, we set off through the crowded oasis carrying bergens weighing just over eighty pounds. A camel spat furiously at me, the green slime all over my sun cap, running down onto my bare shoulders and making me reek of bad camel.

We started steadily across the loose stones of the valley. I soon slipped into a routine, moving easily, picking a firm route away from soft sand and gravel along the many dried-up water courses of the wide valley. We followed the footsteps made by the others two weeks earlier, to find where they had clambered from the valley floor up onto the crumbly terraces above the meanders of swiftly running river.

Henry's party had marked their route with cairns. Unusually, I was ahead and missed the first climb up onto the river terrace. From below the route looked dangerous; part had crumbled away, so I carried on, looking for another way through. The others followed the cairns up onto the cliff. I shouted to Nick to be careful coming down.

They took Henry's route and got down all right, which left me stuck at the bottom of a nine-foot cliff. I shouted for a rope to pull up my bergen so that I, unencumbered, could climb up. Irritated, Nick stuck his head over the cliff:

'Didn't you see the cairns? Go back and walk around like we did.'

He muttered about my getting ahead, and how I'd been grumpy when he and Robbo had done just that, and that he wasn't going to throw a rope or do anything to help me up. I was not immediately sure what he was talking about – until I remembered how, a fortnight earlier, I had told Robbo and Nick off for pushing ahead with the tripod because it prevented me from filming.

As I started to explain, John poked his head over, threw me a rope and he and 'Rad pulled up my bergen. There was no belay point so I couldn't clamber up to join them. I trotted back, up and over the cliff feature, rejoining them on top of the terrace ten minutes later.

As we munched biscuits and chocolate, Nick made a point of being friendly and conversational. The spat was forgotten. Maybe I would find out why some of us irritated one another so much as the trip unfolded. However, we also seemed to be establishing a mechanism for defusing the aggro – at least I hoped we were.

We pushed on, again having to climb and traverse the valley walls above fast, grey waters where the river flowed hard up against the valley side. The second detour was much harder than the first, a moderate grade rock traverse, but over a mile long and carrying our heavy bergens. Our toes, calves and forearms were very tired by the end.

By 2.30 P.M. we had reached the beginning of the traverse over a saddle into the Sarpo Laggo glacier valley, a shortcut used by Eric Shipton in 1937. We had been walking and climbing hard and were tired. The 500-metre climb and descent would be a fair day's walk, so we camped at the base of the gully below the saddle, washing our clothes and bodies, eating and sunbathing.

I was suffering quite badly from a lack of diversion, the result of leaving all my books on the camels to keep the weight of my load reasonable. 'Rad kindly lent me his Wilbur Smith, which I hoovered up like a child seeing TV for the first time.

A very strong wind blew suddenly along the valley, lifting clothes and equipment anchored by heavy stones. I abandoned my read and rushed around catching trousers and sleeping bags, while the others walked some way along the valley in the early evening.

We had done well that day; with heavy bergens, twelve kilometres as the crow flies. We could have hacked over the saddle and done the two days' march in one, but we had rations for three days and the left-over rations would have been extra and unnecessary weight to carry.

I noted in my diary:

'There is nothing like real, shared hardship to get people together. We should have had a tough day under our eighty pounders like this at the beginning of the trip – to pull everybody together.'

Our training week on the Eiger would have achieved this, but the bad weather had prevented us from doing any routes. We had not been able to see one another under pressure, so had not had the chance to develop that vital mutual respect for the others' abilities.

I felt that I was becoming acclimatized and fit: yomping along quite well, although with a certain amount of back pain – the legacy of too much military parachuting.

The effects of altitude were always there. Over-exertion caused breathlessness and chest pain, the sort you get during a hard run on a very cold day – a dry searing that cleared completely after a short rest.

Going uphill tired us all. You have to go slowly at your own pace, stopping if breathing becomes too heavy. A steady rhythm was essential, pulling us slowly upwards, out of the valley towards the horizon. Scrambling and floundering on loose rocks when climbing hills was particularly exhausting, as it destroyed the vital rhythm.

Forgetting to breathe, or breathing too shallowly, was easily done, and quickly disastrous. You had always consciously to breathe deep through the mouth. At night I still tended to breathe through my nose, starving myself of oxygen, causing dreadfully realistic dreams of suffocation and consequent panic awakenings. At first, this constant breathing through the mouth made my throat and mouth very dry and sore, but I got used to it.

I was still counting the days left to endure in the mountains, wakening early in dread of getting up. It was not the ice crackling on the outside of my sleeping bag or the cold wind that frightened me, but simply the new day. I was beginning to have flashes of looking forward to tomorrow, to the mountains and to the challenges to come. But in the dread of each early morning, I had no choice but to accept the challenges as something to be endured as stoically as I could.

As the day ended, the greys merged into blues. The browns faded, the grey stones of the valley becoming darker and more pronounced. The blue sky grew pink in the east as the sun dropped below the rim of the mountains. In our camp site, all was quiet and deserted. The wind died down, leaving a mild warmth and mellow calm. Nothing intruded between us and the peaks towering over us.

We were now in the highest region of the Karakorams. Around the corner of the valley were the north faces of K2 and, to the west, the Crown, towering over the surrounding massifs – the rocky spine of the highest mountains in the world.

Amid the blank grey of the western sky it seemed we were isolated from the rest of the world.

The next day, the early morning sun illuminated the far side of the valley, lightening the sky and dimming the bright pinpricks of stars. We picked our way slowly upwards among the rocks of the waterfall at the start of the 'Shipton' 500-metre short-cut.

We started slowly, taking very small steps, warming to the task, keeping well below the point where we might become overstretched and puffed – which would mean constantly stopping, and thereby wasting time, making the hill seem endless. The path wound upwards, sometimes a six-inch cut into a vertical slope which felt very exposed, or a gradual bluff.

We stopped every hour for five minutes, and after several false summits made the top of the saddle by lunchtime. Our hopes of seeing the Crown were thwarted; it lurked unseen, several nautical miles away. Instead we could see an unnamed 6,060-metre peak, a number of ridges and two lesser peaks swathed in cloud.

We walked down a smooth, rounded gully which steepened into a dry gorge. Traversing left towards K2 we had to negotiate a series of very steep, high scree slopes, ending in cliffs that dropped vertically 1,000 feet to the valley floor. We back-tracked as the cliffs became impossible to climb wearing bergens. The rock was very rough, like coral, tearing the skin of our fingers and palms.

Gradually we traversed south-west along the valley side and plunged down long scree runs amid clouds of dust on a very hot afternoon. Above us, far along the side of the valley, cloudless and dominating, loomed K2.

Immediately ahead, appearing to be mere foothills of K2, the 20,000-foot Chongtar Group looked serene and interesting. The main Sarpo Laggo valley, very wide and boulder-strewn, with several water channels flowing south to north, disappeared south-wards towards the awe-inspiring 23,880-foot (7,280-metre) pillar of Mustag Tower.

The northern K2 glacier river thundered grey and powerful along several courses through a steep-sided cut and out into the valley through a narrow gorge. Before we could camp with Jin Jun and the LO we would have to cross this cold, angry torrent.

Having descended to the valley floor and tramped along the rough boulder surface, we arrived at the water's edge. After dumping the bergens by the river, we wandered up and down looking for a place to cross. I was very dehydrated and drained a water bottle in one.

The first three sections of the crossing, onto boulder islands, were cold and wet, but although it was hard to retain our footing, we made it all right. My legs, shins and feet were excruciatingly cold, numbed at first – a deep blue in colour with fine trickles of blood (as my circulation returned) from the tiny cuts made by slivers of ice. After a few moments on the other side, the return of feeling was a painful experience.

John and Nick walked up towards the K2 gorge entrance, to cross the last section of the river. Nick, up to his waist in grey water, was pirouetted around by its force, managing to grab a rock on the far side. John fell in the centre of the channel, fortunately forward into the flow so the weight of his bergen countered the force of the water – which flowed over his head. They both managed to get to the other bank, then carefully secured a rope to rocks to help 'Rad and me across.

As I went across, the water came to chest height, in spite of my keeping sideways to the flow. Two-thirds of the way across, its power increased suddenly. I had to haul hard on the rope to keep my footing, and after a very cold scramble, Nick grabbed and pulled me to safety. 'Rad crossed in similar style – or lack of it.

We walked the last two kilometres to K2's northern base camp, a small green patch by the river with a tattered white tent pitched in the lee of a small hollow, where Jin Jun and the LO were camping. They came out to greet us, extending an invitation to supper later on.

Knowing how we felt, they whipped up an immediate snack to damp the edge of our appetites: jasmine tea, smoked and salted vegetables – which I have to say were disgusting, even after weeks on Army 'compo' – and fried cakes, the latter delicious. Jin Jun cooked partly on a primus and outside in a wood-fired oven. They had a mountain tent each, pitched inside the main tent which housed their kitchen and dining area.

While we waited hungrily for the promised fresh food feast, the Chinese Army caravan, with the bells of two nights ago, arrived. We had taken the precaution of setting our very modest camp in the best spot, which clearly annoyed the camel drivers who stopped their animals close to us and stared for ages as if we were from another planet, trying to psyche us into moving. Our cooking pots were in the camp fire place – and that was that.

The Chinese caravan seemed to be partly army and partly scientific. The army officer wore cotton Number Two dress complete with splendid peaked cap.

I asked one of the scientists, a ludicrously smartly dressed young man in jacket and tie, pressed trousers and white sunhat, what they were doing. He answered, airily, that they were doing geography, botany, meteorology, geology, seismology, surveying . . . a tour de force of every 'ology known to man.

The camel drivers eventually became bored with looking at us and, receiving the message that we were not going to move, shifted themselves fifty metres away. Each of the scientists put up a green and orange striped tent. John was not impressed with the senior Army officer:

'He took over fifteen minutes to get that tent up.'

And the British Army squatted in the dust, filthy and deeply tanned, wearing shorts (mine a very faded Union flag pattern), boots and little else – and not a tent between us.

Jin Jun's scoff was fabulous: fresh vegetables and a rabbit, shot by himself early in the morning and done chow mein style, rolls and more fried cakes. We ate and ate – it was delicious.

We set off the next morning feeling heavy and over-indulged. After the river crossing, an hour's walk should reunite us with the others. We were very keen to find out how far they had got up the mountain. I also wanted to be with the others again, to be part of the team.

We imagined the others walking in without heavy bergens, crossing the rivers perched on the camels' backs. We felt a little superior, having covered so much ground, exploring new territory whilst they were trekking gently to the foot of the glacier with the camels. We were complacent, a condition that was to be short-lived, for harmonious relations within the group were strained by the highly dangerous crossing of the Sarpo Laggo river. Although we did not yet fully realize it, the river crossings were as dangerous, if not more dangerous than the mountaineering. The others had already lost a donkey. John Day was clearly determined to get to the mountain as fast as he could, not prepared to surrender even one day's delay in the interests of safety.

As he had said at an earlier river crossing:

'If you walk away from it, then in my book, you did it the right way.'

As we walked from that river, I thought how desperately lucky we had been to get away with that crossing. Presumably John was thinking that because he had got away with it, he had made the right decision, thus proving my objections to be wrong.

I don't know how he regarded himself, but I felt small, frail and insignificant: a timid little creature hoping not to be noticed as he crept through this implacably powerful and frightening environment.

After struggling through the Sarpo Laggo river, John coiled the rope and we wrung out our socks, put on warm clothes and ate lunch, shivering as strong southerly winds blew thick clouds of sand into our faces and onto the luncheon meat. Base camp was only two kilometres away. As we drew closer we saw one orange and two blue tents at the base of a small hill slope. The site was deserted.

A long note from Henry, pinned to the floor in the centre of the largest tent, explained what we were to do. We were two days earlier than he had expected, so the instructions needed interpretation. In the meantime I slumped mindlessly on my bergen for about an hour, then tried out the solar shower the others had set up on a bamboo stand.

The camp looked as though it had been a mess; two months' use by the Japanese had left litter with squiggly writing everywhere, which the others had obviously tidied up as best they could. A large rock had been set for peeing, another further away had shovel and loo paper; there was a water point for the jerry cans, and a fuel point (petrol for our cooker) away from fire danger to the tents.

At K2 base camp, Nick and I had admired Jin Jun's water-boiling oven, and decided to make one here. We dug a hole, revetted it with stones and set into it a large water pot. I mixed mud and sealed the pot into the fire hole and made a chimney from an old tin can, while Nick did some expert dry stone walling to make a hearth and cooking area. Once alight, it drew well and soon we were sitting happily beside it, smelling like camel drivers, huge mugs of tea in hand and admiring our handiwork as the final touch of darkness fell across the valley.

The next morning, we lay in our sleeping bags until 8, before getting the fire going and boiling water for breakfast. Nick and I examined the performance of the fire critically and a Mark Two variant on the oven was designed and constructed, the fire powering a pan-cooking section as well as the water boiler.

After a wash we wandered up to the camel dump, half an hour's walk towards the glacier. John commented that by this stage more equipment should have been carried up the mountain, and that the dump was not very well organized.

We gathered together our own gear. I was pleasantly surprised; the camera gear and film had been put together in a hollow and carefully shielded from the sun by large boulders and hessian sacks. In Henry's instructions, he 'allowed' us one carry up to ABC for all our personal mountaineering gear. This load would be very heavy – over seventy pounds.

'Rad and I sauntered back discussing risk taking and the lack of Karakoram experience in the expedition. We wondered whether there was enough expertise for the group to be able to take properly calculated risks. I completed 'Rad's Wilbur Smith whilst lying in the sand beside the 'dining area', oblivious to alternating sun, wind and rain.

Henry had left a second note, written on a large cardboard sheet. John was analysing and decrypting it. We had been a little scornful of the timetable in Henry's first note, whereby we were given two days to get our gear up to ABC, going to the dump on the first day and to ABC on the second. With the same arrogance with which we had thought of the others walking in behind the camels, we imagined we could do it all in one day. However, on closer reading it seemed that there were two dumps, the one we had just visited and another near ABC at the top of the glacier. It might turn out to be rather harder than we had first thought.

Henry's schedules were very carefully worked out. With climbers working above ABC, bedspaces in the various camps became critical. It was vital that we followed the timetable rigidly, not only so that we ended up where there was space in a tent but, more importantly, so that the various camps were resupplied with food and fuel at the right times.

The day had become windy and cold. The Crown was still enshrouded in mist; none of us had yet seen it. We had no idea how far up the others had progressed. Time was passing and soon would be slipping away very rapidly. It was 9 September and we had only until the end of the month to get to the summit. Back in the UK, Henry had talked of 'two weeks on the mountain'. Once we had done our load carrying up the glacier to ABC, two weeks was all that would remain.

John and Nick were now firmly teamed up together, Nick admiring John for his mountaineering knowledge, and John, happy to be admired, attracted by Nick's strength and physical fitness. They were very impatient to get on to the mountain.

Although we were bored with sitting around, 'Rad and I felt we should keep to Henry's instructions and wait at Base Camp until Nellie and Jerry came down from ABC to guide us to the upper glacier dump.

Also, we did not feel the compulsion to get onto the mountain that seemed now to be driving John. Our crossing of the Sarpo Laggo river had seemed foolhardy and illogical. It seemed equally illogical to push off blindly onto a huge, unknown glacier when instructed to wait for guides.

So, without any discussion or disagreement, Conrad and I decided we would remain at Base Camp and John and Nick try to find ABC. The next morning, they pushed off onto the glacier with very heavy bergens, while 'Rad and I settled down to another quiet day. I had collected books from the dump and continued with *Lord of the Rings*. We fried up luncheon meat, garlic and biscuits for lunch, had a sleep and, at 6 P.M., started preparing supper.

As I was squatting in the smoke of the stove, two bronzed and very fit-looking figures strolled round the corner – Jerry and Robbo came down off the mountain to guide us up the glacier. It was great to see them.

They had seen John and Nick's footprints on the glacier – but going in the wrong direction. I threw more food into the pot, an all-in curry cooked in ghee with garlic, dehydrated mutton and beef, four fresh-ish apples (left behind by the Japanese) and oxtail and vegetable soup. The starter was pomme mixed with peas and oxtail soup. I had worked out how to cook the rice: a small amount of water to steam rather than boil it, sealing the top of the pan with plastic for the last ten minutes. Two sachets produced vast fluffy quantities of the stuff – much more than even we could eat.

John and Nick had taken the second radio. At 8 P.M., the time for the nightly radio check, we tried to raise them – without success.

Jerry and Robbo told us of their meeting with the Japanese. With Jerry, Henry had walked out ahead of the camels and the LO, in order to be the first to speak to the Japanese. Henry needed to find out if they had climbed the mountain and then ascertain whether the southern route was feasible. If they had climbed the southern route, or if it was not feasible, he wanted to persuade the Japanese to declare the southern route impossible, and to argue for our trying the northern route, ganging up on the LO when he arrived later with the camels.

The two strode forth with umbrellas like missionaries contacting a long-lost tribe. They found the Japanese bitterly disappointed at having to leave 'their' mountain unclimbed, in tears the next day as they left. They had spent one complete month before even venturing onto the mountain, humping stores over the glacier to ABC, making the journey in three days rather than one. They had left lots of interesting oriental food dumped in various places along the route, which now everyone was trying out. Robbo and Jerry thought them very sporting and generous, passing on useful photographs and equipment, giving us as much information as they could about routes and the mountain.

A whole new system of life had evolved on the mountain – to which we would have to conform: routines of going up and coming down, load carries, the schedules for the next few days being passed hand to hand as pairs of climbers passed each other on the routes, using the correct ration box menu each day . . . We were now part of the big team, no longer a small, independent group wandering in the middle of nowhere.

The four of us had split into two pairs, one fiercely keen to get onto the mountain – and now lost on the glacier in their enthusiasm – and 'Rad and I, looking forward to being reunited with the others and, in our mountaineering innocence, wondering what on earth we had let ourselves in for.

CHAPTER 10

Reunion on the Mountain

I was like a boy going to a new school: no idea of what it would be like, a new set of rules to be learned and many new things to get right. The certainty of serious mountaineering – of which I had only read – was altogether more serious, bringing my boyish enthusiasm to heel.

Judging from Henry and Robbo, the others seemed very confident about climbing the Crown. Just as I was, they were also counting the days before getting out and back to civilization, our expectations of civilization beyond the wilderness lessening daily. Gilgit now counted as a serious metropolis filled with mischief. I decided to keep quiet about the realities of social life in Moslem states.

The message from the mountain – Henry speaking *ex cathedra* from Camp Two – was that we were going to stay until we had got to the top. The camels, when they arrived to bring us out, would have to wait.

A tremendous amount had been done while we had been tramping up the Shakesgam Valley. The huge, uncharted Skamri Glacier had been breached, and the hellish labour of stocking the camps from the camel dump had begun. The boys had been going hard, carrying over half the 1,600 kilos of kit up the glacier and onto the mountain.

The day after arriving at Base Camp, Henry and Andy had set off to investigate routes from the camel dump across the Skamri Glacier river. In the sliding confusion of ice and debris they had got onto the wrong side of the torrent. As night fell, bringing the risk of death by exposure, they had risked their lives making a wet crossing back again.

The others had come from Base Camp searching for them. They met in the darkness, Henry and Andy stumbling badly, shaking with cold. With supreme stiffening of the upper lip, Henry had airily dismissed their concern as hysteria, demanding supper.

The next day Robbo and Jerry had set off to find the route across the lethal no-man's-land of the glacier to Advanced Base Camp. They could not cross the river to the other side of the valley – and the steep ravine that led onto the Crown. Unable to retrace their steps in the darkness, they were forced to make an emergency bivouac within binocular-sight of their destination. They shivered away a very long, cold night in only the clothes they had with them for the day, at first reservedly huddling on their own, then unashamedly wrapped around each other for warmth.

Everyone had been doing load carries; back-breaking, ankle-turning hard labour, learning the twists of the glacier intimately, timing reaching each turning point to within five minutes over the thirty-mile, ten-hour round trip. The loads were made up according to what was most needed on the mountain, from a master list compiled by Bob Wood. Before leaving the UK, Henry had laid down a maximum weight limit of twenty kilograms for loads across the glacier – bearing in mind the altitude and the need to conserve mental and physical energy. Everyone was ignoring the limit to get the stores onto the mountain as fast as possible, packing whatever they could manage to carry. They were bored rigid with the monotony and the pain of it.

When Robbo and Jerry left ABC, the team were doing well on the mountain: Bob and Andy had carried a load up to Camp Two (6,300 metres), and people were sleeping, and therefore acclimatizing, at Camp One (5,600 metres). Advanced Base Camp was 4,850 metres above sea level and we were now at 4,200 metres. The summit of the Crown was now thought to be 7,295 metres.

As we went to sleep that night, we wondered where John and Nick had got to. They were taking their chances on a glacier that even the experienced load-carriers found hard to navigate across –

in spite of red-ribboned bamboo marker wands placed every few hundred metres at the turning points.

Friday, 11 September:
'This was by a long chalk the worst day so far.'

It started early, 'Rad and I walking up to the camel dump and packing all our personal mountaineering kit into one huge load. Our bergens were huge and distorted, Koflak boots and helmets hanging at the sides like tinkers' kettles and weighing well over sixty pounds – but lighter than the ones we had carried in.

The four of us ('Rad, John, Nick and I) had thought that the difficulties of the glacier described so graphically by Henry in one of his notes were exaggerated. However, as Conrad and I were about to discover, the glacier was unbelievably dreadful. Henry's note, with its Edward Lear mis-spellings 'mindles and murdous', which became a catch-phrase, turned out to be an understatement.

It was a terrible combination of physical pain, the need for constant concentration, and grinding boredom.

The route started on the left hand-side of the glacier, up a steep water-gully lined with large boulders. The gully emerged onto the lateral moraine – the cracked rock debris squeezed out of the sides of the glacier. The route, taking the edge where the glacier cut into the valley side, took us up and down steep hills covered with loose rocks, following stone cairns, bamboo wands and red ribbons (some placed by the Japanese and some by us). The route seemed completely and totally without logic, a mad, constant and exhausting winding and doubling back on itself. Every footfall was loose. We had to balance with our sixty-pound bergens, from boulder to boulder like acrobats, a broken leg the reward for a second's inattention.

After two hours of stumbling we came down onto the centre of the glacier, where the river flowed unseen below. The ice creaked as we walked across ominous open spaces, past dirty grey nunataks and followed a deep blue channel carved in white blue ice where the main river emerged from the darkness. At the crossing place, an aluminium ladder bent into a twisted curve by ice movements over the past two weeks was held firm by ropes and pitons hammered into rock. We stepped across the bubbling water to the base of a long, steep moraine slope. Very loose rock was thinly laid over the ice. It was easy to slip on the greasy, melting ice, slipping back and losing height, legs, toes and feet desperate to find some purchase.

The next two hours were soul destroying. We stumbled along the medial moraine, up and down steep hills of shifting debris, following the elusive red-ribbon markers. Some were decoys luring us onto trails abandoned after the frequent shifting of the glacier had made them unusable. There was an occasional encouraging footprint where the debris was particularly fine.

Eventually, the route went off to the left and down onto the bottom of the northern lateral moraine. There was another steep climb, and more stumbling on greasy ice until we reached a flat spot endorsed with a brown tent – the so-named British Dump.

Amid this eternal builders' yard of rubble, the brown tent was an event, a momentous monument looked for anxiously and greeted with a surge of morale.

The afternoon had grown cold and windy and I was becoming very tired. I began to experience stabs of unease. The glacier seemed organically part of the mountain, a heartless entity waiting patiently to absorb us. It frightened me.

The nightmare of serious injury returned again. A casualty could only be got off the mountain through these dreadful moraines. Our extreme isolation and dependence upon one another were crushingly re-emphasized. What on earth would happen if someone were injured? How would we control pain? What would it be like helplessly watching someone fade away before the camels arrived? I worried that despite all the assurances of the competence of Nick and Robbo as 'medics', without a doctor in the team we were very vulnerable.

However, what could a doctor do if something serious happened? As a lightweight expedition, we had insufficient supplies to enable a doctor to do business. The actual value of a doctor, by virtue of qualification alone, was that his or her presence would save the rest of us from responsibility for any casualties. Nick and Robbo were nominated as the ones responsible in that terrible event.

From what Nick had said during his medical lecture back at Yechung, I reckoned in a medical emergency he would do whatever he could, then shrug his shoulders. Robbo, I thought, was rather different – a tough Welshman with the true gentleness that stems from real self-confidence. He was, however, a key climber. With nothing to be done after an emergency, the climb would probably continue. Robbo's talents would be wasted tending the injured while we waited for the camels to arrive.

A real doctor would have been completely and utterly responsible for a casualty: no-one else would then have had to worry. I was the photographer, and certainly no-one else worried about the filming. We were a little compartmentalized. I didn't worry about the climbing; I just did what I was told to do in that respect.

All my thoughts on accidents and medical problems were the product of my insecurity. They were nightmares and could achieve nothing. They were best forgotten – or buried away, deep below conscious thought. Most of us seemed to have similar worries from time to time, and came to the same conclusions. Whichever way you looked at it, we were on our own; there was no point in worrying about it – and that was that.

Conrad and I dumped our personal kit inside the brown tent at British Dump, bidding farewell to Jerry and Robbo. We hoped we could find our way back down to Base Camp. They carried on, to ABC.

The journey up, carrying heavy bergens, had taken five and a half hours. The return journey, downhill and unladen, took just under five hours as we were exhausted. I ended up stumbling along in the gathering dusk too tired even to speak.

At Base Camp we cooked a huge supper. As darkness fell, John and Nick, also tired out, flopped down beside the cookers. After a hard two days and an enforced bivouac beside the river, they had found their way to ABC and dumped their personal climbing gear. Like us they had found the glacier very hard going. Luckily, their bivouac had turned out to be not too far from ABC. They had found the way back to Base by following the elusive bamboo pole markers. I doubled the helpings of food and produced a massive meal. We ate voraciously then fell into a deep sleep.

In Henry's plan, on 12 September John and I were to carry film and all the camera gear up to ABC, while Conrad and Nick carried a load each to British Dump, returning to Base Camp.

It was a grim day that started badly. John had been very pushy, trying to get us to leave Base Camp at the time he had determined – 9 A.M. I had to make certain that we took all the camera gear necessary for the mountain. I needed to think it through carefully, taking no more than necessary, but taking all the vital odds and ends. I resented John's haste, which seemed unnecessary and somehow authoritarian. What was so special about 0900 hours?

At nine John made a critical comment about Conrad's not being ready – as he (John) was strapping the tripod onto the top of his bergen. I riposted:

'It does look as though we are waiting for you,' I said – an outrageously ridiculous statement.

'That's a bit rich,' said Nick, stabbing back in protection of his 'partner'.

'Only a joke,' said I. 'It's what's called a sense of humour.'

I knew John could not tolerate any humour, or attempts at it, at his expense. There was no humour in any of the swordplay. It was very bitter.

Without a word or glance John shouldered his bergen. With Nick in tow, he strode out of camp, along the boulders and sand towards the far spur and the gully of the camel dump. 'Rad was still packing – ignoring John and Nick – so I waited, and the two of us set off in their footsteps.

We left the camel dump at half past nine. After the exhaustion of the previous day, I was determined to go steadily. However, John and Nick were deliberately pushing out ahead at a cracking pace. He and Nick got extra rest as 'Rad and I plodded in after them, then chivvied us to get started again. This regime irritated the patient and ebullient Conrad to the point where he spoke to John about it.

In the afternoon Nick proposed that as he and 'Rad had to

return to sleep down at Base Camp, they should push on to the dump and avoid finishing the journey in darkness. They moved off.

John and I continued at my speed. This split separated John and Nick and slowed things down to a sensible pace. After stopping briefly at the brown tent at British Dump to pick up some of my personal gear, we reached Advanced Base Camp in good time at 4 P.M. – five and half hours' climbing plus all the rest stops and the dallying that had irritated John so much.

The final approach to Advanced Base Camp was down a steep scree slope, a final river crossing on a tyrolean rope traverse (hanging upside down pulling yourself across), then along the river terraces to where a large gorge cut down into the valley.

ABC sat on two terraces above the river. Up through the narrow sides of the gorge, the summit of the Crown could be seen, huge, snow-covered and awe inspiring. At the other side of the river, thousands of tons of debris and the black cliffs of the glacier rose up from the fast-flowing waters.

Jerry came out to greet us as we stumbled in.

The Japanese had left three tents, loads of food and impressive medical supplies. The food was interesting and would make a very welcome change from the monotony of Army rations – but didn't seem to be very nutritious. The tents were useful – but the medical supplies were the cause of an extraordinary exchange.

We were looking through the boxes of pills, syringes, glass vials and highly coloured capsules. Everything was in Japanese with only a few names duplicated in English. The English was medical jargon and only a few words were understandable.

About three or four items were identifiable – appearing to be pill or capsule tonics rather than anything really useful. The large box of injection vials seemed to be some strange selection of oriental fluids – perhaps to boost the flagging performance of tired mountaineers. The Japanese team included a doctor, to whom all this stuff would have made sense. Also since their leader (and sponsor) was the head of a drug marketing company, these were probably his products.

As we looked through the several large boxes full of glittering foil sheets, bright cartons and expensive-looking tubes, John became quite heated, talking angrily about the money the Japanese had spent on their expedition, how much they had wasted and in particular how disgraceful it was for them to have left 'thousands of pounds' worth of medical gear at the foot of the mountain'.

I found myself unable to get excited about the money they had spent – apart from being jealous of their sponsorship – because they had humped all their expensive gear across the dreadful glacier. No amount of sponsorship money could have done that for them.

John's diatribe continued. In a world where medical supplies are invaluable, it was disgraceful to abandon all this gear:

'You have not seen how desperate they are for medicines in Africa.'

I was fed up with John's insistence that he was always right, so, unwisely, I argued; my devil was in the ascendancy. I couldn't imagine anyone humping all this stuff back down the glacier at the end of their climbing so saw nothing wrong in the Japanese having dumped it – and I said so.

John then launched into how unnecessary all the medication was. As most of the labels were in Japanese and none of us were doctors, we couldn't judge the usefulness or otherwise of what they had left –although some of it did look a bit dubious.

John now warmed to his theme and announced that we should destroy the lot as it was a danger to the camel drivers, who would eat all the pills and inject themselves with the fluids. He spoke bitterly of his African experiences, where similar things had occurred.

The idea of destroying medical supplies annoyed me. Some future expedition with a doctor – or the Japanese if they returned – might need these supplies in an emergency. The camel drivers were very unlikely to flog all day up the glacier for a drugs party. The Turkestan drugs scene was probably limited to marijuana and I could not see them mainlining cough linctus on the off-chance. Anyway, if we didn't tell them of the drugs cache, how would they come to know of it? And even then, I doubted whether they would be physically capable of making it up the glacier.

This anger that had flared up inside me was stupid. I had allowed myself to become drawn into something that was unnecessary. My devil overcame my common sense, and I spoke when I should have retreated into silence.

John exploded. He shouted, staring at me with the anger of a parent goaded beyond all patience by a naughty child:

'Listen, Hugh, I'm TELLING YOU. Those camel drivers will be up here as soon as we have gone . . .'

Robbo, who was with us sifting through the boxes, said:

'Does it really matter?'

Catching myself, and mentally thanking Robbo for his intervention, I extricated myself from this fracas:

'All right, John, yes, you are absolutely right.'

I raised my arms in mock surrender and moved away, resisting the temptation to be any more sarcastic, sending my devil back to his sulphurous cloister. The whole episode had taken my breath away with its suddenness and irrational ferocity. I wrote in my diary:

'John worries me. He *has* to be in charge – which is fair enough; he knows mountaineering and has become second-in-command. However, it seems that he has always to be right and that disagreement is not allowed.

'Today there were no proper laughs from him. He and Nick – a partnership – joked with each other, but there were no laughs for anyone else. It was claustrophobic and unpleasant – and very lonely.'

I was worried and perplexed after this incident. After a suitable cooling-down period I approached John and told him that my laughing at him (as I had at the end to defuse the situation) did neither of us any good. I worried about future conflict.

'What should I do?' I asked him. 'How do you advise me to behave in the future to prevent this sort of thing happening again?'

He looked grim and turned away:

'Don't worry about it, Hugh,' was his reply.

Jerry was in Advanced Base Camp when we arrived because he had been forced to abandon a load carry up to Camp One with Robbo. Weakened by diarrhoea, he had found himself unable to climb the fixed ropes. Robbo returned shortly after we arrived, having made the climb on his own. He reported that the others were reasonably well, Bob with diarrhoea, Nellie with sore hands and Andy suffering from heartburn and indigestion. They were having problems finding a site for Camp Two, trying to find a way through several steep and very avalanche-prone gullies.

The mood was optimistic. The barrier of the glacier was breached and a route up the mountain was being created. The potentially time-consuming reconnaissance phase had ended and the team were committed to a realistic southern ridge-line route on an unknown mountain. The camels would arrive on 4 October, in twenty-one days. We had three weeks to climb about 1,700 metres – which, expressed thus, seemed a reasonable task.

That night, in the communal mess tent, after the aggravation of the day, we talked away the evening together in the flickering light of candles and primus stoves. Stories were told of Henry's previous expeditions, their 'epic' qualities – when events escalated into high drama or hilarity, the ambition and off-beat style of them: Henry 'nipping' down from an alpine climbing hut for a few bottles of beer and having to make a serious ascent in pitch darkness to get back – with the beer: chatting to an RAF officer in a bar and ending up being flown to Bavaria in a VIP jet with a pile of climbing gear on an airforce 'navigation exercise': of talking people out of US sheriff's jails and terrible practical jokes, usually involving slipping heavy weights into other people's rucksacks.

We had never talked like this before. Everyone was making an effort to be sociable, listening to stories, contributing and encouraging others. The atmosphere was warm and friendly. Supper was huge: delicious Japanese noodles with dried fish (and monosodium glutamate flavouring), soup, curry and peas.

I wrote in my diary of that evening:

'My interest in the expedition and in learning more about mountaineering was rekindled. After the weeks of travel and work, and in the daunting face of the mountain, my enthusiasm had gone. My patience was to the fore, a tired, suffering form of resignation without any spark, foundation or motivation – other than enduring and seeing the thing through.

'I now want to get up onto the mountain and see what it is all about – and learn what I need to learn in order to do that.'

The next morning Robbo got up early to make breakfast in the mess tent. We joined him and huddled together around the cookers, sipping hot tea and spooning down sweet, watery porridge. I washed up last night's pots and pans in cold water to save valuable fuel. The water kept freezing as I swooshed it round.

We loaded our rucksacks with the shopping list from the mountain; thermo mats, bivvie bags, food packs, curry powder, loo roll, etc, then set off up the ravine towards the first of the Crown glaciers.

It was cold and dank.

After an hour of upward toil we came to the bottom of the first fixed ropes – and emerged into warm sunshine. We followed the bamboo poles steadily upwards along the side of the glacier and cut across the base of a massive ice fall. It rose in baroque splendour like an inner-city cathedral, its white walls grimy with debris. The steep ice slopes were not the usual exhausting scramble, the rocks still giving purchase as the sun had not yet melted them loose. We had to squeeze through narrow gaps between massive white pillars, carefully avoiding using our hands for support as the ice surface was razor sharp and finely pitted like exposed coral. A blue tent appeared incongruously planted at the top of what looked like a massive gravel pit, zippered up securely with no signs of life.

Camp One was perched amid huge piles of frost-shattered gravel at the top of the icefall, at the foot of a towering spur. The glacier vanished upwards into oblivion like a frozen river tilted suddenly and dramatically into a seventy-degree angle.

Our load carry from Advanced Base Camp had taken three hours.

John and I dumped our loads and set back down, arriving in ABC one hour later, to scoff a complete packet of Japanese 'Cigar' biscuits with our morning coffee. With empty bergens, we walked to British Dump to collect the rest of my personal gear and the cine film.

British Dump had originally been called 'English Dump' to

differentiate it from a Japanese dump in the same area. Robbo, a staunch Welshman, had quite properly objected to this Anglo Saxon chauvinism.

As it had been on our first trip up the glacier, the river was high, so we had to cross on the rope traverse, hauling our bergens across attached with karabiners. This trip took just over three hours.

With our two load carries for the day completed, I went to get water, refilling our jerry can – strapped into a rucksack back-frame for ease of carrying – from the river, a half-mile scramble down several steep river terraces. I then cooked a huge supper of noodle soup with dried Japanese prawns, mutton stew, peas and more of the delicious noodles (our absolute favourite) in a sauce.

In the gathering gloom, John took the radio for the twice daily radio check with the mountain. This was done standing beside a bamboo marker pole, which experience had shown was the only place from which we could communicate with the higher camps. In the centre of the steep valley with the Crown towering overhead, the wind swept straight down from the glacier, making dawn and dusk radio checks a very cold chore.

John came back into the mess tent with the news. The climbers had reached Camp Two but were making slow progress finding a route up the very steep gully above it. They were having to hack footsteps through heavy icing and dig out fixed ropes where they had been left by the Japanese. There were several gullies, each had to be climbed until they found one that was not a dead end. It sounded laborious and disheartening.

They were all suffering the effects of the high altitude. Despite this, Henry had decided they would persevere on the mountain for another forty-eight hours for further acclimatization. This would enable them, after a rest, to go higher more quickly without such debilitating symptoms.

That night, John, very conscious of missing out on the mountaineering, talked of the unfairness of this decision of Henry's. He said that by making the others stay too long on the mountain, Henry was denying us the opportunity to acclimatize higher up, which would in turn lessen our chances of reaching the summit. John was quite honest about his absolute determination to get out of our novice group and join the climbers on the mountain as fast as he could. When he talked about 'our' chances of reaching the summit, he meant his own.

I was feeling very dirty and smelly – to the extent of developing sore patches on parts where walking caused skin to rub. The only concession to health and hygiene available to me was to put on a pair of absolutely brand new socks – sheer luxury.

I was excited by the prospects ahead. The Crown loomed over us every time we poked our heads from the tent – a massive, cold and very daunting problem, to be overcome if we had the guts, luck and skill to do it. And the day had been enjoyable. With the mountain as our goal, everyone seemed to be much more at peace, getting on with the job.

On the morning of Monday, 14 September at 6.30, after a very restless night, I had to leave my sleeping bag in a hurry. Digestive problems had returned yet again – although not badly. John, Conrad, Nick and I did another load carry up to Camp One, Robbo and Andy having gone back up the mountain on Sunday.

As had become usual, Nick pushed ahead on his own up the gully to Camp One, leaving us marching steadily behind. On the flat place above the first fixed ropes, we caught up with him for a break. My bergen, top-heavy with camera tripod, toppled over and the spike of my ice hammer, strapped to the outside, ripped the leg of Nick's trousers. Luckily his leg was unscathed. He was furious and my apologies were to no avail. John, recognizing the need for a little tuition, spoke calmly and generally about taking care with ice tools – which was helpful as none of the rest of us had ever used them.

Nick then stormed up the glacier with John in his wake, irritating Conrad and me as they were soon too far ahead to be able to help if we had an accident. 'Rad was feeling dizzy and ill, having to rush off behind rocks, so I stayed with him. I was suffering from similar difficulties. We were both disgruntled at being left behind.

I wondered whether Nick was competing for a 'place' on the summit of the mountain – as the fittest and strongest of the novice mountaineers. I wrote in my diary:

I think Nick uses an exterior of calm and organization to conceal something. He gives nothing away, and often degenerates into back-biting and sarcasm – or sides with John, whom he seems to admire and respect. They have mutual friends from the past, and John's mountaineering expertise and his position as second-in-command make him worth courting.

Load-carrying brings out the worst in me. I start thinking Black Thoughts. I imagine people to be racing me, or deliberately going too slowly.

Perhaps all these Machiavellian intrigues are part of the Black Thoughts syndrome, existing only in my imagination? Am I being far too cynical?'

It was a clear, sunny day and the mountains were free of cloud. We dumped our loads at Camp One and slithered and slid back down to Advanced Base Camp. 'Rad and Nick left for British Dump to pick up their climbing gear while John and I tidied up the camp. After refilling the water jerry can, we washed our clothes – and then with great briskness washed our bodies in the bitterly cold Skamri Glacier river.

We then prepared a huge supper of dried fish, noodles, mashed potato, curry with lots of garlic and my best effort at boiled rice so far – very dry and fluffy.

'Rad claimed great hunger. To my delight, he admitted defeat after four very large helpings.

During the evening radio check, Henry asked for us all to come up and stay at Camp One for two days' acclimatization. He had decided to come down himself, to allow John to get onto the mountain. With the remaining three of us, Henry then wanted to finish carrying the rest of the food and equipment from the Camel Dump up the glacier to Advanced Base Camp. This was a dreadful prospect as by now we all loathed the Skamri Glacier.

We sat in the orange tent talking, then filed out into the darkness to our smaller two-man tents to sleep. There was no moon, but the outlines of snow and rock could be seen in the cold, clear light of thousands of stars. The mountains opposite, with the splendid southern branch of the Skamri Glacier flowing majestically down towards us, were dark and terribly empty.

The stars were so bright; the Milky Way seemed to issue forth from the mountains, from a dark fire deep inside the heart of rock giving off as sparks the thousands of tiny bright stars. Star-smoke flowed upwards from the horizon, over our heads in a broad, wind-driven band.

Outside our thin tents the river roared and thundered, and occasionally a fall of rocks and glacier debris rattled down the black ice cliffs. We felt safe, high above on our river terrace.

After this relatively easy day, and the huge curry and total, much-needed wash, I felt relaxed and comfortable. Conrad and I lay in our sleeping bags, writing diaries and reading, the light of head torches throwing a warm glow through the double skins of the dumpy, domed mountain tents. In spite of the prospect of days of load-carrying across that dreadful glacier, we were at peace.

In my diary I reflected upon the pain of isolation, and the joy of teamwork:

'The heavy physical work of load-carrying makes everyone very grumpy. Any small lack of consideration – for example the failure of one to offer his water bottle to everyone else when he has drunk from others' at a previous stop – can become a big personal issue as the march proceeds. None of the reactions of others are predictable because each person may be boiling away at some dark and imagined injustice.

'The best days are when we all stick together on the march and chat – while we still have the breath. Communication between everyone in the group leads to overall good spirits.'

I suffered yet another disturbed and anxious night, twisted up in my sleeping bag. In order to end it, I got up before dawn and took photos of the Crown. In due course everyone else got up. It was well below zero and I was using long time exposures and the tripod. Nick poked his head out of the mess tent flap and shouted across that breakfast was ready. I replied that I would be five minutes packing up. His laconic response, that it would be cold by then, made me grind my teeth with rage; it seemed that he simply couldn't care less.

I dug a pit for the film – to keep it cool and out of the hot sun –

covered over with a spare tent sheet. We set off yet again for Camp One, intending to film the route – a process that made the climb twice as long as usual.

I had a chat with John on the way up. This started when, coming over a crevasse, he refused my helping hand. I told him that he was too independent for his own good. He agreed, explaining that he saw mountaineering as a challenge and as a series of techniques to be perfected. My helping hand was not the correct way for him to overcome the obstacle. By taking my hand he would learn nothing. I talked about the effect on other people of his rejecting their help – about how they would feel personally rejected. It seemed to me at the time that he wanted, at the end of the expedition, to be able to say that everything he had achieved he had done by himself – and certainly without the help of someone as inept on mountains as myself. I wrote:

> He [John] is disturbingly intense at times. I try not to get upset by it all but the coldness and seeming lack of humanity is now very hard to ignore.
> . . . I would be reasonably happy climbing with John as he knows enough to be safe, but not with Nick. He is very fit and strong, but seems to have no sense of caring for the less strong. He seems totally concerned with his own progress in mountaineering, looking only after himself (and his mentor John) and to hell with anyone else. 'Rad and I, the self-confessed novices with no pretensions to mountain skill, are in addition to this handicap also saddled with the filming. Doubtless, to the other two we seem very inept. Nick is now making no attempt to conceal this, not deigning to even speak to us. It is very depressing living in this sort of company.
> Conrad has another problem; John and Nick keep making little quips to him like 'Come on, 'Rad, smile so we can see you.' He turned to me and said:
> 'How am I supposed to react to this? It's not as if they are good jokes, but ones I've heard millions of times before. If I object then they'll think I'm being over-sensitive, that I can't take black-man jokes. I'm just sick of having to pretend to find it amusing.'

We arrived at Camp One just after 4 P.M. Henry and Nellie were there to greet us, 'H' bearded and confident. The team were finally reunited. Apart from scabby, sun-burned earlobes, they looked well, happily adjusting to the altitude – going through the hangover symptoms, resting, recovering then going on higher and repeating the process, a cycle we were going to enter once we had completed a last terrible bout of load-carrying across the glacier.

I wrote in my diary:

'The transformation in Nick when we met Henry was significant; talking respectfully to him and ignoring 'Rad and me. John is completely one-track minded; the mountain is the only consideration – and to hell with anything else. Nick seems to be the same, also wanting desperately to get up it. He is the least experienced climber so is trying very hard to appear capable. He seems to feel superior to 'Rad and me – and does not waste his time with us. He has "collected" the Shakesgam Valley and now wants the Crown. Underlying all this, could he possibly fear that he does not have what it takes?'

John took Henry to one side and started trying to persuade him to replace Nellie with Nick on the mountain. As things stood John, replacing Henry, would get Nellie (an excellent climber) as his partner. and Nick would stay with us.

I knew that one of Henry's aims for the expedition was to get Nellie as near to the summit as possible because, being the youngest and a very technically able climber, Nellie seemed to have the most promise for the future as a mountaineer. John's proposal ran contrary to this aim.

I was pleased to note that Henry was not swayed.

Thermos flasks are vital for that first brew of the morning – made with water boiled up the night before and consumed from the warmth of the sleeping bag. Conrad and I found we had only one flask, whereas John and Nick had a *third* thermos in their tent. This discovery had been for me the final straw of their selfishness that day.

My bad mood was broken by 'Rad pointedly asking John and Nick if they would mind letting us 'borrow' their third flask. John professed not to have noticed and handed it over. We wondered whether maybe Nick knew they had an extra one – it was visible for all to see:

'The surrender of the thermos pitchforked me out of my black mood. Such small things make a great difference in the scaling of unclimbed peaks!'

That evening, before dusk set in, Henry led us down from Camp One, from the pile of moraine, across the glacier to where we could see up the ravine towards Camp Two. Quietly, he was showing us his mountain.

From the glacier, on the left there were several steep chutes cut into a shoulder of rock, down which we could hear rocks and ice chunks rattling. The route went up one of these chutes. One-third of the way up the ravine, a blanket of white snow covered the brown and grey of the exposed rock – the permanent snow line of the mountain. Above the shoulder of rock, to the right, a huge snow-filled bowl hung cracked and crevassed, filled with millions of tons of ice and snow, poised to avalanche.

Above this bowl, the summit of the mountain appeared to be dome-shaped – like Oxford's Tom Tower eroded down into thousands of sharp ridges and gullies. The route from Camp Two went across the rock shoulder and the top edge of the snow bowl, then up into the crenellations of the eroded dome. From fifteen miles away, in Eric Shipton's photograph of the Crown taken from the west, the mountain had a classic sharp triangular shape to it. From our position directly below, this classic and awe-inspiring shape seemed to have become severely foreshortened. From close up, however, the power and ferocity of the mountain took over completely from its beauty. It became malevolently squat, snow swirling in its crenellations.

Henry reflected that, by his reckoning, the Japanese had got the heights of the various camps wrong, that the mountain itself was foreshortened and we were therefore further up it than we thought. However it was not possible to be certain. His recalculation of these heights seemed to produce different answers. One reason for this variation was that our altimeters were barometric – and thus affected by the weather. Even a series of readings taken by these means could only indicate approximate heights and the total height of the mountain was also in dispute. Nevertheless, we were not about to disagree with anything that put us closer to the summit.

* * *

That night 'Rad and I, cosy in a small, two-man tent on the rock rubble of Camp One, were suffering from Cheyne-Stokes breathing: panting and gasping through lack of oxygen, continually waking in a panic, then making the conscious effort to breathe deeply and steadily in order to calm down again. At one time I felt as if my whole body had swollen up leaving me lurking inside it, as if I were floating inside a huge balloon. I tried to remain stationary on my back. By my distressed rolling around, I was tying myself up in my cotton liner inside my sleeping bag and disturbing Conrad.

Before retiring, we had placed the cooker and pans ready for breakfast in the doorway. When I had to get up for a pee (after trying to ignore it for a long time) they became an obstacle course to be negotiated in order to get out of the tent. At 2 A.M., standing outside the tent wearing nothing but underpants, it was cold – but the constant tossing and turning had made me hot so I didn't notice. I was so sleepless and depressed that as soon as it grew light enough to read (the night was endless) I picked up a dog-eared thriller, a boring tale of the rescue of some American businessmen from a Tehran jail.

At 10 A.M., Henry, Conrad, Nick and I clattered down to ABC, me carting the camera gear, where we sat around drinking coffee and eating Japanese biscuits. We found we could polish off a huge catering-size packet in seconds. We were delaying starting on the interminable trek to Base Camp.

After a few miles, Nick, wanting to move faster, offered to take the Bolex cine camera – which I relinquished to him with grateful haste. Travelling unladen (apart from my camera gear), we made fast work of the glacier, chatting as we stumbled along the tortuous route. I was relieved to have Henry to talk with; thinking and talking made crossing the endless miles of boulders and slipping, frost-shattered rock seem to go much faster.

The weather was changeable; a series of fronts coming down the valley with mist, cold winds and some snow. Just after we arrived at Base Camp, and while Nick who had gone to fetch water from the river was a tiny dot in the distance, it even poured with rain.

We had been lucky with the weather; Eric Shipton had suffered days of cold rain that had slowed him down and made life miserable. Nick returned soaked.

'Rad and I cooked – a huge curry made with ghee (melted butter – in tubes, provided as part of Gurkha Army ration pack and thrown in with our special rations), and the chocolate custard that Conrad had developed as his speciality. I managed to spill all the garlic onto the tent floor, scraping it back into the frying pan when no one was looking. By the end of the meal, I was covered in rancid butter and custard powder.

I found that the end of my right thumb had split, the wound lengthening and deepening every day, which hampered my tying knots and doing up buckles. The dry atmosphere and the high altitude kept wounds from healing as quickly as they would at sea level. The healing process seemed to stop completely further up the mountain. I was treating this irritating sore by sucking the thumb until the hard skin had softened, then filling the crack with Cicatrin antibiotic powder.

Henry had suffered quite badly from the altitude at Camp Two, particularly from lethargy and hangover type sickness. He told me the lethargy had worried him most; he thought it dangerous, that it seriously affected his judgement. He had decided to take the drug Diamox if he felt that way again.

'H' was not happy with the way the climbing was going. He confided to me that, in his opinion, Andy and Bob were a bit too relaxed. He thought their late morning starts were partly to blame for the delay in finding the route from Camp One to Camp Two.

On Thursday, 17 September we each carried eight rations and two litres of fuel up to British Dump – which weighed just over twenty kilogrammes each. We left at 8 and stumbled back into Base Camp just before dusk, at 6.30. That night, I cooked a huge meal of fried rice with luncheon meat using Japanese 'Golden Cock' lard, followed by curry and rice. We were almost too tired to eat, having to force the food down.

On Friday we carried loads all the way to ABC, with me filming the process. The camera gear was heavy and the day very long and wearing, lasting from 9 until 7.30. Conrad changed the film in the camera for me – which gave me the chance to think about the shots, take the still photographs and have a rest – while the others sat around, bored and wishing that we could get on to the food and rest of ABC.

The glacier seemed to have moved significantly since our last foray. The ice had humped upwards near the ladder across the river and a huge, deep lake had suddenly emptied, leaving a black serrated hole like a vast rotten tooth socket.

At the very end of this dreadful day, as the sun dropped behind the mountains, I asked everyone to pose silhouetted against the sky. I calculated the aperture very carefully then started filming. Halfway through the shot I asked them to point at some object on the distant horizon – to introduce some movement and draw the viewer's eye. Nick pointed vertically up into the air. It had to be Nick, and of course I immediately assumed he had done it deliberately.

The shot was ruined. Afterwards I was galled to see that the exposure was perfect and it had come out beautifully – except for an arm waving inexplicably at the early evening stars. This incident destroyed what little there was left of my frayed patience, causing me to explode with anger. Conrad, appreciating the moment, was overcome by hysterical laughter, and Henry saw only what had happened without realizing how I felt. Unfortunately he did not back me up – or even just say nothing – instead chided me for my lack of sense of humour, which made me angrier still.

I packed up the cameras, refused to take any more shots, and we stumbled down to the tyrolean traverse, across the swollen river and along the terraces to ABC. At our last rest stop I offered boiled sweet peace offerings all round – which were accepted. Our evening's eating, cooked by Nick (noodles with everything in the huge pot) was congenial.

I was sharing a tent with Henry, who got up at 7 on Saturday to make breakfast, prompting me to get up for the pee I had been trying to ignore since 5.30. He was trying to clean up a gunged-up primus cooker, repairing the split pin that allowed the valve to regulate the petrol supply.

We boiled up the water and listened to the cassette machine.

There were only a few tapes; Whitney Houston, the sophisticated night music of Jean-Michel Jarre, Vivaldi's *Four Seasons*, Feargal Sharkey and 'Atmospheres' — a collection of evocative instrumentals that was played the most.

By 9 we were en route back to British Dump, to pick up the loads from the last two days and film the tyrolean traverse. I was still angry with Nick so I tried to leave him out of frame whenever I could. When we were all across the river and I had finished filming, the other three pushed off towards ABC leaving me to pack the camera and tripod into my load.

In my fit of annoyance at being abandoned I took the wrong river terrace twice, having to retrace my footsteps each time, arriving at ABC half an hour after the others and in a foul temper. Henry was washing himself in a large battered aluminium bowl, Nick (as he seemed always to be doing) was carefully packing his kit and Conrad was making a brew for everyone else.

'Rad seemed rather vague, with an air of distraction. I asked him what he was doing. He scratched his head vacantly:

'I was going to wash my private parts,' he explained, 'but I decided to sweep out the tent instead.'

We found some Japanese toffees in the food tent and had three each with our morning coffee.

After lunch and several cups of tea, we set off for Camp One with heavy loads — me with camera gear and the others with rations, fuel and sleeping gear. We went quite fast and the climb was very tiring. Conrad plodded steadily at the rear using a ski pole as a walking stick. For the last bit, up the loose scree at the top of the glacier, Henry, who also had a ski pole, lent me his. The last forty minutes seemed to last for ever, staggering slowly upwards until the blue tents of Camp One appeared over the last pile of brown, cracked slates.

Henry cooked and we crammed into one of the blue tents to eat. For some strange reason, we ate raw garlic and I fried a whole onion in ghee to enliven the dehydrated beef stew. On the radio we heard that Camp Three was not yet occupied. They had endured another heavy day struggling to free ropes already laid, but iced-up. They were having to rest today to recover.

I wrote in my diary:

Henry is excited because his whole team is at last on the mountain —
and we are happy for the same reason. All the frustrations of
humping kit up the valley has fallen away and we are being very
cheerful and considerate with each other.

I think the bad temper arises from worry and fear of the mountain
— AND not being on the mountain, and thus not able to get on with the
climbing.

I hope I don't have any more of the panic breathing tonight that I
had the last time I slept up here (at 5,600 metres).

I feel contented and calm, for the first time wanting to get on with
it, and looking forward to all the things I have to learn — like wearing
crampons for the first time.

CHAPTER 11

High Altitudes

On Sunday, 20 September I started a new phase in my life – as a real mountaineer. Henry and I breakfasted inside our tent, then crawled from warm sleeping bags to sort out our climbing equipment.

We checked the batteries of our personal radio beacons – which, if we were to be engulfed by avalanche, would emit a signal to enable the others to locate where we lay; adjusted climbing harnesses, with a screw-gate karabiner and several clip karabiners – a clip to secure ropes and slings and through which ropes can run yet be disconnected easily; slings, builder-style helmets, an ice axe and hammer each, crampons and three prussic loops.

The latter, sounding like a form of colonic irrigation used in cases of arsenic poisoning, is actually a clever looping of rope which allows a climber to move safely up a rope secured by the 'prussic'. On falling, the loop tightens, forming an effective brake.

We left Camp One at 8.45. Wearing double-thickness trousers, thick pile jackets, walking a little awkwardly in quilted leather inner boots and high-tech plastic shell outers like ski boots (to which crampons would be strapped), we moved across the glacier to the bottom of the rock shoulder and the ravines. In our bergens, we carried the previous night's order of stores for Camp Two. We planned to rendezvous with Nellie and John at 'Nellie's Ledge'. They were to come down from Camp Two, and would carry the groceries the rest of the way. Henry and I, Conrad and Nick were then to come back down and spend another night at Camp One.

At the bottom of the ravine we put on helmets and crampons.

Rocks and chunks of ice rattled down without warning from the unseen slopes above. Henry sent me off onto a fixed rope at the foot of the ravine, coming up below, offering advice.

The fixed ropes were like handrails, ascended using a jumar – a ratchet device that allows a heavy pull on the rope, then a free slide upwards on the ratchet in preparation for another pull. The true nature of my mountaineering knowledge became apparent. Although I had heard the others talking of jumars, until starting up the fixed rope, I had no idea of their purpose and so hadn't asked Bob for one. 'H' gave me his then followed using the much slower prussic loop method. There were few footholds and I made much use of my crampon toe prongs, elbows, knees, chin and anything else that I could apply to the rock.

To Henry's quiet prompting, I climbed steadily upwards, through the rock chutes and onto the steep snow slopes. The bright orange fixed rope looped from belay to belay, each fixed securely into the rock with ice screws, across the snow slope and steeply upwards out of sight. At every stop, with relief we shrugged off our bergens, clipping them onto the fixed rope lest they tumble thousands of feet onto the glacier below.

Temperature varied greatly. The sunshine was uncomfortably hot and the shade like a deep freeze, a strong, biting wind carving through the more exposed places. The traverses, where the route went across the scree faces, were very exposed to rock and ice falls from above. Boulders were loosened by our movements on the fixed ropes, skittering down on us as we pulled ourselves upwards. The helmets were very necessary.

At the rest stops Henry and I talked of the stresses in the team, and of inconsiderate behaviour during the expedition. Henry thought the mountain the root cause of this, generating tension and pressure in each of us.

I found myself starting to understand the intense satisfaction, excitement and challenge of mountaineering. Having been pitch-forked into the sport at a fairly advanced standard of endeavour was something like making a first parachute jump from 24,000 feet (as opposed to the usual 2,400 feet) and there was no alternative but to enjoy it.

The physical feelings and raw emotions – of fear, satisfaction, joy, camaraderie, and sheer accomplishment – were intense. I felt I could understand John Day's attitude if the frustration and the tension that he displayed had been generated by not being on the mountain. For my frustration and tension I could claim no such excuse. My bad temper was not so much generated by the mountain as by the general situation – and in particular occurred in response to the tension and ill humour of others.

Henry warned me that there would be more bad temper as the higher altitude took its effect on people. He was nevertheless sanguine. For the moment all was well, and he felt the challenge of the situation on the mountain was keeping everyone occupied.

Using crampons is like climbing with skis. Using only the toe points rapidly exhausts the calf muscles so you have to 'herringbone' or 'duck-walk' up the steep bits, feet splayed outwards, placing the boot down flat so that all the points dig in. A variation, to rest the ankles a little, is to climb sideways, feet across the line of the slope – again trying to kick the points flat into the snow, parallel to the angle of the slope. The crampon tips become clogged with snow, making the feet appreciably heavier, and the consequent reduction in grip causes the foot to slip and the climber to fall. This happened to me frequently, the fixed rope stopping my fall, stretching downwards in a 'V' shape as I scrambled to my feet and climbed laboriously back up onto the route once more.

At each belay point along the fixed rope we had to stop and go through a vital ritual. As well as the jumar, we clipped ourselves onto the fixed rope with two karabiners. At each belay the rope went through a bolt. We had to unclip a karabiner then replace it onto the rope above the belay bolt. The jumar was then unclipped and similarly re-attached. Finally the second karabiner was unclipped and reclipped above the bolt, giving safety to the potentially dangerous process of moving the jumar above the belay. There were hundreds of belays, some a few metres apart, others fifty or a hundred feet apart.

The slope was growing steeper. Our footholds were formed in the snow by the careful placement of boots and crampons – unstable snow-steps which frequently collapsed. We slid back down until the rope stopped us. With the heavy bergens, keeping balance was exhausting and often impossible. Falls were frequent.

The altitude made everything much harder. Lack of oxygen was now painfully apparent. I tried to compensate by taking deep breaths, then after a few minutes of reasonable movement and feeling all right, would be overcome by lack of oxygen and the sudden debilitating build-up of carbon dioxide.

As I couldn't yet climb properly with crampons, my movements were very uneconomical. I was making myself much more tired than necessary. I could see that a nice steady rhythm was required.

The last few hundred metres of the climb were extremely tiring. I had to stop every few metres, panting heavily with my head spinning. The crumbling snow and loose scree caused me to slip frequently – minor disasters of wasted effort that seemed almost unbearable at the time.

After about three hours of hard work Henry and I reached Nellie's Ledge. The last hundred feet, with the ledge in sight, were painful and seemed to take an age. Finally I crawled over the lip, clipping onto the belay and slumping exhausted onto my bergen for several totally mindless minutes.

I felt sick – but as I recovered, the impact of the scenery began to penetrate my exhaustion. Perching on this narrow ledge high above the glacier, looking out across the Changtok and Chongtar Groups of mountains where K2 lay enshrouded in mist was exhilarating. Looking down without the painful distraction of oxygen debt, the sheer drop up which I had climbed was suddenly frightening.

In the void above the glacier, far below my snow-covered boots, I watched a single black raven using air currents, circling relentlessly upwards, gaining height until he reached our altitude. As the airflow swooped up and over the brown rock ridge in whose shadow we were sheltering, the bird vanished suddenly above our heads.

This seemed to be the same raven that had followed us from the Shakesgam Valley. We were the only source of food for miles around and the bird seemed drawn to us by the finely tuned antennae of his desire for survival. How far had he come? He was something elemental, part of the power of the mountain, more like a wraith or a spirit than flesh and blood.

Henry and I sat quietly looking out across the mountains, then watched as the other pair moved slowly up the rope. Finally Conrad arrived, crawling painfully up to Nellie's Ledge, to slump beside me, miserable with exhaustion.

I forced myself to eat some biscuits and a slab of luncheon meat. At Camp One this meal would have been delicious, but here and now the meat seemed greasy and disgusting – another effect of altitude.

'Rad was not interested in anything – in food, the splendid view or anything at all. He told me later he felt panic, sickness and lethargy and that if he was going to feel like that again he did not ever want to return again to this altitude.

These feelings were classic symptoms of mild altitude sickness and were extraordinarily powerful and very difficult to resist. They affected your personality and corrupted your willpower and desire to succeed. Judgement became unbalanced by apathy.

After half an hour together on the ledge, the four of us (Henry, Nick, Conrad and I) started back down to Camp One. Nellie and John had collected the 'shopping' and were making their way back to Camp Two. Henry gave us a quick lesson on descending using a fixed rope. You twist it round your wrists and run forwards down the mountain, arms stretched out behind, braking and using your woollen dachstein gloves to absorb the heat of the friction. Crampons were unnecessary. We slid and stumbled swiftly down the pitches that had been so painful and slow to climb, pausing only at each belay for the karabiner ritual.

We stopped at the top of the rock chutes, needing to abseil down through them. There was a brief moment of confusion as Henry realized that I did not know how to tie or use an 'Italian' – a method of twisting the rope through a karabiner so that it formed a safe brake for the abseil. Henry tied one for me, and told me how to brake. I stepped off the top of the rock shoulder and bounced cautiously down the chutes, through to the surface of the glacier.

Back at Camp One, I cooked supper, chatted with Henry and

listened to Vivaldi. I lay on loose slates of glacial moraine outside our tent, staring westwards up at the snow-covered ridge and its thick snow cornice. The sun had vanished behind the ridge, making radiant with gold the underside of the white clouds that moved behind the saddle, and behind the snow and ice massif of the Crown itself.

The mountain was so pure – hard but clean. The cold, clear, blue skies; rock, ice and snow; uncompromising and simple.

Henry took that night's radio check, walking up and down the piles of loose rock until he found a position from which he could communicate with the others.

We had expected Bob and Andy to have reached Camp Three – however, they reported more problems with iced-up ropes. All six of them were back at Camp Two again. This was disappointing as time was marching on. When they did reach Camp Three, judging from what had happened at the other two camps, they would have to rest for at least one day before pushing on again, using up even more precious time.

We estimated that getting to the summit would take at least four days from the time we occupied Camp Four. The Japanese said that they had been defeated by a one-hundred-and-fifty-foot ice wall above Camp Four – and this might itself take several days to climb.

Although philosophical and optimistic, Henry was worried about a lack of drive up front; whether the second pair of climbers were getting up in the mornings, packing a load and following on in the footsteps of the lead climbers – who climbed with the bare minimum of gear. The second pair should dump their loads at the point where the first pair decided to call it a day. All four would then return to the previous camp.

If this process was taking place the delays were not so critical, as the food and equipment necessary for the higher camps was being carried up the mountain – even if the lead was proceeding slowly.

Henry rightly regarded himself as the man with the experience to solve the mountaineering problems, and the drive and determination to implement them. He wanted to get back up to the work face as soon as possible to find out what was going on.

* * *

That night, Monday, 21 September, was misery:

I shared a small tent with Henry who snored abominably.

If he rolled onto his front there was blissful quiet. After a period of peace he would roll onto his back and produce terribly fluidy, rending-membrane noises. These would build up from sudden isolated snorts until his nasal-maxillary volume level was at its unbearable maximum. I tried sharp nudges, deep sighs and noisy rearrangements of my own position, jostling him so that he resettled onto his front in delicious peace and quiet. These ploys had some success, but at 2.30, in spite of being dog-tired, I was still horribly awake.

For the rest of the long night I snatched brief moments of sleep while Henry was on his front. Early in the new day I established a policy of aggressive slumber, breathing firmly and regularly, ruthlessly ignoring Henry's snoring, getting on with the business of my own sleep. Sadly, although this policy was beginning to work well – helped by my exhaustion – it was interrupted by Henry's wrist-watch alarm peeping reveille.

For a person who had been the object of so many ill-intentioned wishes, Henry woke that morning remarkably unscathed and refreshed, with great sighs and much self-congratulation at how long and how well he was sleeping:

'What will I do when I get back to the UK without this nine and ten hours' sleep every night?'

Our cooker was being pathetic, taking ages to heat the water for brews and rolled oats. I dozed grumpily for the first ten minutes then started the balancing act of eating and drinking breakfast, and dressing without getting out of the sleeping bag until the very last minute.

Henry shouted at the others (Conrad and Nick) to start walking before us. We needed at least a twenty-minute interval between our two groups on the fixed ropes. The bottom pair could pull the top pair off, or at least make their progress difficult. Conversely, the top pair could shower the others with rocks and ice debris.

I got up and packed the Bolex camera, five one-hundred-foot rolls of cine film, three lenses, the tripod attachments and some personal survival kit – which came to a little over fifteen kilos. Henry and I set off across the glacier at 9, coming round the shoulder to the bottom of the gorge to see 'Rad walking slowly back. He had wrenched his neck and shoulder, could not do the climb, and returned to Camp One for a lonely, boring and painful day.

For my second time up the fixed ropes, I resolved to get into a steady rhythm. It had been snowing all night and fresh snow covered the rocks, hiding the holds. The steep cliffs looked impossible and I asked Henry if we were on the same route as yesterday. Henry commented that we were, but that as I was learning my snow and ice climbing the hard way – at 20,000 feet carrying fifteen kilos – I shouldn't get downhearted.

I struggled up, trying not to use my knees as they were very painful – skinned raw during yesterday's climb. I managed to slip into a steady pace which got me going on relatively easily.

Henry told Nick, who was without a partner as Conrad was injured, to carry on and wait for us at Nellie's Ledge, where we would all have lunch together. Nick vanished upwards and we pushed on with the occasional five-minute stop.

A rattle of stones from above warned of the arrival of Bob and Andy, who swung into view down the gulley, en route to ABC. We stopped for a twenty-minute chat. I had not seen Bob and Andy since we split to explore the Shakesgam Valley. They looked lean and fit and it felt good to be with them again.

They had found the going from Camp Two to Camp Three very hard indeed – and a very long way. They, like Henry, reckoned the summit was much closer than it looked. They thought that after Camp Three, the ascent flattened out a bit.

I commented in my diary:

'I know that Himalayan peaks are supposed to be very steep initially, with a walk to the summit. As the Japanese were defeated by this part of the mountain, I wonder if the supposition will hold true for the Crown. Could it just be wishful thinking on our part?'

During our rest stops, Henry and I chatted about personalities.

In the planning stages of the expedition, quartermaster Bob Wood had taken a long time to produce the expedition kit list – which had irritated Henry. However, once started he had worked very hard to produce a well-researched and almost faultless list. Bob was quiet, long suffering and very sensible, but seemed to Henry to be too cautious, inclined to wait until conditions on the mountain were perfect. As tends to happen to perfectionists in most walks of life, conditions rarely prove perfect, so fleeting opportunities are often missed.

Henry knew Andy Aspinall, Bob's partner, very well indeed and knew that he would take his lead from whoever he was with. Henry's worries over the delays on the mountain were based on these assessments of character, from which he suspected that Bob and Andy might not have gone really hard for Camp Three.

Henry and I concluded this discussion on Nellie's Ledge. By this later stage of the climb, as on the previous day, my initially rhythmical progress had collapsed into a series of stumbling gasps and long rests — often bent forward with my forehead resting in the snow.

The second last piton before Nellie's Ledge was particularly memorable. It was hammered high into a rock wall, where the rock was firm and safe. The fixed rope looped up to it at the end of a long, steep climb, without the respite of a knot or belay.

In order to clip on above this last belay, we had to climb the rock face using fingers and crampon points. The alternative was to unclip completely and climb round to the ledge, relying only on an ice axe and crampons — which would be stupid. I had to stop for more than two minutes' hard gasping before I had enough breath even to climb up onto the rock from the snow.

I finally made it to Nellie's Ledge, clipping myself and bergen onto the fixed rope. Henry was still plodding steadily up the long bit to the last belay. The ledge was deserted. There was no sign of Nick, who seemed to have pushed on ahead of us.

I was so exhausted it took me over ten minutes to get out my lunch, find a place to sit and organize my ropes. Down the valley, falling snow obscured the mountains. Henry organized himself beside me. Fine, cold ice crystals blew into our faces as we munched luncheon meat and I tried to prevent my precious chocolate bar from skating off the icy ledge and down the steep slope over which we were perched.

Robbo arrived from above, enthusiastic, friendly and capable, to say that Nick was up at Camp Two. He took my load, to save me the additional two hours' climb to their camp. After a chat and bite to eat, he departed upwards on the orange rope.

Nick's absence from the ledge, in spite of Henry's having told him to stay and have lunch with us, prompted Henry to express disappointment with his performance – saying that he did not seem to be showing the qualities that had won him a Commando Medal (awarded on the Commando Course for team work, selflessness and the like). I offered my theory: that Nick had adopted John as his model and was trying very hard to be regarded as a contender for the summit.

Henry's hope was that Nick would imitate Andy Aspinall – who, as I had discovered during the basketball match against the Chinese Army, is excellent and caring when confident of his own abilities and position. Henry believed John to be an unsuitable model for Nick because, although a capable mountaineer, John was a soloist, and when under pressure on a mountain would make decisions that were correct for him – within his own capabilities and desires – but not necessarily correct for the group. I described the river crossing episode. Henry said that like me he would not have crossed as John had done.

Henry told me of his batting order for the ascent to the summit: Nellie and Andy first, John and Bob, then me to film – with the others after that if there was time. He was giving the honours for the first to go to the summit to Nellie and Andy as the ones with the most to gain from the experience. Despite having done the lion's share of the organizing work, Henry did not consider standing on the summit himself to be terribly important.

I became cold sitting on the ledge. I demonstrated to Henry the correct tying of an 'Italian' abseil knot and started back down into a freezing gale of fine snow. Henry went up to Camp Two, his rest at lower altitudes over. Halfway down I removed my crampons to speed up the descent.

Abseiling on my own through the rock chute gave me a few anxious moments. I wasn't certain I was going down the correct one as ropes were laid down both. Then I used the wrong fixed rope and had to karabiner onto a belay and tie another Italian onto the correct rope. It was becoming a little over-technical for one so inexperienced. I kept wondering if Nick would come bouncing down bringing a landslide through the narrow chute onto my head.

Fifty feet above the glacier, the cliff eased out into a steep slope. I came off the rope and scrambled down onto the glacier with a sigh of relief. I was concerned about Conrad, who had spent a long day on his own. He was hunched up in his sleeping bag, uncomfortable but otherwise all right.

Conrad was unhappy, a direct continuation of his altitude-induced depression at Nellie's Ledge the previous day. He talked of not wanting to go to the summit of the mountain, as if the strain and sickness of the previous day had psyched him out of it. I was reminded of what one of the great early Himalayan mountaineers had written.

'He said that you must really, really want to climb a mountain,' I told 'Rad, 'because by the time you get near the top, all your motivation will have been eroded away by the altitude. You needed a vast amount of enthusiasm and commitment before you started, so that there would be a small amount left to enable you to get to the summit.'

I urged Conrad – if he could – not to dwell on the situation. He should stay low until his shoulder was absolutely right again and he should not worry – as that was what he seemed to have done for most of the long, lonely day.

We cooked supper, and an hour or so later Nick arrived from Camp Two. He was chatty and interesting – much better company than he had been. I wondered whether this might be because Henry had spoken to him.

I made the 7.30 radio check. They needed another tent at Camp Two so we dismantled the Phoenix (the tent Henry and I had been occupying) for delivery to them on the morrow. I moved into a smaller one. I welcomed this glorious situation, anticipating a much needed night of snore-free, undisturbed slumber. But, without a second warm body to heat up the tent, my night of glorious isolation was very cold. I had to get up twice for a pee – on a freezing clear, starlit night. Nick and 'Rad, in the next tent, were enjoying the fug of their collective warmth. They muttered 'Poor bastard' every time they heard me stumbling and fumbling into the deep freeze wearing only vest and Union Jack shorts.

By dawn the cold had forced me into my thick mountain shirt and woolly hat. I was still shivering and should also have put on thick trousers and socks. As on our first night at Maza Dala, in the illogicality of idleness I preferred to be cold rather than get up a third time to don trousers in order to be warm.

The next morning (Tuesday, 22 September) I set off twenty minutes before Nick to get a start on the fixed ropes. I felt terrible: very weak and sick, my pack too heavy even for the walk across the glacier. In my daze I walked past the bottom of the gully and had to be whistled back by Nick, who was following. I did not think that I would be able to make the climb and was preparing to give up and go back to Camp One.

To lighten my load, I dumped the cine camera tripod – tying it onto the end of the fixed rope so I would find it later. After putting on climbing harness heavy with hardware and helmet, my pack felt manageable.

Rather than go back to Camp One, I started climbing the rock gully, to see how I would feel. I had no commitment, enthusiasm or determination. It was sheer awkward bloody-mindedness that made me go up the rope rather than back across the rubble to my tent. I couldn't have cared less which I did.

The first steep climb – about seventy feet of chimneying – seemed very hard. I tried to establish a rhythm and soon found myself up at the first of the two traverses – where I stopped to wait for Nick. I ate my peanuts and raisins, and after twenty minutes went back down to look for him. He was at the Japanese Dump (at the top of the rock chutes) emptying rations from his pack – which, with the tent as well, he had found to be too heavy.

We both felt dreadful.

From the second traverse we continued upwards, me keeping one pitch ahead so that we would not interfere with each other on the rope, moving steadily. Around a bend in the first narrow ice gorge, we encountered Jerry. He was stumbling down the steep slope wrapped up in his salopettes, Red Liner jacket (a super-warm high altitude life-saver), and Aztec-style woollen balaclava. He had altitude sickness and was making a painful descent, face puffed and swollen, his speech badly slurred. He said that having come down a thousand feet or so he already felt better. He looked dreadful. After ten minutes' chat with us, Jerry gathered himself and his equipment and continued downwards to safety.

Nick and I made Nellie's Ledge by 1.30 – me literally on hands and knees. We chattered about options for military careers. Nick was considering applying to join a more extreme part of the Army about which I knew a small amount. We talked over the implications of this, and how he saw his career as a Royal Engineer developing.

We ate lunch and, after a most congenial hour, pushed on.

The next bit, up to Camp Two, was new to me – but not to Nick.

After a vertiginous traverse over a steep, very exposed slope that swept downwards for several thousand feet, the route continued up a steep exposed face covered with soft snow. I had to learn snow and ice climbing very rapidly – as well as how to use the prussic loops issued to me three days earlier as our jumars were slipping uselessly on the icy rope.

The altitude was beginning to really bite. After each terribly short pitch between belays, we could not even speak for several minutes after the karabiner clipping ritual. We slumped forward in the soft snow, panting desperately, trying to suck in oxygen.

Each step was a major effort; kicking the snow from the crampons, then lifting the boot from the deep snow and aiming to place the crampons firmly into the ice to obtain a good foothold. Often the snow gave way, and a laborious, energy-sapping step forward turned into an uncontrolled exhausting slide, halted by the fixed rope. Regaining the lost height was heart-breaking.

We waited for each other, chatting while the other regained the ability to speak, then enjoying really whole-hearted conversation until it was time for the leader to plod upwards once more. We were both totally physically and mentally committed to what we were doing. There was simply no other way for us to get up the mountain; any less commitment and we would have been forced to go back down again.

This day with Nick was for me the best day of the whole expedition. Afterwards Nick told me plainly that it had been the best day for him too.

I found it a remarkable experience: of pain, fear, determination, intense, high pressure learning of half-remembered mountaineering techniques, good humour and immense satisfaction. In statistical terms, we climbed from 5,500 to 6,200 metres, and took from 9.35 to around 6.30 to do it – seven and a half hours of climbing, with many stops.

As we crawled over the last belay and along the short traverse to Camp Two a small figure was descending through the rocks from the mists above. Inside one of the three tents, Nellie was ill from the altitude, shouting a weak greeting as he heard us arrive.

The descending figure was Henry bearing good news. They had made it to Camp Three and John and Robbo were to stay there that night.

Camp Two looked very cramped, perched on a narrow ridge of snow between the snow face up which we had climbed and a steep, rocky ravine. Henry described Camp Three as very much worse: cut out of a steep ice slope with very little space for anything other than a couple of tents. It was a long way – over 700 metres vertically in height. Henry was considering placing an intermediate camp somewhere in between to shorten the days and thus conserve energy. From Camp Two, when Henry pointed it out to us, Camp Three looked to be almost at the top – a very long way up the mountain.

Henry also talked about staying on the mountain and continuing the effort even if the allotted time ran out before we reached the top. He thought the rations left by the Japanese would give us the extra time. The snows would make the planned overland trip through the Kunjerab Pass – to fly from Karachi – impossible. We would have to walk to Maza Dala, fly to Xian and from there to Hong Kong.

This idea caused much concern. Some people were worried at the prospect of additional expense. I was in two minds, wanting to climb the mountain, but aware that winter could catch and imprison us if we stayed too long. But Henry's determination was contagious – although his declaration of intent to stay worried some who felt they should have a say in this important decision.

I wondered later whether the idea of staying was a leadership ploy to generate a bit more commitment from the team, rather than something that might actually happen. Henry could be devious in his motivation of others, putting forward ideas that were impractical to see how others would react. I was not sure whether the staying-on idea was genuine but spurious enthusiasm, or a calculated but somewhat ill-advised manipulation.

At the time, I reacted positively to the idea at face value, welcoming Henry's lack of inhibition. His 'ill-advised manipulation' worked very well on me.

Nick and I shared one of the two tents at Camp Two. Unfortunately the floor was flooded with over an inch of icy water, from condensation and ice melted at night by body heat. The heat of sun on the outside of the tent kept the water from re-freezing during the day.

I lay on two thermo mats in the pool of water, taking care to keep my highly absorbent down sleeping bag inside my waterproof bivvie bag. A wet sleeping bag could be fatal.

Nick and I were feeling very dehydrated and so cooked a huge watery stew. I remembered (for the first time on the expedition) to take a pee bottle to bed with me. There were two reasons for this precaution; apart from the extra cold ($-10°$ centigrade and less), the cliff up which we had struggled was only four feet from the tent entrance. I did not wish to return prematurely to Camp One whilst having a sleepy slash in the middle of the night.

Although not soaked by floorwater, I had a terrible night. At first I could not sleep at all, and then when I did drop off, suffered peculiar dreams, then Cheyne-Stokes breathing – waking with the panic of drowning and suffocation.

The very dry atmosphere and deep and constant breathing through the mouth (so as to suck in enough oxygen) evaporated off all saliva and moistening fluid from our tongues, mouths and throats. It was very unpleasant trying to generate more moistening saliva in a sore, dry mouth and throat. By morning my mouth was coated with a thick layer of gunge left after the evaporation, which I had to scrape away with teaspoon and handkerchief before I could speak.

And it was cold; we both slept hooded, fastened into all the special heat baffles of our sleeping bags, me wearing thermal vest, woolly hat, double thickness trousers and socks. In the morning the inside of our tent was thick with fine frost that covered us with cold, icy powder if we moved the tent walls. The water on the floor had acquired a dry surface of ice, and my two thin thermal mats had protected me from getting wet.

I was depressed, with a headache and no desire to do anything. For the latter part of the night I had ignored increasing bladder pressure as I had forgotten that I had a pee bottle with me. Eventually the pressure overcame my desire to remain in the cocooned warmth of my sleeping bag, and I crawled from the tent into the wide, wild world outside.

Above, the Crown was clear, the summit a small pinnacle above its serrated dome of rock and ice. The precipice at either side plunged downwards, the view clear and sharp, unimpeded by mist or snow. My reaction was to wish that the others would hurry up and climb the mountain so we could all go home.

We stripped out the tent, laying everything in the sunshine to dry. Henry left for a lonely load carry up to Camp Three, Nellie went down, and Nick and I, acclimatizing, lay about in the weak sunshine resting, reading and drinking brews.

Time was getting tight; we had seven days left on the mountain, up to ten at a stretch, before we had to start back across the glacier for our rendezvous with the camels. Henry's idea of extending the period in order to conquer the Crown had serious knock-on effects and there was less than universal approval for the idea. My thoughts at the time (in my diary) were that such a departure from the plan could only be justified to get one pair to the top (rather than all of us) and only then if there was some certainty of getting up within a very limited time period. We were becoming increasingly anxious, not only about the growing danger of the mountaineering, but about the amount of time left to us.

It was now essential to identify as quickly as possible the ice wall that had stopped the Japanese, and either get up it – or round it.

The solitary black raven had returned, circling high above in the area of Camp Three. I cooked supper perched on the lip of the narrow ridge on which the three tents stood. I could not understand how the raven was managing to live in this wilderness; perhaps it had come with us from the Aghil Pass, then up the Shakesgam Valley eating our silty rice, following us to Base Camp then ABC, and was now investigating our latest camp, high above where I was now cooking.

The next day Nellie arrived back up from Camp One. He was knackered. Henry appeared from Camp Three, where John and Robbo were feeling all right and would push upwards from there tomorrow. He described the situation up there; the higher altitude was more debilitating. Weight limits for load carries were very much less than to Camp Two, two rations was the maximum load, in a bergen light enough to lift with one hand. Henry said he had taken the best part of an hour getting ready to come back down – putting on helmet, belt harness, crampons and bergen. His confidence was, as always, undiminished. We would make a summit attempt in a week – or so.

I suffered another bad night (Thursday, 24 September) with a continuous, meaningless dream that rotated round and round in my head with inescapable, hysterical and panic-ridden boredom. I had also developed a haemorrhoid – another usual but less well-chronicled aspect of high altitude mountaineering – which was quite painful, especially as the rations were causing much passing of wind. In the early hours I was driven to use my pee bottle in earnest, an interesting experience resembling wetting the bed. In one go I filled my one-litre bottle to the very brim – a masterpiece of fortuitous precision that could easily have gone wrong.

Nick left at 8.30 for Camp Three. Henry, Nellie and I breakfasted then went down to Nellie's Ledge to film and pick up supplies from Bob, Andy, 'Rad and Jerry. This time we were able to jumar back up (rather than use prussics) as the sunshine had melted the snow and ice from the rope. I managed to establish a good routine for myself, taking two or more heavy breaths in between each careful movement. However, in spite of this care, I was often overcome and forced to stop, bent forward, head resting in the snow, panting furiously.

Conrad had overcome his depression, illness and injury and made it to Nellie's Ledge. On our return to Camp Two, he continued up with us. He found the going very hard indeed. With painful slowness but absolute determination he plodded upwards, slumping forward into the snow after a few paces, sucking the air into his lungs then pushing on again.

'It was the hardest thing I have ever done,' he said to me afterwards. 'And I admit that I cried during the last bit.

'I asked God to help me because I did not think I could carry on. I promised to believe in him. It was at that moment I looked up to see you grinning at me from a few metres away over the top of the ice lip. I think you said something about having just made a cup of tea.

'My prayers had been answered instantly.'

Having now seen for himself how the lead climbers were getting on, Henry was disappointed with Bob and Andy and believed that they should be split up. His suspicions seemed to have been justified; Andy was taking his lead from Bob – who 'H' thought was being over cautious.

Henry had never been prepared to tolerate any comment or suggestion he thought to be in any way negative – even if it was meant to be helpful. He would snap back with a demand for an alternative solution to whatever was being criticized, or with a lecturette about unhelpfulness. Now Bob and Andy, already in Henry's bad books, had adopted a rather carping attitude, seeming to be unimpressed by everything that anybody else did; complaining about the way others left the various camps, being generally critical and having an evident lack of pleasure at what was being achieved. Their attitude irritated Henry, an irritation exacerbated by his doubts over their efforts – which left us lower on the mountain than he thought we might otherwise have been, and short of time.

It had been a beautiful, very cold, clear day. Cold winds had blown fine powder snow across the void between Camp Two in strange shimmering columns of flickering light like dancing spectres. The view stretched out across the top of the Karakoram range, to the south and deep into Pakistan and to where K2 stood squarely dominant amid streaks of white cloud, against the fierce blue of treacherous skies.

That night on the radio we heard from Camp Three that Robbo, fed up with sitting around because John, his partner, was unwell, had gone off on his own, reaching the bottom of the ice cliff, the point where he reckoned the Japanese had given up. He had looked carefully at the rock band and ice cliff and commented that 'it didn't look too bad'. Robbo was a very good and exceptionally strong technical climber, so I didn't know whether to regard this judgement favourably or not. Henry decided to go up the next day with Nick, to stay at Camp Three and 'push the route' as far as they could.

John Day was coming down. He had been sitting around at Camp Three consuming rations without doing much, the altitude having hit him hard. He had been taking Diamox, one capsule every night. Because it is a diuretic, Diamox is usually taken in the morning – so that getting rid of the retained fluids can be managed easily. Taking the tablets at night must have given him plenty of opportunities to use his pee bottle.

Despite the drug, John still felt ill – to the extent that Nick reported his motivation to be 'badly broken'. Knowing John's strength and resilience, I believed that he would recover after a rest at ABC.

I was feeling better myself than I had the previous day. There is a theory that you can only acclimatize by working hard at altitude, that simply resting would only acclimatize you for inactivity. I thought the climb back up from Nellie's Ledge had done me good. The two-hour climb, after a day's rest, seemed ideal – to the extent that I was looking forward to having another day of filming on the morrow.

However, after another night of broken sleep, wearing too much and being hot, and then becoming cold, I crawled out into another new day with a headache and severe symptoms of boredom. Nick and Henry left for Camp Three after a strange discussion in which Henry insisted that the mountain camera cassette film I had packed with the camera was in fact cans of 100-foot reels for the Bolex. He did not like being told (very politely, hesitantly and gently by me – after a moment of self-doubt) that he was wrong.

'Rad and I pottered about making breakfast and brews. He was very slow, and I was impatient, taking over many of the tasks.

At around 10 I heard the crumbling crack and slow roar of an avalanche. A train of ice, powder billowing like smoke in its wake, rushed down one of the small high glaciers below our camp, the sound (being slower to arrive) seeming to emanate from the wake of the ice cloud. The debris vanished around the corner onto the glacier – where Bob, Andy and Jerry, who were load-carrying up that route, would be walking.

Over 2000 feet above, making a cup of coffee and watching the ice crashing down from the couloir, I hoped that they had made a prompt start from ABC and were actually climbing – safe in the rock shoulder gorge.

In fact, down on the main glacier, Bob, Andy and Jerry had heard the avalanche coming. They had managed to run into the lee of the rock gully, avoiding a lethal wave of thousands of tons of moving rock and ice to emerge completely covered in very cold powder ice.

Andy had been carrying a portable stereo, with small speakers tied onto the top of his bergen, playing Whitney Houston. After the noise of the avalanche, the soundless roar of a featureless limbo descended upon them as the whiteout blanketed off all sound, all colour and all shape. As the noise subsided, the music became audible. After several minutes the ice cloud cleared until they could see one another – covered in Christmas frost. For a few of those moments, they assumed Miss Houston to be even more of an angel than she looks and sounds.

My hopes for their prompt start had not been realized. As usual they had been late leaving camp, but not so late that they were still safe in Camp One, nor late enough to have been caught in the middle of the lower glacier into which the avalanche swept, away from the shelter and safety of the rocks.

In life, timing is everything. In this instance, a minute or so had been the difference between life and death.

At 1 P.M. Conrad and I set off down to Nellie's Ledge with the camera. A hundred feet or so from the ledge we erected the tripod on a precarious rock outcrop. As Bob, Andy and Jerry came through with their loads, we filmed their laborious progress.

This was a very cold, exposed business. Loading the camera became especially difficult; fresh film had to be fed through the gate and onto the ratchets inside a light-proof black bag. This required the removal of the camera from the tripod, and undoing one of our karabiners from the belay. Parts of this delicate task meant removing gloves and needed much coordination of effort between the two of us.

I decided that rather than film mountaineers, someone should make a film about those who film mountaineers. In order to get good, hairy-looking shots, the camera has to be in an even hairier position.

Conrad and I had so many karabiners, slings and ropes holding us onto this wind-swept cliff that it took several minutes to work out which ones to undo when reloading the camera. At one point I asked Conrad to stop everything while I checked the ropes – to find that some sixth sense had registered that in the confusion of slings securing everything else, I was not actually clipped on myself.

John Day came down to Camp Two but decided on arrival not to go on down to ABC as he thought his altitude sickness was a little better. I was sure he was making a big mistake and that he should go straight down and join Nellie at ABC for a proper rest. Perhaps, having been so high, he couldn't face the thought of climbing all the way back up the mountain afterwards.

After resting at ABC and then Camp One, Andy, Bob and Jerry were now returning to the mountain. They seemed to think that in their absence we had not been doing things as we should. Bob tried to tell me off for leaving some pans dirty, and Jerry and John spent hours clearing out the flooded tent in which we had spent the last three nights. They moved in shovels full of gravel in an attempt to get rid of the floor water. Unfortunately they collected this gravel from the camp's urination spot. I hoped that when the tent warmed up it wouldn't smell too disgusting.

At Camp Three, Henry had drawn up a schedule for each day until the end of the month to get everyone to 'Camp Four' – his euphemism for a point from which the summit could easily be taken. John reckoned that his optimism was well placed and that the lead climbers would find a route to the top very soon. Over the radio Robbo announced that he, Henry and Nick, with an early start the next day, would make the first attempt on the summit.

Everyone seemed to be peeved and irritable. Altitude was affecting us all: bad temper, shortness of breath and subtle alterations of judgement. We needed all the good news we could get. My diary notes:

> For the first time I feel that I am degenerating; not too badly, but definitely going down physically and, to an accompanying extent, mentally.
>
> I ate supper this evening with the square, plastic end of an orange washing-up brush, used to scrape snow from the soles of boots before entering the tents. I knew my spoon with the blue cord attached was safe somewhere, but couldn't be bothered to find it. I found my spoon later in the pocket of my jacket.
>
> 'Rad has just made some hot chocolate and I am sitting on my sleeping bag inside the puddle of water. We are melting bum-shaped holes at night which fill up.

I spent the morning with John in his tent. He stayed in his sleeping bag most of the day, drinking brews and resting. I was quite worried about him; he seemed to have lost all aggression and determination, not being bothered about anything. My diary continues:

It takes ages to make hot water from snow; quicker if you have some water already in the pot and add snow to it. I really do feel odd; lackadaisical and weak in head and body.

Saturday, 26 September: feel like shit; splitting headache, slight nausea, depression, lethargy and breathlessness. I've had enough and am going down to ABC tomorrow morning. No-one up here is interested; when 'Rad asked Andy and Jerry who would take over the filming from me, they said no-one was bothered. They will wait for Henry to order someone. But by then I will not be available to advise – which is disappointing.

Sunday, 27 September: By 1.30 A.M. I could no longer endure the appalling headache that was ripping my brain in two. Outside, a snow storm was raging. I got up and went into the storm and dug around in the snow drifts that had built up against the tent to find the medical pack. My head-torch batteries faded into nothing in the intense cold. I crawled back, half into the tent, to ask Conrad to help me as I was at the end of my tether.

  While I stood shaking outside, he fumbled with fresh torch batteries, passing the head-torch out, enabling me to continue with my search. Thank God the medical pack came quickly to hand. The Brufen and Diamox were at the top, but no aspirin.

It was as well that the aspirin were not to hand. I would have taken several, which would have eased the pain but not stopped the build-up of fluid that was causing it.

The Diamox capsules were in several frozen lumps, the plastic capsules split by the cold. I took one Diamox and stumbled back into the tent. Conrad solicitously positioned a pee bottle to hand for when the drug started working – getting rid of the build-up of fluid that was causing my severe headache.

I was in hell. Inescapable, bad head pain, active depression – a vacuum absence of anything good or pleasurable with that total rewiring of personality that turns life into a terrible and unbearable burden – and a complete lack of interest in mountains and mountaineering. The Diamox started working after an hour, the headache fading until I fell into disturbed and sporadic sleep, with bad dreams and oxygen deprivation – requiring constant, deep, fast breathing.

In the morning, although I was far from well, by contrast to the night before I was so much better. I was a real person with a purpose again.

I resolved to go down, and briefed Jerry on the filming as I lay in my bag. At 10 I got up and set off back down the ropes. Although Conrad offered to take me down, I knew that he did not want to come and that the effort of coming back up would be very hard on him. I insisted on going down on my own as there was no-one else to come with me.

I had bad pins-and-needles in my face, hands and feet and I was very tired. Fresh snow clogged my crampons and I kept slipping on the steep slope, hanging grimly onto the orange fixed rope.

I could not swallow as my mouth and throat were so dry and my throat muscles did not seem to work. This induced a slight panic. I had to stop at belays to suck in air, bent over, head in the snow, for several minutes each time.

I was descending mechanically, falling over and hanging limply at the end of the rope until I regained my breath. My method of using two karabiners, one always clipped on when unclipping at the belays, saved me on several occasions.

A re-run of yesterday's avalanche came thundering down the valley – but by that time I was safe at Camp One. I spent over an hour there making a brew.

On the glacier, avalanches and ice movement had altered the route radically. I lost the red bamboo markers and had to find my own way across the ruptured earth and huge heaved-up ice walls.

As I walked along, hearing my footsteps crunching and echoing amid the dripping water and barely audible creaking sounds, I heard human voices, talking gaily, calling out and laughing – sometimes with music.

Whenever I stopped to listen they stopped too – leaving me in silence.

By the time I reached ABC I was very tired, moving slowly from rock to rock. I did not relish going again all the way back up to Camp Two, then from there to the summit.

Desperate for real human voices I tuned into the World Service of the BBC to be cheered up (along with the rest of the English-speaking world) by the gentle humour of Rabbi Lionel Blue. The daily service came on – from St Paul's – and I sat on an upturned cooking pot in the mess tent thinking of Sunday mornings in deserted City streets, the impeccable civilization of Morning Prayer and the warmth and humanity of the busy pub afterwards. I resolved to make the effort to go every Sunday morning when I returned.

As I congratulated myself on my return to a relative sort of normality, the radio degenerated into various sorts of static, in all modes and on all frequencies. It felt like a phone call with an old friend being suddenly cut off.

Far above, the mountain was clear. Every hour or so I was compelled to walk from the tent to the edge of the river terrace and look up the glacier for people coming down. I kept thinking I could see two figures, but because of the huge scale of everything, I couldn't decide what I was looking at.

The 7.30 radio check revealed more progress on the mountain. From Camp Three it took seven and a half hours to get to the bottom of the rock band wall. The wall had now been climbed and fixed ropes were being installed. Problems on the ridge beyond the rock band had slowed the impetus. Henry was planning for a second backup team to put in more ropes to allow a summit team to scoot through all the difficult bits and hack their way to the top.

Robbo was coming down, having shot his bolt. On his own he had forced the route up to the foot of the rock band. On the rock band, he had led what in Scotland would be described as a difficult Grade Four ice climb. This meant being totally dependent upon crampons, ice axes and ice screws, a strenuous climb for experts only. At 7,300 metres above sea level, on a virgin rock face, the difficulties were multiplied until they became awe-inspiring.

The summit of the Crown lay just along the ridge from the top of the rock band. Robbo was naturally very disappointed at having missed it by such a small margin. Despite his determination and physical strength, the altitude had taken its toll on him and he had no choice but to come down.

Time would now be very tight indeed. If we were to leave on schedule, there were only three days left in which to reach the summit.

On my own, I was bored and lonely at ABC. I sat down and read the camp log.

Two nights ago Nellie had discovered a large rat-like animal which enjoyed being chased. It continually presented itself for morning and evening games so Nellie obliged. He cornered the beast and in the hand-to-hand combat that ensued was severely bitten, but saved from injury by the thick wool of his dachstein mitten. His prey made good an escape.

There was time to reflect. The expedition was not what might be called fun but a huge mental and physical challenge, at times worrying and frightening. There were moments of humour, camaraderie and achievement, but they stood out as special incidents. The reality was uncomfortable, sometimes boring, mostly unwashed, often hungry with dull and insufficient food, and either feeling unwell or, often at the same time, irritated by the unreasonable behaviour of others – who I am sure thought exactly the same of me. The prospect of all the work to be done to get off the mountain, all the mindless load carrying back down to the Camel Dump for 4 October, did not even bear consideration. I wrote in my diary:

We are now convinced our ascent is a foregone conclusion. Getting to the top of the Crown myself has so many unknowns that I fear rather than look forward to it. My experience of altitude sickness has not exactly made me enthusiastic to push on above the 6,200 metres of Camp Two, let alone to the top at 7,400.

I reckon Henry has abandoned the idea of getting us all up, concentrating on getting one pair to the top. I don't think I could do it now that I am back down here with bad pins and needles in my right arm and hand. I am in two minds about going back up to Camp Two again in two days – as suggested by Henry – although I would dearly love to make it to Camp Three to film the view. Time has certainly run out for me.

There was not time for me to recover and get back up the mountain to go on to higher camps. Defeatism had taken over and I had given up – an attitude of mind that was very unfamiliar to me.

I woke just after 9 after my first good, sound night's sleep for ages. I still had pins and needles, unable to use or even clench my right hand. I could not face rolled oats, so had coffee and decided to make some Australian-style damper bread using Japanese flour. I tried various mixes of flour, water and peculiar monosodium glutamate Japanese salt seasonings. The cookers required some cleaning and the use of my extra-strong penknife to butcher the flame-control shaft into turning.

After trying the complete range of different consistencies of mixture and thicknesses of dough, of temperature and speed of cooking, I came to the conclusion that I needed to read up on unleavened bread technology. None of my efforts would rise or cook in the middle – but the experimentation passed the time admirably.

I was not feeling normal (whatever 'normal' might be). I had no interest in mountains or expeditions, only in getting away from piles of boulders and cliffs of dirty ice and broken rocks.

I wanted to be home, where the sea rolls onto long, sandy beaches, where seagulls swirl in salty winds and tractors trundle across rich, turf-hedged fields beside slate roofed, granite-walled farmhouses. King's Road on Saturday afternoon would do just as well: delicious schoolgirls waving handbills for trendy hairdressing saloons, tight bottoms in black leather promenading up and down and tourists gazing in astonishment at punks halo'ed with spikes and rainbows.

I had lost all the spare flesh around my middle; even my waist 'handles' had been burned away by the cold and fierce exercise. I had spells of light-headedness and blurring of vision.

On the mountain, John and 'Rad, having both had bad days, were coming down, bringing all their kit with them. I should be seeing them today (Monday).

By mid afternoon they had not yet arrived. I was becoming

increasingly anxious about them, taking to lying outside the tent on the rocks looking along the river terrace towards where they would come. I dozed in the sunshine, to be jerked into wakefulness by a loud, heartless croak. The raven was circling thirty feet above my head. I clapped loudly to show I was still alive and the huge, malevolent-looking bird unhurriedly turned away, settling on a cliff one hundred feet away casting baleful stares in my direction.

I came out of the tent on several occasions convinced I could hear people walking around. Several times I walked to the bed of the river to where I could see up the glacier, to look for them climbing down the fixed ropes.

Even my attempts to obtain the World Service met with static. I was on my own.

At 7 P.M. the sunshine gone and the cold of dusk setting in, I retreated miserably into the orange tent. After ten minutes I heard more crunching of feet outside, but these were real feet – not the spectres of my imagination. Conrad and John arrived, very tired after a late start from Camp Two and a slow, heavy carry.

The radio check told of bad weather at the top of the mountain, of a rest day on the morrow and two tries for the summit on the 30th and the first.

It was a seven-hour climb to the foot of the rock band so they were going to make 'alpine starts' at 4 A.M. Although making a very long day, an alpine start would get them above the rockband with enough hours of daylight left to take the summit and get back down to Camp Three safely.

Outside it was cold, snowing freely. The summer was over. Autumn and the breath of the savage winter was upon us. We all longed to be away. Conrad desperately wanted to have a bath. John wanted to be clear of all mountains by whatever means and to eat tinned sausages in fresh bread rolls with tomato sauce and mustard.

I wanted somebody different to talk to.

CHAPTER 12

Racing Against Time

It was now 29 September. The camels would arrive at Base Camp on 4 October, our march-out beginning immediately they were loaded. In order to be ready for them, we faced several days of load carrying back down the glacier. Those still on the mountain would take two days to get themselves and equipment back to Base Camp.

We had two days in which to climb the last ridge of the Crown and take the summit.

In the meantime, if the tents and most of the mountaineering gear were to be got off the mountain, the load carrying had to start. The weather was deteriorating, every day becoming increasingly colder, with flurries of snow even at ABC. The autumn was early – which would affect the rivers and high passes we had to cross in order to get out.

Delays now would knock-on into the next month. Time was tight. Everything had to go like clockwork.

We had first to escape north, from the remoteness of the Chinese Karakoram, travelling into the onset of winter to Yechung. We then had to re-enter the Karakorams, crossing south by road over the Kunjerab Pass into Pakistan. Because the heavy snows made it an impassable death-trap, the pass closed on 16 October until spring. If everything went to plan, we would cross on the 16th. If we were delayed – especially by bad weather – we faced the very real prospect of wintering in the high country of Chinese Turkestan.

I woke with snow sliding down the tent. I was cold. My inflatable thermo mat had punctured on a sharp stone. I had been needing a pee since 5.58 but had been trying to ignore it. There was a neat little headache burrowing into my skull, just behind my right eye.

At 0559 hours precisely (as for some reason I looked at my digital wrist-watch), I stuffed my salopettes underneath the sleeping bag as compensatory insulation. Drawing cold legs up around my chest, I dozed fitfully until 9, when daylight and the warming effect of the sun melted the thick layer of snow on the outer skin of the tent. The noise of ice and crystallized snow slipping from the nylon flysheet finally got the better of my desire to remain safely cocooned against the outside world, and I got up.

After a breakfast of rice, rolled oats and apple flakes (we did not open any ration packs, scavenging the camp for odds and ends in order to save food for the walk-out), I sat in the sunshine reading while the others washed socks and bodies.

I was feeling tired and empty. Up at Camp Three they were having a rest day – a shame as the sky was completely clear all day, indicating ideal climbing conditions. After packing loads, we set off unwillingly for Base Camp.

As we walked towards the tyrolean traverse, Conrad suggested trying to follow the river rather than make the meandering, 'mega-flog' across the glacier. Previously the water levels had made the river impossible to cross. But the levels were much lower now than they had been a week earlier – and very much lower than during the team's first reconnaissance of the glacier.

I was willing to give it a try. Apart from saving us much pain and boredom, the river route could halve the time we would otherwise need to get the equipment off the mountain. John Day, however, wanted to go over the glacier. He refused to have anything to do with 'Rad's idea. The discussion developed in the usual acrimonious fashion.

'Rad cut any further discussion short by shouldering his bergen and tramping off downstream. I followed in his footsteps, happy for once not to have been a lone voice of dissension against John. I also felt rather smug. Although confident that we would find a route now the water levels were so much lower, I could not be blamed if we failed.

John's situation amused me. Without Nick to back him up, he had two choices. He could stick to his guns and hack across the glacier on his own – seven hours' solitary with hard labour, and the pointless, additional danger of being on his own.

His alternative was to follow us.

If we spent all day scrambling around on the ice or wading helplessly in the river without finding the route, John would suffer along with us. If, however, 'Rad was right and we got through, John would have been proved wrong by one of 'us novices' – to the detriment of his mountaineering pride. From his point of view, neither option looked very good.

'Rad's idea was much more important than anybody's pride. If he found the shorter route, the load carried from ABC to Base Camp and the 'empty' return trip could be done in one day – a vital element in our race to get out of the mountains.

I walked ten metres behind Conrad. After a few minutes I looked back. John had decided to come with us after all.

In my disorganized retreat from the mountain I had retained a strange mixture of clothes. My only trousers were over-sized, high altitude salopettes. To keep cool I had to undo the utilitarian open-crotch zip. With my lightweight, baseball-type trekking boots, I felt like a big bouncing baby wearing a romper suit.

We made swift if inelegant progress, suffering anxious moments when a narrow gorge, through which the river ran as it cut through the 4,400-metre contour, looked to be impassable. The ice walls of the glacier overhung some of our route, rocks plopping without warning from its surface 100 feet above our heads. 'Rad was convinced these boulders were 'going for him'.

After three and a half hours' steady walking we emerged at the snout of the Skamri Glacier, having halved the time of the old route. After crossing the river, we walked to the end of the glacier's snout – in case there were more water courses to be crossed. We could see the orange tent of Base camp across the boulder-strewn valley floor.

Our change of direction, with home apparently only twenty minutes' walk away, turned out to be premature. Half a mile further on we came to the top of a steep slope, at the bottom of which a second wide, strong river – grey with silt and ferocity – ran from the base of the glacier. After walking upstream to where the river emerged from the glacier snout searching for a better crossing place, we stopped and removed our boots, socks and trousers. That poor donkey, swept away during one of their crossings on the way in came to mind. I had the strong feeling that maybe rivers were more dangerous than mountains.

John Day, whose bravery in the face of powerful rivers remained undiminished, removed his clothes. Wearing on his feet the plastic outer shells of his mountaineering boots with gaiters over the top and with bergen straps tight, he set off into the torrent.

This crossing did not look nearly as adventurous as some of our previous epics. Even so, John nearly fell twice. In his last fifteen feet he was completely knocked over, saving himself by scrambling furiously in the shallows and hanging onto rocks on the far bank.

Having watched John's progress carefully, I thought I saw a slightly better route and followed him into the freezing water. I fell in the first six feet of the fifty-foot-wide river, the cold of the water a severe and debilitating shock to me. In the centre, I fell for a second time – the force of the water tipping me forward onto my front so that I was thundering downstream head first, pushed down by the weight of my heavy bergen.

'Rad's initial reaction to my plight, he told me afterwards, was to laugh – an emotion that swiftly changed to concern as he realized it was his turn next! He plunged into the water to try to help me.

Through sheer panic I managed to regain my feet and stumbled onto a narrower underwater sand spit. The water was only thigh deep, and I could do nothing but lean exhausted and soaked against a large rock. Conrad shouted, 'Are you all right?'

I could only nod my head up and down – shaking with cold, breathing like a welter-weight between rounds. I meant by this to convey: 'No, I am not.'

If I stayed any longer in the middle of the river I would never make it. Unwisely I had changed into my large, loose, mountaineering boots for the crossing and they were hard to move against the surge. I kept my footing by bracing them at odd angles against large boulders on the bottom. I had to lean well forward into the freezing current, fighting against it at every step. The water was up to my waist.

I could not find a secure place for my left foot, which the water took, spinning me round and back into the torrent. I leapt desperately for the bank as I went over, grabbing a rock in the shallows, finishing sitting in icy meltwater up to my armpits.

I found I could barely stand. My knees were completely blue and peculiarly wrinkled. For fifteen minutes I could feel neither my fingers nor my toes. Totally sick from the cold and exertion, I gasped my words in between heavy panting:

'I don't seem to have the same strength as on our previous river crossings.'

'I felt that,' said John, who was changing into warm clothes. 'We don't have the same will to resist as we had coming in.'

I was stumbling aimlessly about, trying to get a towel out of my bergen, putting my head into the armholes of a shirt and wondering whether I was so cold that my clothes would only keep me that way in the watery sunshine and cold wind of the afternoon. In the meantime 'Rad had got across with only a wet midriff – wearing his Mickey Mouse cartoon underpants and very expensive glacier glasses.

I was exhausted into a total numbness by this near escape, very glad of my 'toddler' thermal dungarees, walking slowly behind the others.

There was no water at Base Camp. I took the 15-litre jerry can and walked up a scree slope to the usual stream, finding it dry. The main river was one and a half miles away across the boulders. The full jerry can slopped against my thighs.

The insignificance of our presence here and the triviality of our activities struck me. In comparison to the grandeur of our surroundings, we were rather pathetic. Base Camp was an orange dot at the foot of huge scree slopes. The sun set behind The Fangs, its last rays blinding me through the woolly brim of my mountain hat.

'Rad had thrown every oddment of food he could find into a pot. As we cooked and ate, we talked about the firemen's strike, when the British Army had manned fire stations and achieved the ambition of every small boy, and most soldiers: putting out fires, rescuing cats – then, after a nice cup of tea from the grateful granny, running them over reversing from the drive. John's fire station had been near where I used to live – Oadby in Leicestershire, a coincidence that allowed the conversation to expand into talk of life before the Army. John had been brought up in darkest Dorset – which I know reasonably well from being stationed at Royal Marines Poole for five years. We also discussed life at university and how the human race would cope with a third sex.

We left Base Camp at 10 A.M. on Wednesday, 30 September and, disinclined to again risk crossing the river, wandered along its southern side. The idea was to cross on the glacier after the river had buried itself in the ice. We clambered up onto the glacier snout – the debris like the ruins of some massive, ancient castle.

We stumbled for two hours – up, down and across in all directions, sometimes finding cairns and red marker wands from early attempts by ourselves and the Japanese to find routes to ABC. Eventually we found a way across; where the river vanished under the ice, we were able to cross over a small, rubble-filled gully.

There was no water on the rock-strewn ice so we became thirsty. Also we had only two lunches between the three of us. The conversation was therefore exclusively about food, English pubs and what we would do when we got back. Somehow, every planned activity ended up with a huge, blow-out meal.

More practically, Conrad and I were planning a feast for that evening, using oddments left behind by the Japanese.

We needed to get down to the main river, cross and so get back onto Conrad's riverside route. There were two options: a scramble down the ice ridge which had conveniently cracked into several slices allowing us several forty-foot scrambles down onto the river bed; or a more sedate descent after a tramp up a boulder ridge. We were tired and chose the closer, more dangerous, first option. Both meant going through a huge ice cavern – down a steep slope and under a seventy-foot slab of solid ice.

John slithered down into the darkness of the cave. 'Rad and I followed, finding ourselves in a hall of mirrors: huge, curved sheets of transparent ice several miles thick, smooth-surfaced and filled with air bubbles the size of one pence pieces. Water dripped and flowed, and stones slid without warning from above, rattling down the black ice walls into the vault. We ducked under the ice overhang, walking close to the smooth, concave ice wall. We shivered in the refrigerated wind that sucked through the ice tunnel.

Safely down on the river bed, we refilled water bottles, absorbing several litres of cold fluid before setting off up the winding, rocky valley. We were exhausted, especially 'Rad.

John and I were delighted to amble along behind him, heads bowed looking at his heels, placing our feet exactly where he placed his. He could have walked over a precipice and we would never have noticed until we too had fallen.

Conrad was stumbling. His wooden staff made him look like an Ethiopian Moses. I fantasized; he had carelessly lost the Chosen People, then became severely geographically misplaced trying to find them again.

We had become too tired even to finish planning our huge evening meal.

The walk to ABC seemed to take hours. We took frequent rests, finally arriving at 6 P.M.

There were others living there now. On the stone table, a telescope and tripod were trained on the mountain. We saw Jerry first – in his Aztec hat, then Bob, Robbo, Nellie and Nick. They had come down from Camp Three the previous day and sorted out the remainder of the kit for carrying back down.

There was a strong atmosphere of 'us and them'. 'Rad said he felt like an outcast.

'They' cooked supper for themselves and 'we' had to wait outside the tent until they finished – although I was able to start cooking on a spare stove. John went into a sulk, stamping about, poking the kit, complaining bitterly about not being able to locate various bits of his own stuff – and about the others not vacating the communal tent. I made some dough batter for nan bread – for the meal 'Rad and I had been planning all afternoon.

When we got into the tent and cooked our meal (noodle soup

with nan, curry and rice with nan, and coffee) the others were very curious – especially about the nan:

> It was very good – and filling. The others wanted some – tough shit.
> Nick stuck his head in, demanding to know how to make nan – wanting to have some of ours even though he had just finished a full supper. After a noncommittal reply from me, he returned with the flour bag.
> I said that if he left it, I'd make enough for everyone tomorrow night – but that if he mucked about tonight there wouldn't be enough for everyone tomorrow, and whatever he made probably wouldn't be very nice.
> Exit Nick in an ill humour.
> The three of us had a great meal. Tough luck on the rest.

As we washed up and organized our loads for the morrow, the drama on the mountain reached its climax.

Henry and Andy were together going for the summit. Teacher and former pupil were risking their lives on the last ridge of an unknown mountain.

Nellie, Henry's first choice for the top, had been unable to overcome his altitude sickness – younger mountaineers being more susceptible – and was therefore not finishing off his education in quite the style Henry had intended. Instead and, to my mind, very appropriately, Henry was with Andy Aspinall – the man whose surface bravado concealed strong feelings of inferiority.

Ian Roberts, who sadly had been forced off the mountain after his heroics on the ice wall, had a very strong inner strength that would never let him (or anyone else) down. Robbo knew what he could do and was quietly confident. I was certain Andy had the same depth of character and strength inside him. The extreme challenge he and Henry were now facing would bring this strength to the surface. If they survived, Andy need never again doubt his own capabilities.

Robbo, who had been monitoring Henry and Andy's progress through the telescope, announced that he had seen them abseiling off the top ridge.

We were relieved. This meant that Henry had decided against

staying the night up there in a snow hole in order to be well placed for a final, last-minute stab at the very top the next day. Such a desperate measure would probably have been fatal. Although we now knew them to be safe, we did not, however, know whether they had made it to the top.

Later, when they got back to Camp Three, Henry told us over the radio what had happened.

Along the final snow ridge, the rock was crumbling and badly ice-shattered and the snow rotten from the summer's good weather. They had therefore been unable to obtain any belay protection — fixing ice screws, pitons or whatever into either the snow or the rock along the final snow ridge.

Even though the final knoll was only three and a half rope lengths away (seventy metres), because of the very high risk of falling they had decided not to go to the top. The final ridge was literally a knife edge with a six-thousand-foot sheer drop at either side. With crampons and ice axes, they could have walked up, but in the high winds and with unstable snow underfoot, the chances of returning to the fixed ropes of the rock band without a disaster were slender.

Henry would see us all tomorrow.

And that was it.

After washing up we gathered in the tent, drank tea and chatted for several hours: about mountain sickness, the Japanese, about the actual height of the mountain being higher than on the map (7500 metres rather than 7270), about going home . . . but very little about failure. There was a tremendous, underlying relief that Andy and Henry were safe.

Robbo, the most justifiably disappointed after having done so much and being so close to the summit, was philosophical:

'Now, getting to the top doesn't seem to be so important. It would have been the icing on the cake.'

The doing, and the effort itself, were really the things, rather than the result.

Robbo and I shared a tent that night:

'I fart a lot,' he warned me.

'What do you reckon we did wrong in the planning of this expedition?' he asked.

'Nothing', I said. 'But I've learned a lot of things for a future trip – like bringing a good cook to be responsible for all the rations and the cooking.'

'I wouldn't say it's been enjoyable,' he said, 'because it hasn't. Challenging and hard work certainly. What have you made of it?'

I said that I wouldn't be able to answer that question for months afterwards; moments of fun and enjoyment – but few and far between. It was simply not that sort of experience.

Rations were now short, hence six lunches between eight of us. We were load carrying. The rocks along the side of the river were covered with ice, and the shorter, but nevertheless tedious trip down to the near side of the river at the glacier snout took over four hours.

Everyone was keeping out of one another's way, within well-defined little groups. The 'in crowd' comprised Robbo, John and Nick. Nellie stuck with Bob, but walked with me for a time, talking about returning to his squadron and probably having to do very ordinary tasks like clerk's (errand) runner. Jerry strode along on his own, saying how aggressive he felt – screwed-up and wanting to have a fight with somebody. I talked with him for a bit, then, as he really did want to be on his own, left him sitting on his bergen by the side of the river.

At the end of the walk Bob, Jerry and I had finished up together. We reached the river, dumped our loads well above the waterline in case the river rose – and not at the very edge as the others had done. After a long sit, we started back up to ABC. Bob looked terrible, his face blotchy and sun-burned, moving very slowly.

The return trip to ABC, even without loads, took five hours – and seemed without end. We were all very tired, having to take a sleep in the sunshine.

Bob and I finished the last few miles together. We made efforts to talk to each other, wanting to find out how the other was. Having been in separate groups for several weeks, someone different to talk to was a real break. I had a feeling that Bob was to an extent a kindred soul – feeling a little apart from the others, and therefore lonely. He was certainly 'non-aligned', keeping away from the 'in-crowd'.

Bob's mind was with his fiancée, planning a future now that he knew he had one, wanting to lift himself from the drudgery of our reality through conversation. As usual, the conversation was bizarre; about buying personal computers, living in France, of the pitfalls of running a restaurant (food again) and setting up a small business.

Bob and I would, like Captain Kirk of the Starship Enterprise, quite happily have been 'beamed-up from the hostile planet and transported' back home.

That night I cooked the promised pancakes. Mouths had been watering all day in anticipation. I spent the whole evening in a position of tremendous personal power, crouched behind a blazing MSR cooker with everyone lusting for seconds.

Halfway through this meal, Henry and Andy arrived from the mountain looking cheerful but tired, to a surge of good humour. There was no talk at all of the mountain, and we went to bed at 10, tired out.

Henry and Andy slept in the empty stores tent next to Robbo and me. That night I overheard them talking as they lay in their sleeping bags. They had been worried about our reaction to their not having gone those last few metres to the summit, that we would blame them for the team's not having managed to make the first ascent of the Crown. It was a quiet, reflective conversation between two people who were delighted to have returned from somewhere so alien to their previous experience that it might just as well have been another planet.

In spite of being reassured by our response, they were still concerned over the decision they had made – to leave the last short ridge and get back to the relative safety of Camp Three before it was too late. (A night shivering in a snow hole up there would almost certainly have been fatal.)

They were also worried about money. Because the mountain remained unclimbed, our huge debt of more than £50,000 would be less recoverable from sponsorship. During their attempt, especially when deciding not to continue, they had been concerned that the rest of us would blame them. Our reaction to their return seemed to have eradicated that worry.

'I must say,' said Henry, 'I thought they were bloody good about it.'

We left ABC for the last time on the morning of Friday, 2 October. Loaded up with every last thing, for one last, monstrous load carry, we looked like tinkers. Cooking pots, ice tools, tents, ropes . . . were strapped onto the outsides of misshapen and very heavy bergens.

John got a very expensive fire going: the remainder of our fixed ropes, spare cooking gear, the Japanese medicine (to thwart camel drivers) and, in the last moments, the Epigas canisters and one of the Japanese oxygen cylinders.

We left ABC to several small explosions, then one quite large one, which echoed (like our presence) briefly about the ice walls, leaving the place untouched by human hand – and ourselves forgotten.

On leaving, the emotional atmosphere was peculiar: tense and irritable. John Day's usual tension and slight bad temper was greatly ameliorated compared to when we first arrived at ABC – although one would not describe him as having 'mellowed'. Overall we shared a great sense of relief at leaving a godforsaken spot.

Minds in neutral, we stared at the ground two paces ahead of where our feet were treading, or at the backs of the heels of the man immediately in front. The day was cold, 10° centigrade in the sun, noisily melting the face of the glacier – and a chill wind blew. It was definitely autumn.

We stopped every hour to chat: whether our cars would start when we got back, what we would do for Christmas, how glad we would be not going on the bloody glacier again. We ate four-fifths of a Mars Bar each. Because someone had eaten a whole one I got only two-fifths; chocolate brings out the worst in many people.

At the snout of the glacier, close to where I had nearly been swept away two days earlier, Robbo had set up a rope haulage system across the river. The equipment was pulled across in one of the plastic drums and the rope gave a handrail for us to use when wading. The water was freezing but I made it across without difficulty.

At Base Camp 'Rad cooked supper and we sat until 10.30 chatting over arrangements for the future, everyone very relaxed. My diary notes:

'I can't help thinking that we could have achieved a similar atmosphere throughout the expedition if certain people had behaved differently. (I dare say some would include me on that list of names.) Tension affects some folk like that. If I had known more mountaineering and therefore been a person that the others respected more, I could have helped establish a better atmosphere.'

These thoughts may have been pious regrets after the event, but nevertheless they were genuine. When stress is eating away at people, I believe that good manners and considerate behaviour become essential to team spirit.

I was somewhat taken aback when Henry told me that, in comparison to other expeditions, relations on our trip were remarkably harmonious. I had seen examples of people improving their behaviour in his presence, which could account for his evaluation being at odds with mine.

By the same logic, as people behaved well in his presence, perhaps they behaved badly in mine – in response to me? Perhaps also the writings of other climbers and explorers have been sanitized, the tensions referred to but not given full substance.

Or perhaps Henry was right, and other expeditions were fraught with serious aggro? To my knowledge, we had not come to blows – which maybe happens between the lines on other people's trips.

Saturday, 3 October was feast day, eating the box of goodies donated to us by Ann. We had been looking forward to it for weeks.

'Rad and I got the Moore/McManners patented cooking machine stoked up with a roaring fire – producing a cauldron of boiling water. By mid afternoon we had made a large curry and rice hors d'œuvre, ten litres of spaghetti bolognese, grilled sausages, soups and lots of coffees and teas. We were disgustingly full for the first time in weeks, ending up inside the orange mess tent drinking Nellie's Orkney whisky.

The camels arrived a day early, as the feast was beginning. Henry sent them away, back across the Sarpo Laggo river to K2 base camp.

At midday on Sunday, the camels returned. Drivers and Liaison Officer went through our rubbish heap, opening every plastic bag, spreading junk over our carefully cleaned site.

After gathering up and setting fire to the rubbish, we delayed leaving. Ann's box provided strawberry jam and sardines for lunch. We made a brew.

With strange reluctance to leave, finally we walked away from it all, the mountain resplendent in bright, white snow, perfectly clear on a beautiful warm day. At the Sarpo Laggo river we sat quietly in the sunshine waiting for the camels to catch up. John Day stood with his bergen on, looking at the water. Then, too impatient to wait for dry, safe carriage on a camel's back, he strode up river. Followed by Nellie, John crossed the river on foot, pressing on towards K2 base camp.

That night Jin Jun invited us to one of his superb meals; seven o'clock sharp, warm shirts and shorts. As we did not wish to appear rude and greedy by gobbling it all down, we ate an early 'compo' meal to offset our appetites.

Bearing pan lids and frying pans as plates, we arrived exactly on the hour and sat looking wantonly at a full table of different dishes, waiting for the last two to be cooked. There was bully beef and potatoes, rabbit in cabbage (rabbit shot by Jin Jun), omelettes in tomato sauce (a 'western dish'), tinned fruit, tinned fish, scrambled eggs, peanuts and chili . . . and more, plus half a can of Tsing Tao beer each. It was excellent.

There was then a pause while the noodles were cooked in the pressure cooker outside. Wang (we were now calling the LO by his name) nipped out to release the pressure valve and managed to tip the contents onto the ground. Through the tent flap, we spotted Jin Jun surreptitiously salvaging what he could with a shovel.

The noodles were perfectly cooked, served with a sauce of oil, onions, red chilis and garlic – very strong, very hot and very good. They kept coming. We regretted our earlier meal. One by one we left the table. I began to feel ill at my third helping of noodles, leaving Henry, Jerry and Bob still eating.

Manners were not good; there were adverse comments about dishes, grabbing, and John (sitting next to me) kept farting loudly. The first was possibly a mistake, but the rest were so blatant that Jin Jun, as the perfect host, had to pretend to smile, to regard John's loud raspberries as a peculiar western joke.

Nick stalked out after the first dishes had been consumed, not waiting for the noodles and without a word of thanks to Jin Jun. Jerry commented afterwards that Nick had been rather odd since being forced by sickness to come down from Camp Three.

Bob, Henry and Jerry were the sole survivors at the end of this wonderful meal, defeated only when Wang handed out Chinese cigarettes which Henry, a staunch non-smoker, refused. The other two accepted – and regretted it.

I found blowing up my thermo mat difficult. I could only get to sleep by lying carefully on my side, knees drawn up towards my chest – which relieved the pressure of the food in my stomach.

The walk-out started late, at 11.30 on Monday, 5 October. I joined Jerry and we walked briskly north along the Sarpo Laggo valley to get around the corner into the Shakesgam Valley.

Jerry wanted to get this boring bit over as fast as possible. We talked of the north of England: Manchester and Sheffield where he had been brought up and trained as a jeweller before joining the Royal Marines. He was less hyped-up now, happy to talk, but wanting to get on with the walk.

At the junction of the two valleys a large island of rock stood in the middle of the flat alluvium, separated from the southern point of the bifurcation, left behind by Shakesgam flood waters. Once out of the colder north-south Sarpo Laggo valley, the Shakesgam was noticeably warmer.

After numerous shallow-water crossings of the many channels of the Shakesgam river, we reached the camp site. When Jin Jun arrived he declared that we should camp further along because of the strong winds that could strike us on this bend in the valley. Robbo had just removed the nail from his frost-bitten big toe. We tried using this as an excuse to stay where we were. No-one was inclined towards another hour's walk.

None the less, Jin Jun was adamant. Robbo had to suffer the indignity of travel by camel. That night I glued the soles back onto my walking boots for the sixth time, then slept.

After breakfast the next morning, it became apparent that we were not going to move for some time as there were no camels. During the night, the drivers had not bothered to tether them and seven had wandered off into the darkness – which way no-one could tell.

The drivers split up, east and west, to recapture them. The little man wearing a green Chinese Army combat jacket, who rode the donkey, lay around indolently in his immaculate baseball boots. He appeared to be the supervisor. Wang, wearing three pairs of trousers and three jackets, slept like Monsieur Michelin.

'Rad cooked spam, corned beef and noodles for lunch and we made brews. Henry finished reading *Porterhouse Blue*, releasing me from the purgatory of Alistair Maclean's *Santorini*.

Henry was in an odd mood, snapping very sharply at Nellie during a discussion about the performance of mountaineering equipment we had brought with us (details for our final report).

At 3.30 Issac, well-practised by now in the art of camel recapture, returned with his three, so we started, our essential gear loaded onto them.

The walk took several hours, and included a long wade through a pleasantly cold, clear channel. Andy and I chatted about his career as an Army physical training instructor. He was thinking about the future, wanting a new direction and more of a purpose in his life.

Our next camp site, at the foot of the Aghil Pass, had our cached food buried under bushes and rocks. It was undisturbed. There would now be one ration per person per day. We could eat well.

'Rad and I cooked a huge curry – quantity being all important. My diary notes:

'They wanted quantity. Morale always improves with a huge feed and the selfishness relaxes. Everyone becomes more friendly with 'Rad and me, thanking us for our efforts. Nick and Robbo spent several minutes fixing my head torch, which gave up as I was trying to write this. It seems that by cooking, we non-mountaineers can achieve a parity with the rest.'

I had discovered that the camels came from villages ten days' walk away, and were now used only for expeditions into the mountains. Otherwise they grazed and the drivers farmed. They regarded these trips as money-making jaunts.

The camels had no monetary value in that they could not be bought. The drivers bred them, making them work from the age of four until they died, at around thirteen years. They needed to be fed every day, to have lots of rest days and, judging from the corpses along our route, were not too happy to be overloaded.

I had wondered why the drivers seemed unworried about the weight of our equipment. I had expected, as we had brought well up to the maximum the beasts could carry, that there would be much sucking of teeth at loading time. The reason for their sanguine attitude became clear. For our purposes the camels were valued at between 800 and 1,000 yuan (an unheard-of amount locally), depending on sex, age and size. If a camel died, said Jin Jun, we paid.

Our agreement with the inscrutable CIST specified that we would not have to pay for dead camels – but I doubt if we would have been permitted to leave without providing the cash. I was not surprised to discover that the camel drivers received only a small fraction of the daily rate that CIST were charging us.

I remembered also that we had paid for the empty camels to return to their home village after taking us to the Crown base camp when in fact CIST had carefully arranged that these camels would carry out the Japanese, who would have paid the higher rate for full camels.

You only learn these things when it is too late. And then, when we got back to Yechung, we had the deferred row over filming fees to resolve, in time to be allowed to leave China before the Kunjerab Pass was closed by the winter.

Wednesday was to be a long day, over the Aghil Pass and down the other side. The day's walk would take us back to the populated part of the region, and end our sojourn in the absolute wilderness.

Maza Dala, the village at the end of our journey, could not really be described as civilization. It was on the absolute margin of human habitation, made viable only by Chinese Army vehicles bringing in supplies to their patrol-base camp.

The camels stayed with us (hobbled) that night and we got away in good time the next morning.

It was a beautiful clear day. At the top of the Pass, beyond the three dead camels, the grey and brown rocks of the southern side blossomed unexpectedly into vivid green with specks of red lush mosses and grass. In the distance, in the long, gentle saddle of the pass itself, a shallow lake was ringed green-blue as winter ice formed from the edges inwards. We rested out of the wind behind a large rock.

I walked down with Robbo, talking of his home in Wales, of his desire to organize expeditions himself, and of what Pakistan would be like.

'A change is really essential now,' I noted in my diary. 'Everyone is looking forward to home – and even to Pakistan. Robbo admitted to dreaming of the Tube journey from Heathrow to Euston!'

The old man and his family, who had been herding the summer pasture just below the top of the northern side of the Aghil Pass, were nowhere to be seen. The pastures were abandoned for the winter, their stone hut and sheep pens empty.

When the sun dropped behind the mountains all warmth went too. We had no wood and only one stove worked properly. I installed myself behind a windbreak, and against the tent wall, to cook ten litres of spag bol, the pot perched precariously on the small cooker. Faces were grey with cold and tension, anxiously and hungrily watching me cook. John Day expended some of his pent-up emotion on me. As always this was upsetting, but I managed a mild, gentle response which sent him storming back into his tent.

The next morning 'Rad and I let the others go on ahead. We wanted to keep to ourselves.

By the narrow gorge, a small, white, long-coated kid with innocent head was tethered to a stake by the side of the path, bleating as we passed. The camel driver with the military jacket, who had bought it from the villagers on his way in, untied the cord.

The goat trotted behind him like a puppy, bounding and leaping at his heels, then sometimes planting all four hooves in furious but hopeless resistance.

On the far side of the huge crumbling valley, two red-shawled girls and a father holding hands with his wide-eyed toddler son were herding rough-coated brown and black sheep in a swirling mass – from one crumbling terrace down to the next, bringing them to the river for the night.

It was the end of a long day. Everyone was tired.

The camel drivers had tried to ignore loads that were slipping, one to the extent of falling onto a camel's neck. With much complaining from the beasts, ropes were pulled tight again, but with little enthusiasm or care.

Our camping ground for that evening was a flat bed of gravel with a raised area of beautiful green grass, surrounded by tinder-dry thickets of tough, hard-leaved bushes five feet high. There was plenty of good, dry wood.

Conrad and I, our eyes streaming as always from the wood smoke, made a huge curry, with care because of the danger of causing a bush fire, and with many brews of tea as we worked.

When I was alone, John Day came over and apologized for his outburst of bad temper while I was cooking the previous night.

'I was completely out of order,' he said.

I was considerably cheered by this generous act, as the incident of the previous evening had thrown me into depression. The apology restored my faith in humanity and boosted my flagging self-confidence. I shook John's hand, thanking him for what he had said – and slept soundly that night, despite Nick reading on, loudly crunching boiled sweets until the early hours.

We walked through bushes and grass, north into the valley of the bridge. The shallowness of the streams, in the sunshine of the wide valley, made their water sweetly warm.

We bathed and ate lunch, lying on mossy banks where six weeks earlier we had camped. I walked up the road and across the bridge, leaving Nellie and Robbo to the tranquillity of the deserted camp.

The camels had passed by thirty minutes earlier. I walked along in isolated and optimistic reflection. The path wound steeply up the side of the basin, past the bridge where the valley narrowed into a steep gorge, then downwards over boulders and stones to the river. The water was deep and very powerful, a beautiful, glowing shade of blue.

The camels were swaying steadily just ahead. I caught them up and marched on to where Wang and the cameleer were riding the tiny donkeys, the white kid still bleating at the end of its long tether. A larger donkey was trotting towards them, ridden briskly by a man in a black fur hat, dirty grey coat and embroidered carpet saddle.

A chance encounter on the road – with a stranger – was as good a sign as any that we had returned to civilization.

Our last campsite was a group of juniper bushes by the river. It was a warm night – uncomfortably so. Restless, we stood outside chatting and drinking tea 'til late. Nick again lay in bed unable to sleep, reading and crunching boiled sweets.

Thoughts were of home, of making the transition back to normal army life – officers being 'Sir', working parades every morning, the RSM . . . and of doing ordinary, mundane, comfortable things like going shopping on Saturday morning or having a beer in the pub.

Nellie would start life in the Army proper; his first two years had been at Apprentice College. From being an equal member of the team he would suddenly find himself a very junior private soldier; running errands for his Squadron clerk, standing guard on the main gate and trying to fit in with soldiers of his own age whose greatest adventures took place on Saturday nights after the buses stopped running.

Andy Aspinall would go back to the routine of training junior soldiers in the gymnasium, trying to keep his hard-bitten, Scouse CQMS reasonably sweet. John Day wanted to live as quiet and as normal a life as possible; Jerry needed to get on with being a platoon commander; Nick and Robbo wanted to get back to Plymouth, Bob and Henry to see their fiancées and Conrad to sort out his ailing marriage.

In coming on the expedition, we had suspended our normal lives for an indefinite period. Now we could think realistically about taking up where we left off.

Henry and Robbo were in a slightly different situation from the rest of us. Before we left, they had heard they were on the short-list for the Army's Everest expedition the following spring. Once we reached Islamabad they could telex the Ministry of Defence to find out if they had been selected.

Henry, freshly engaged, was considering refusing a place if it were offered. Although Everest is the ultimate ambition of most mountaineers – and before we left the UK he had been raring to go, he thought differently now. Everest offered danger but less of the challenge of the Crown.

On the Crown, Henry had sensed the fragility of his own mortality. He had turned down his chance to be the first to stand on its summit because there were other things in life that he wanted to do.

Robbo felt differently. Annoyed at having been forced off the mountain, he would probably jump at the chance to climb on Everest if it were offered to him.

Trying to find sleep in the darkness, I started feeling peculiar – similar to how I had felt one night at Camp One.

My rib-cage started to expand like the bones of a large whale until I felt enormous and very tense – like a cleverly stressed building. The feeling was overpowering and frightening. I felt lost inside my huge, bloated carcase, a peanut on the floor of an empty aircraft hangar.

Everything was becoming too much, the peculiar feeling took on the shape of an allegorical dream constructed by my imagination to illustrate my mental condition. Having had the sensation before, I abandoned myself to it and tried to relax and enjoy its bizarre, almost drug-like reality.

I got up and re-built the fire, made a brew and sat thinking. My desire for travel and adventure seemed undiminished. I calmed myself by sketching out a plan to cross America by Harley Davidson. The moon was half obscured by clouds and the stars were indistinct. The camels shifted somewhere in the darkness and the poor, lost kid bleated pathetically. The camel drivers had tethered it well away from their shelter to gain some peace – and it was lonely.

On that last morning, I walked with Andy and Conrad, talking of the expedition and how we felt about the outcome of the mountaineering. For the first time, Andy talked about his feelings on having been so close to the summit:

'Going from Camp Three to what we called Camp Four – the base of the gully, the final barrier before the summit – was sheer hell. Going above seven thousand metres, into what Mesner calls the Death Zone, something in the Lake District that you'd womble up in less than an hour, took over three hours. We'd go for a few steps then stop, and every ten steps collapse, face down in the snow.

'It all gets to be really, really strenuous. By the time we arrived at the foot of the gully, I thought that would be as far as I would be able to go. But after half an hour's rest and something to eat and drink, we'd be ready and fit to go again.'

While Henry and Andy had been preparing for the summit attempt, everyone else was stripping out the gear from the other camps, loading it up for the carry down to ABC. Four people were still on the mountain, Bob Wood, Jerry Slack, Henry and Andy. Jerry Slack was struck down by altitude sickness, a cerebral oedema so painful that he was in tears and had to get off and down to ABC rapidly, at night, with only moonlight and the beam of his head torch to guide him down.

Andy continued:

'We had only three days left. Getting up to the gully that first time was one of the most strenuous things I have ever done. Having pushed it that far, we came back down and had to rest the next day –so creating a make-or-break for the last day. Bob Wood got very bad altitude headaches as well and had to get down in the teeth of a serious storm, the temperature less than minus thirty degrees C.

'That left Henry and me as the only ones at Camp Three, with the pressure really on.

'The night before our summit attempt, there was no way I could sleep. Everything rested on our shoulders. The debt of the expedition would be easier to recover if we succeeded on the mountain, but the feat ahead seemed impossible. I had thought I could go no further than the gully, but to climb the mountain, we had to go much further: up the gully that Ian Roberts had led and onto the final ridge. It would take some seven and a half hours of hard work to get to the bottom of the gully – a full day's work in itself.

'We got up at four thirty, starting off in the dark. Most of the climbing up to the gully was done in darkness. It was quite spectacular watching the sun rise at that altitude, something I'll not forget.

'We followed Robbo and Henry's route to the end of the rope. It was my turn to take the lead, under a large cornice – in the shadow, out of the sun. I came up the other side of the cornice until I came to what I thought to be a bit of level ground, which was actually a wafer-thin ridge of snow. I had to go back down and come up again along this ridge for another try. I was getting further and further away from Henry, and as the snow was poor, the protection wasn't any good. Looking back towards "H", and getting further and further from the protection was pretty frightening.

'Henry had only a few ice screws holding him on, and it was far from wonderful as he was perched underneath this massive cornice, which might come down on both of us at any time. I managed to climb the full rope's length, but because the snow was like alpine summer snow – all crystally – I couldn't get any ice screws in. I had to go over the other side of the ridge, make myself a seat and use my body weight and the length of the rope tied to the screws where Henry was as a belay. Henry was about forty-five metres away.

'We were on the final little knoll of the mountain, the ridge leading up to the summit itself. Henry followed me up on a jumar, passed me, then led a pitch to the base of the final face. This was risky because every kind of piton he tried to hammer in shattered the rock. He was relying on me, and the belay under the cornice, one hundred and fifty foot behind me.

'By the afternoon we were moving seriously slow; I was totally exhausted, but even so, the sight of the top, being so close, spurred us on. The weather was fairly bright but cold, minus twenty in the sun and less than minus thirty in the shade, like walking from a sunny day into a refrigerator. There was no wind.

'Henry was in a small hollow under the final face, about four rope lengths away from the summit. We felt good about getting to the top; it was three thirty in the afternoon with stacks of time left. I came up to Henry sitting in his gully, with the only protection he could give me coming from his body weight – his ice axes and crampons dug into the snow around him.

'I led another rope length up a gully, which was to be the last pitch on the mountain. There was absolutely no protection at all along the forty-five metres of that last rope, from Henry's anyway-precarious position. The slope itself was only a one-in-one, the sort of pitch that in the Alps you'd solo up with your ice axe; but there was the altitude, and a sheer drop either side, three thousand feet down to a very gloomy end on the valley floor.

'I was happy going up the rope, but when I got to the end I was trying to bang pitons in and the rock was shattering like chalk. I got one lousy screw in, but I wasn't really happy; I just didn't feel safe.

'I cut myself somewhere to sit and dug my ice axes and crampons in, then brought Henry up to where I was. We were three pitches from the top, about seventy-five metres, and the protection was desperate. It was really disappointing, like one of these competitions with the time ticking away, the wind starting to get up and the temperature dropping.

'It was only a forty-five degree slope to the summit and I would have been quite happy going there, in spite of the lack of protection. It's just whether we would have got down or not – a sixty-forty chance, I would guess, of having a serious accident.

'We were both exhausted, and rather emotional. The lads had done all that work and we were lucky enough to be up there, so close. We were both desperately depressed. The pressure to get to the top, especially with the money situation, was great. However, we both had too much to live for, to risk walking back down that slope in those conditions. We sat there for some time discussing possible options, but we both knew that we'd come as far as those snow conditions would allow.

'We abseiled off. Henry managed to fall thirty feet, held by the ice screw at the base of the huge cornice – proving that it worked. I had a narrow escape with two pitons, one of which came out in Henry's hand as he followed me down the rope.

'We never spoke to each other at all that day or the next, apart from a few words of reassurance that we'd made the right decision. A front of bad weather came through, the temperatures dropped to minus thirty and forty with lots of spindrift snow and high winds.

'It was pretty lonely.'

Our last couple of hours of walking, to the truck at Maza Dala, passed quickly with everyone doing for the camera exactly as I asked – for the first time on the whole trip. Our caravan came steadily round the last bend in the Yarkand river and over the stone bridge to where the truck was supposed to be waiting.

Three round-faced, red-shawled girls carried huge piles of cut grass across the river to a store room in the mud and stone building – winter fodder for their large herd of brown and black sheep. There was no sign of the truck.

We spent the afternoon eating delicious nan bread, from a large wok over a mud oven – courtesy of the drivers. Conrad handed out polaroid snaps, to the delight and amusement of all. Then the truck arrived and we departed, shaking hands all round and smiling.

The army camp at Maza Dala seemed deserted. The garrison had moved north over the high passes to winter in the marginally less depressing Quei. Inside the dingy gates, decrepit mud-walled buildings with broken windows stood on packed earth, a small stream diverted through for washing. The walls were daubed with huge red-painted symbols:

'By serving and guarding the Chinese People, we make the Karakoram more beautiful and noticed.'

On the wall of the cookhouse, several instructional texts urged 'Order and Beauty through Cleanliness' and that all soldiers should 'Take to Heart the example of Lay Fung' – the well-known paragon of military virtue who never took any leave or holidays, his splendid example brought to the attention of the Chinese People by Chairman Mao.

We camped on worn mattresses and shaky beds in dirty dormitories. Wood stoves were effective – but the chimney pipe fell off and the room filled with smoke. We ate compo as the last handful of soldiers clearing out of the camp had little food.

At breakfast the next morning, Robbo waved at the orderly supervising the series of disgusting pickled and salted dishes that remained of the garrison's victuals. He went over and muttered something in Welsh, which miraculously resulted in hot cooked rice and steamed bread/dough rolls being served, fresh from the pressure cooker.

We had two more high passes to cross before we were safely out of the mountains. Already to the south, the valley up which we had walked was grey with gathering storm clouds.

As we drove slowly and uncomfortably upwards in the battered lorries, snow started falling. Our driver had no experience of these treacherous conditions and soon we were sliding around corners and having to get out to push on hairpin bends. This incompetence particularly irritated Nick Moore, a very experienced arctic driver.

At the top of each of the two passes, blizzards raged. Army trucks were parked up, heavily swathed figures huddled over their open bonnets, flames flickering tentatively in the gloom as they attempted to thaw out frozen fuel lines and pre-heat chilled diesel engines.

The army barracks at Quei looked bleak as we passed. The sky was shrouded in dank clouds and all about was grey, damp, cold and miserable.

The foothills gave way suddenly to the flatness of the Xinjiang plain. The woollen suits and bright cotton dresses of summer had been packed away. Folk on the road were wrapped tightly against the driving sleet in corduroy jackets, shawls and fur hats.

As we bounced along, I was trying to read the final volume of *Lord of the Rings*. Gandalf and company had just demolished Sauron's smooth-stoned tower. Everyone seemed to be getting somewhere at last.

We, without Sauron to contend with, had at least escaped the clutches of winter – unlike many who were trapped either side of the Himalayas – in Tibet, on the northern foothills of the Karakoram and on Everest (Chris Bonington and team), during this harsh and sudden autumn of 1987.

With the dangers of the mountain behind us, one might think that our stress-induced fractious behaviour would cease – or at least lessen greatly. In fact, without the unifying challenge of the mountain, we seemed to have become even less tolerant, so the difficulties continued.

We had now to escape from China without being further ripped off by the CIST or CMA, and get through the Kunjerab Pass before it closed. In comparison to what we had already achieved, this seemed very straightforward.

However, our problems were not yet over.

The idea of normal life back at home seemed like a golden idyll, vague but very agreeable. My experience of such homecomings cautioned me against expecting too much. It was just as well.

CHAPTER 13

The Return to Reality

Mud-walled villages flashed past, rain running down ditches at the sides of the rough track, water splashing from pot-holes. The skies were grey and once sun-baked courtyards and streets were now quagmire. Damp donkeys trotted dismally and women wrapped in wet shawls turned away to avoid the splash of our passing. At 6 we entered the concrete compound of the CMA hotel at Yechung — three inches deep in dirty water. By 7.30 we had opened the beers and were eating supper.

Hot baths were now vital.

Behind the echoing hotel, hot water came from the huge brass furnace in a large chimney-house tended by two cheerful young men in green army fatigues. They shovelled the coal from a large, dirty pile in the yard. The fire was roaring.

After comradely cigarettes, they explained that there would be hot water at eight-thirty. By nine-thirty there was a trickle which by ten had increased to a regular flow.

In the darkness, the electricity was off so I wore my headtorch. The floor half an inch deep with seepage from the lavatory, I had my first bath for eight weeks, a delicious and singular moment, as the Japanese say, 'sent from God'.

Monday, 12 October was another day of gross over-eating, from breakfast onwards. After lunch, Robbo and Nellie, who had surpassed my rudimentary efforts and become experts at pancake manufacture, set up a stall in the courtyard with the stoves and the remainder of the flour, dried milk and sugar.

Unfortunately back at the groaning lunch table, Henry, Bob and I had been waylaid with rice spirit by one of the CMA drivers. I escaped with two large tumblersful – and slept until mid-afternoon. Between meals, the pancake stall was doing a roaring trade.

We were over-eating in response to bodily demands for food to replace the weight we had lost. I had lost well over a stone, going down to ten stone from eleven and a quarter. At five feet eleven inches tall, I have very little spare flesh to lose.

In the gathering evening, Conrad and I slipped out for a walk around Yechung, up narrow streets shaded by poplar trees with seven-foot-high mud walls and elaborate carved wooden gates. Inside were courtyards, gardens and the single-storeyed, flat-roofed houses in which these farming people live. The alleys were straight, at right angles to each other, ideal for the ringing bicycles that weaved through uncertain clusters of hens.

Curious gaggles of children stared wide-eyed at Conrad – and perhaps at me as well – then drew back behind doorways with shrieks of delighted alarm if he teasingly growled at the more rudely adventurous.

The outskirts of the town spread out into the market gardens and fields. The brown mud walls of houses gave way to a deep, water-filled ditch. Corn and other crops flourished in well-irrigated fields of two to four acres. The cart-track road, built up by the excavation of the ditches, stood several feet above the level of the fields. The junctions and crossroads were like ramparts – lined with ubiquitous poplar trees.

We walked along behind the main road looking at the back of the wide, 'modernized' shopping area.

The new buildings had bent metal reinforcing rods protruding from their flat roofs, ensuring they never looked finished. A four-storey hotel was being constructed; a thin, ragged man shovelled river gravel and cement into a smoky, diesel-engine powered cement mixer. A wooden ramp of bamboo scaffolding lashed together with twine ran round the building, up which he pushed a wheelbarrow filled with cement. At the first floor, a fearsomely dangerous-looking diesel-powered lift took the barrow to the top where others were hammering in a desultory, disinterested fashion.

That night I became ill. Between spectacular bouts of bodily evacuation I finished the third volume of *The Lord of the Rings*.

The next morning (Tuesday, 13 October), me ill with stomach cramps and overpowering lunges for the lavatory, we quit Yechung. The six-hour drive to Kashgar seemed to take for ever, punctuated thrice by my requesting urgent stops.

Another and creatively dreadful driver piloted the Datsun very slowly at the head of our convoy – until the other vehicles passed him. Then, without detectable driving ability or experience, he put foot flat onto the floor, bouncing outrageously past donkey carts – which pulled over into the ditch in terror – his frightened passengers pushing hard on the roof to remain seated.

Outside Kashgar, six Chinese Army staff cars – huge limousines with immaculate white lace curtains – cruised quietly. The army were much in evidence: scruffy soldiers smoking cigarettes, tunics undone and caps on the backs of their heads and officers smart in green gaberdine raincoats. One officer was briskly pedalling a bicycle, an old, ragged man perched on the luggage rack.

We entered the town through a series of road repairs, over a bridge below which men were shovelling river gravel into lorries.

Although a grey, miserable day here on the plain, in the distance, from time to time, we could see the snow-capped Tien Shan Mountains – a glimpse of another world.

After a day and night of not eating, much of the time doing the opposite, I felt much better – just as well because the day started early with loud and very dreadful loudspeaker music.

The noise was so awful as to be funny: martial, classical music, tinny and distorted, followed by a woman's voice shouting out numbers and commands in time. Whistle blasts sounded from unseen instructors and the record changed abruptly – from the middle of one to the middle of the next, some of the music indistinguishably distorted.

Like a Chinese war torture, the noise was punctuated by

disturbing periods of silence – then erupted once more from a tension of anticipation. Then there were voices – an authoritative woman and smooth-sounding man.

In the hotel complex there were four different compounds, each with separate cook houses and restaurants – for foreigners, Moslems, government officials and Chinese. The cacophony came from the Ugyar part of the hotel. I asked Jin Jun what it was all about; he had no idea. He understood as much as the rest of us.

After one hour of this terrible noise there was a permanent, blessed silence.

I managed breakfast without problems. A group of Japanese tourists at the next table were lacing their hot water with exactly the packets of monosodium glutamate soups we had sampled on the mountain. Well-heeled teams of middle-aged Germans, a posse of Chinese American journalists from the USA, and a Japanese ladies motorcycling team were travelling the Silk Road.

The morning was bright and clear with the lines of poplar trees straight, yellow and green, the fields with ripening corn and clean water gurgling along their irrigation ditches. I flagged down a donkey-cart taxi and, legs trailing over the side, trotted briskly up a long, straight road, past cyclists and walkers, the bells on the donkey's harness jingling in time with the hollow clop of the hooves.

The Abakh Hoja Mosque (the burial place of a Moslem saint) sold entry tickets and charged 80 Yuan (over £20) for video photography. Three immaculately dressed Chinese Army officers doing some sightseeing of their own seemed puzzled by the interior which, as the building is a tomb filled with flag-covered coffins, has no space for worshippers.

We left Kashgar on Thursday, 15 October, with no time at all to spare before the pass closed for the winter. The Ugyar early-morning exercise session ensured a prompt start and Wang wished us a fond farewell – which we reciprocated politely.

After two hours of diversions around culvert repairs in the road, through the back streets of small villages, we were halted by a small lake – formed from a stream dammed by a blocked culvert.

Already three lorries were stuck up to their axles, including the one carrying our equipment. Our driver couldn't get the Nissan through because he did not know how to lock the two front axles into four-wheel drive.

Like moths dive-bombing a Calor gas flame, more lorries entered the water – and stuck. An attractive, red-shawled woman did better than most of the men, extricating herself by driving through the water to an undisturbed piece of river bank.

It took two hours to get our lorry through.

Across a dry, stony desert, the K'un Lun mountains appeared, brown and white-ridged. In mountaineering terms, they looked 'fairly comfortable'. We entered a long valley with pale red and green rock foothills. The road alternated from good dirt and tarmac to appalling switchback; rocks had collapsed from the cliffs above, and the road edge had crumbled down into the fast-flowing river.

The roadside was busy with work gangs, some with plant, but mostly shovelling dirt from lorries into the pot-holes by hand. Some of the road gangs were army engineers, others civilian – possibly prisoners.

Grim camps of circular, padded wool tents sprouted bleakly along the road. Army camps were distinguished by brick buildings and slogan-emblazoned gateways. Other camps had boulder walls protecting the outside of the wool tents from the savage winter winds. The job of keeping the road open was clearly full-time; rock falls turned long sections into long and spring-shattering crawls over large and jagged boulders.

A long, gradual pass, with lakes and boulder-strewn river banks, reminded me of Norway. The snow was thick on the road and Laurel and Hardy – our two very average drivers – drove as if they had never seen the stuff before.

We came over a pass then back down the other side, snow disappearing from the roads as we descended. Clouds of thick dust followed the lead vehicle. Laurel insisted on following so close behind that the only indication of a disaster would be sudden red from the gloom as the front vehicle's brakes were applied.

Wide valleys with green grass and moss led upwards to snow-covered mountains. Villages had flat-roofed farm buildings, stove chimneys protruding, surrounded by rectangular compounds enclosed behind mud brick walls. Winter fodder was being grown until the last possible moment for the herds of long-coated, curved-horned cattle and long-coated goats and sheep – which would shelter inside the buildings until spring. Shepherds worked on foot or rode horses, sometimes leading pack horses laden with embroidered saddle bags.

It grew dark. The road work continued, lines of desultory shovellers blinking and turning away from the glare of our headlights as we passed. Heavy bulldozers manoeuvred in the gloom, their single spotlights picking out the snow at the side of the road.

After eleven hours' hard driving, we hit a smooth tarmac road and the dark, unfriendly-looking settlement of Tashgorkan. Electric street lights were mounted on modern poles, but remained unlit.

Tashgorkan is said to be the former site of Stone Tower, like one of Tolkien's *Ring* landmarks, the first stop for caravans from Kashgar after ten days of rocky spurs and defiles. Similarly, for travellers from the west, Stone Tower was the first landmark after interminable snow and tundra of the harrowing journey over the Kunjerab Pass.

We turned into a large, decrepit compound, which was totally dark and filled with noisy children dressed as adults. The boys wore coats and peaked caps, or jackets, trousers and shirts. The girls wore red shawls and peculiar flat hats, like dwarfed Queens of Hearts from a psycho version of *Alice in Wonderland*.

The hotel was modern, but dusty and half finished, very dimly lit with single, low wattage bulbs. Reception was staffed by two villainous-looking men smoking foul cigarettes and ignoring the swirl of clientèle, who rotated aimlessly before them to no consequence.

We were to sleep in a seventeen-bed dormitory, but had to wait because the drivers refused to share with us.

Jin Jun discussed a plan to leave very early in the morning in order to get ahead of other groups of westerners also crossing the border into Pakistan. A further advantage of leaving early, which greatly appealed, was to book our freight into customs, then take lunch as it was checked. His plan meant missing breakfast — which in this god-forsaken hole would be no bad thing.

As we stood in the gloom discussing this plan, Nellie said plaintively, as if it were the final straw:

'What, no breakfast?'

It seemed such a pointless and pathetic thing to say, the sort of thought the rest of us were keeping to ourselves at the end of this long day.

To Nellie, not feeling well, it probably was the final straw. However this moved me to a sarcastic and completely unnecessary response:

'Yes, Nellie, no breakfast,' mimicking his tone of voice, that I regretted as soon as I said it. The strain of the endless journey had eroded our resilience to rock bottom.

The journey itself still had my attention, but for the others, some or all of the novelty had long since worn away. They were enduring each day and wanted to be back home. Nellie, the youngest, probably felt this the most keenly.

The kitchen and dining room were across the crowded and heavily pot-holed yard — on their own as a precaution against fire. The food was the worst ever; bad tasting, meagre and cold, served by more authentically bad-tempered Queen of Hearts lookalikes in a dank, dimly lit room filled with smoke from the kitchen fires. It matched our mood perfectly.

Hoping to gain a degree of oblivion and dose my digestive tract with prophylactic alcohol, I went in search of some more beer. Through the kitchen smoke, a sheep's carcase hung, strips cut roughly from its flanks.

Peering at me in the dim light, the surly staff pretended not to have any more beer. I poked around in the store rooms, another education in themselves, until the kitchen man — as the women had given up with me — admitted defeat and found five more bottles.

We unloaded the trucks. Everyone took their own bergens, leaving me to cope with the camera gear — two extra loads.

Tashgorkan was depressing.

The dormitory was huge, dirty and lined with grubby, straw-filled mattresses, plaster crumbling off in huge chunks like a picture of a Crimean War hospital. Next door, men talked loudly for most of the night and children shouted outside in the darkness. I hid under a thick, hard duvet, protecting my head from imagined bugs and lice by wrapping the pillow in my spare shirt – illogical as the latter was much more likely to harbour insect life.

By the first chimes of the early morning radio broadcast, I was awake and walking outside through the building site of the hotel grounds into the tree-lined street – as the sun came up over the mountains.

Our early departure was thwarted by Jin Jun's having been taken ill with a stomach upset and spending the night at Tashgorkan Hospital. He returned, we loaded the truck and were off.

Outside Tashgorkan the tarmac stopped; there was only a mile of it either side of the town. The road was rough and pot-holed, climbing slowly ahead of us into the snow. Herds of goats, sheep and huge, large-horned cattle grazed at the roadside, their herders chasing them off as we bore down, horns blaring.

Camel caravans moved to one side as we passed, walking rhythmically, laden with huge cloth bundles, the drivers in front heavily hooded against the cold. Horse riders with pack animals gave way to us, rifles slung across their shoulders. Even the cattle, in docile lines, were laden with bundles, and had riders on their backs.

One string of long-horned, long-haired cattle were being led by a brightly dressed, red-shawled woman with orange, gold and silver circles of metal chained together as an over-shawl. Her well-oiled rifle was slung ready for use, across her back.

Snow covered the ground and the air was beautifully clear. The herders' villages looked well able to withstand the rigours of winter. Their rectangular houses and compounds were separated by several hundred metres of snow-covered grassland. Women strode about the mud walls carrying firewood and children, wrapped in dark red shawls with white face masks to keep off the cold. The road workers' settlements were fenced and gated, the conical roofs of their padded, felt tents pierced by soot-black chimneys venting smoky stoves into the clean, white air.

We drove past beautiful lakes, pale blue in the bright sunshine, their edges crisp with perfect white ice — expired bulldozers hopelessly bogged into the foreshore. Camels grazed quietly in the snow, beside cattle and goats. The mountains to either side were spread back from the road, the pass up which we were going wide and gentle.

We reached the Chinese border post at 3 P.M., getting through customs with ceremony but eliciting no special interest. They were completely uninterested in whether we still had the cameras, cassette players and other attractive black-market goods with which we had entered China.

Also, there were no telexes from the CMA, CIST or the Xinjiang Autonomous Government ordering that we be held until bills were settled.

Jin Jun was not permitted to go any further with us. We shook hands and left him at the barrier. We had thoughts only for the journey ahead; thoughts of him were put to one side. I expect, as he drove back into China proper, he felt relief that we were no longer his responsibility.

After another barrier, the last in China, ten minutes' drive took us to the actual head of the Kunjerab Pass, where plaques commemorate the opening of the road (the 'KKH', the Karakoram Highway) and a stone obelisk marks the China–Pakistan border, which runs along the line of the ridge. A group of Chinese customs officials were taking photographs of one another, and a lone Japanese cyclist, having pedalled all the way up from the south, was preparing for his hair-raising descent back into Pakistan.

Having crossed the border, leaving Central Asia and entering the Indian sub-continent, the change was immediate. Aluminium telegraph poles and smart signs in English urged us to 'Save Marco Polo's Sheep', and announced the 'World Wild Life Fund – No Hunting', 'Kunjerab National Park', 'Pakistan Welcomes Our Visitors' and advised 'Relax and have a Safe Drive'. The pass narrowed into a ravine as we descended below jagged, high mountains beside a strong river roaring over large, round boulders.

After an hour and more, the narrow road emerged into a valley, to a line of Chinese-made combine harvesters waiting for customs clearance and a group of ramshackle buildings. Cardboard boxes were piled up beside the road and brown and grey-shawled men wandered round sedately, brown and grey chapatti-shaped hats on their heads. A very smart Army officer and a reciprocally scruffy customs official greeted us.

We had arrived in Pakistan, at the village of Soust – the end of the line as far as the Chinese were concerned. Our possessions formed a pile of vulnerable-looking boxes, which attracted much interest from the professional lookers-on, the most persistent a swarthy, unshaven man in tight Bundeswehr combat jacket.

The Chinese lorries roared northwards in a cloud of diesel fumes, leaving us to continue our journey as best we could.

The crate of Tsing Tao beer chinked inoffensively inside one of our dusty boxes as we earnestly denied having any alcohol. Faces became downcast as, in an instant RE and Geography lesson combined, the team realized that Pakistan was Moslem – which meant not only were there no discotheques, but no beer either.

Now safely in the 'Land of the Pure', we started considering what to do next.

The village of Soust is perched high on a series of richly fertile river terraces above the Baltoro River, the road winding through the small houses and guest lodges of this northernmost part of Pakistan. The high terraces rise up either side of the river, yellow poplar trees and smarter houses perched above the road.

Waiting to clear the equipment through customs we heard that the roads south to Gilgit, and from there south to Islamabad and the plain of northern Pakistan, were blocked by landslides and would not be passable for several days – or even weeks. Soust was running out of food and kerosene, and there were said to be thousands of tourists stuck in Gilgit unable to get out, causing similar food and fuel problems.

For all its neat, clean simplicity, and friendly, helpful people – for on first sight, northern Pakistan seemed to be a dramatic improvement on western China – Soust was not the sort of place in which we wanted to be marooned. A sunkissed beach being kissed by sunkissed maidens was more what everyone had in mind.

Gilgit would be a step in the right direction; at least we could try Hunza apricots. Meanwhile a small Datsun pickup truck elaborately decorated like a mobile Hindu temple (odd for a Moslem country) took us in three lifts to a guest house, a low-beamed, very clean barn where we ate spinach and potato curry with dahl and green tea – and were satisfied.

That night, while trying to find out who owned a pair of unsupervised trousers, I again offended Nellie. He was insulted to have been asked by me if he might have misplaced something.

Since my misguided comment in Tashgorkan's depressing hotel lobby, he had been avoiding me. I followed him outside in an attempt to restore reasonable relations. In the gathering dusk, he pushed me aside, telling me to get off his back and keep out of his way. He stormed back into the barn, to the others, in front of whom he rightly assumed I would not continue the discussion.

My comment in the hotel lobby may at that moment have been a final straw for Nellie, but for me this was too much.

As we walked in the darkness along the track towards the communal room of the lodge, I had a chat with Bob Wood. In any other group of people a problem like this could have been sorted out very easily – if necessary by force. A quick scrap, broken up by the others, or stopped by mutual consent, would clear the air and allow normal relations to return. Bob (a sergeant), had he been in my place, said he would have clipped Nellie round the ear and told him not to be so stupid.

However, Nellie and I could not behave in this normal fashion. In spite of our informal chumminess, I was still a major and Nellie a sapper – a private soldier. If I hit him in any way, I would rightly be court martialled for striking a subordinate; and if he hit me, the same process – for striking an officer. I risked losing everything: pension, seniority and rank for dishonourable discharge and imprisonment. Nellie risked only discharge and imprisonment – he had no rank or pension to lose.

Bob Wood's no-nonsense solution showed how the British Army rank structure operates. A sergeant physically makes things happen, while officers decide what those things should be.

An officer is removed from direct working contact with private soldiers by three layers of non-commissioned officers – lance corporals, corporals and sergeants. He is placed on a pedestal and expected to behave differently, earning his pay when everyone else is flagging and some intangible boost of motivation and leadership is necessary, or a critical decision required.

In combat particularly, the officer enables everyone else to do their jobs unhindered. Before going into action, orders and contradictory orders ricochet in all directions, rumours abound and the smell of fear is in the air. The officer must protect his men from these energy-sapping distractions.

And then, some time during their 'blooding', in that terrible moment when everything is in the balance, all eyes turn to him and he is 'on'. The years of expensive training and his character as a man telescope inwards to condition his crucial reaction at that moment. This is why, in the British Army, officers are traditionally a race apart.

However, the credibility of an officer caste of supposedly perfect beings, kept in splendid isolation, would not last long today. One of the benefits of the Army's 'adventure training' is to allow young officers to live with their soldiers, enabling leader and led to get to know one another as people. The leader comes to the humbling conclusion that his soldiers are better than him at many things. In turn, the young officer's platoon realize that he is human and rally round to help him do his difficult job.

Even so neither side would wish to see the barrier completely removed as both understand the differences in lifestyle and responsibilities of the other. Also, both need to be able to get away from the other.

With Henry's informal, non-military system, all this had been thrust aside. No-one really knew where they stood. I felt that, whichever way I played it, I could never be right.

Being older than the others, very much older than some – and used to responsibility, I found it hard to condone what I felt to be wrong. But if I told anyone what to do, or offered my opinion – even disagreed with anyone else's opinion – I was being 'majorish' or deliberately awkward, and was put down. On the other hand, if I bit my lip and didn't intervene initially, either my sense of responsibility would get the better of me or I became annoyed.

When it came to picking up pieces, we were all affected.

My difficult position was a consequence of Henry's philosophy that expeditions were a 'School for Life', he wearing the mortarboard. He left us to find our own positions within the group – and 'ourselves' in the process. He gave corrective nudges only when he felt them absolutely necessary.

On Henry's previous expeditions he had been able to combine climbing with relaxation – in discos, nightclubs, etc. Having a good time was part of the aim of these trips.

The Karakorams are obviously very different from the Alps or the Rockies, and three and a half months a long time. On this trip, having a good time could not be guaranteed. At risk of sounding boring, having a good time was not really on our agenda.

The statistics for the Karakoram are fearsome. Discipline within a team entering such an area is vital, because the stresses on individuals are so great.

We were lucky; being a military expedition we had military discipline as our very high common denominator. When things got tough, like a turbo-charger, that common denominator had come into play. Unfortunately, the rest of the time – on less dangerous and physically demanding occasions – Henry's removing our social structure had left us to find our own codes of behaviour.

I, a crusty old major of some sixteen years' Army service, was in conflict with Nellie, a nineteen-year-old just out of basic training with but a few months' service with his first squadron. Our social backgrounds were very different and the chances of our finding common ground, under the pressure we were both under, were close to nil.

Bob advised me to speak to Henry, which I did, walking up and down the dark road, past groups of well-wrapped Balti men who passed the time of the night with us. Henry was his usual urbane self, offering a degree of support and sympathy.

In his view, my feeling of isolation from the others was partly my own creation; my role as cameraman, director etc had made me sharp with the others. They felt I was ordering them about — which was quite true as the job had to be done. However, because there was supposed not to be any exercise of military rank on the expedition, they resented me for it.

Henry said there had been 'reactions' against me — some reacting more than others. Sadly no-one had come forward and spoken directly to me about it. Had this happened, I could have explained my problems, and maybe cleared the air. Perhaps, despite Henry's rank-free system, they were loath to speak in a forthright fashion to a major and preferred to mutter to one another on the margins.

We had been trying to ignore military rank when, for better or worse, it was always present somewhere in our minds. Speaking with hindsight, it could never have worked. The rank given to me by the Queen was not mine to surrender nor Henry's to suspend.

Henry admitted that he had noticed some of the difficulties I described to him. Unfortunately, he had felt unable to do anything about them, and I suppose, given all the other things Henry had to worry about, this particular problem cannot have mattered to him very much. After all, I was the only person adversely affected. Of this particular incident, Henry felt Nellie had gone 'over the top'. Henry would speak to him.

We wound up the discussion. I knew that Henry's speaking to Nellie would not solve any of my problems. I was certain to emerge even more blackened, having sneaked to the headmaster. However, in my own twisting nightmare of relationships, talking to Bob then Henry had made me feel better.

Robbo and I, still hungry after the potato and spinach curry, sloped off down the street to another eating place — as where we were staying had run out of food. We ate aloo (curried potatoes) with nan bread for twelve rupees.

It was decided, rather than linger in Soust, to attempt to walk through the landslides to Gilgit. The boxed equipment was stored in the back of the guest-house barn for collection later and we packed whatever we thought we would need for the one-hundred-and-eighty-kilometre journey.

Everyone else crammed their valuables into bergens and were able to walk out with virtually all their personal possessions – plus sleeping bags and other survival gear that might be necessary. The idea of leaving cameras and the exposed film in the barn did not appeal to me. The cine equipment was too heavy to carry on my own. I took my still cameras and the exposed film – some forty kilos – warm clothing and a toothbrush, trusting to Providence.

After fifty kilometres in a battered and very overloaded transit van, we were stopped by huge boulders and Pakistan Army engineers with explosives and crowbars.

An hour's walk took us to the far end of the landslides, where we talked with people who had got through thus far from the south.

Nellie was looking very fed up. Henry told me they had spoken at length; about other incidents and attitudes that Henry had noted, not just the one I had reported – to no immediately constructive effect. The poor chap was under great personal pressure.

An ornate, heavily decorated bus stood at the top of a hill, front wheels chocked with stones. During the landslide it had been caught, and was trapped until the Army had cleared the way. We walked on, over more debris, until we came upon a line of minibuses, and were driven to the nearest village.

Karimabad lay on the western bank of the Hunza valley, its corn fields growing strongly on rich, alluvial terraces, the road winding up past single storey stone houses, over the curved top of the alluvial fan and down the hill at the other side. To the north-west, up a steep hillside and towards the far, snow-covered mountain ridge, terraced fields and houses perched among poplar trees and growing crops. Crowds of schoolchildren bearing satchels and large grins meandered up the road, the boys smart and cheeky, the girls in bright blue shirts and trouser suits, some with red shawls around their heads and their beautiful, round eyes emphasized with black ochre.

The road ran to the end of the valley and curved back round to the other side, vanishing grandly into the distance, over a spectacular suspension bridge. On our side it ran high above the terrace on which every available piece of ground was covered with a patchwork of well-tended, stone-walled fields. Across on the other side of the river, the green fields ran up the steep scree slopes to the very tops of the funnels of loose rock from above which made all hope of plant growth impossible.

Where regular landslides occurred, sweeping the road away, the resultant gully had been filled with rubble and a retaining wall constructed on the outside of the road. These parts were accurately labelled 'Dangerous' and named – for example, 'Rakaposhi Slide' –which gave an added piquancy to the basic terror of the drive.

However, on the other side of the valley, in a peculiar sort of reassurance, a terrifyingly winding, exposed scar zig-zagged along, up and down the cliff. This old 'jeep track' was the original and only road before the building of the KKH, and resembled a fairground switchback.

The driver was fast, but had more skill than the Chinese had shown. We stopped above a village as the evening drew in.

Below in the fields, oxen were being brought in for the night, women were carrying scythed sheaves of corn and two small boys were climbing a tree. The men of the village sat in the darkening evening, heads and shoulders wrapped in large grey and light brown blankets, or sauntered up and down the road, conversations interrupted by the strident blare of the minibus as we thundered past. Across the valley, the low buildings of Gilgit came into view.

The bridges on the KKH were built by the Chinese, who placed dragons on every pillar and forbad photography. Before entering Gilgit, the KKH goes over a long bridge across the river, 'Photography Strictly Prohibited', then splits to Rawalpindi. We entered Gilgit, past Army tents and Military Police posts, the sentries in smart red berets with British Army brass badges.

The hotels were either full or had no gasolene for hot water. Ours lost electricity as well, soon after we booked in.

* * *

I went down to the restaurant to write my diary in the candlelight. A Dutch girl came over and asked if she could join me. She was trying to lose her amorous Pakistani guide.

The Dutch girl had been on a week's trek. After two days, anticipating an added dimension to his duties, her guide had dismissed the porter. He was actually a professional polo player, guiding in the off-season.

Tall, dark and athletic, he was a ladies' man. He boasted about his salary; R2,500 a month, twice that of a Pakistan schoolteacher. The Dutch girl was not impressed; she thought the disparity immoral. His wife and family lived elsewhere, on their own for most of the year while he played polo or took parties of tourists into the hills.

The polo player boasted of how he seduced brides on honeymoon after rows with their new husbands. The grooms stormed off or (worse) remained because they could not find their way back to Gilgit. He claimed that his conquests wrote to him to book further love-holidays in the hills of Hunza.

The Dutch girl was no innocent. An experienced traveller, she used her sexuality, or a hint of things to come, to get what she wanted – on this occasion a guide for next to nothing. However, he had her passport and was 'promising' to use his contacts with the local police to get her out on an early plane. She was stymied. I, presumably, was supposed to make him jealous, to spur him on – or whatever.

The next morning, getting up early and sitting in the hopelessly inefficient hotel restaurant waiting endlessly for breakfast, I passed the time of day with a podgy, prosperous-looking young man dressed in traditional white shirt and baggy trousers. We chatted about London and the south of England. He was very interested in English girls, and with many nudges, told me how jealous he was, having seen the Dutch girl join me the night before. He seemed to spend much of his time going round the circuit of hotels in Gilgit where westerners stay, trying to pick up women. He let slip that he also was married with a family.

There seemed to be a coterie of affluent men driving flashy jeeps, intent on slipping the leash of Moslem morality and chasing the unattached or loosely attached western women who came into town. It seemed to be a compulsive activity for them, a gigolo lifestyle without the financial reimbursement for services rendered – or maybe there was financial reimbursement from some.

My replies to his jocular enquiries as to how I had got on with the Dutch girl were deprecating murmurs:

'I've rather forgotten how to do it . . . been too long in the mountains . . . will have to get back into practice slowly . . .' met with back-slapping disbelief.

My Moslem Don Juan believed all Englishmen capable of fulfilling everything that his fevered, repressed imagination could conjure up. I lived in London, carving a cool swathe through hordes of lascivious nymphomaniacs; I must know everything there was to know about women. (He refused to believe I had not seduced the Dutch girl.) He preferred his dreams to the reality of the west, where women are fully fledged individuals, and where AIDS makes his sort of snatched immorality very dangerous.

The Dutch girl wanted my attendance at the polo, so she could flaunt me to the polo player, who was watching rather than playing that afternoon. The game was on the practice ground, through a network of back streets behind the bazaar.

The pitch proper was situated just out of town and had a wooden grandstand and proper markings. The practice ground was probably where traditionally the game had been played for centuries. It was a dusty street, five hundred metres long, a narrow entrance at one end and a small field at the other, and about thirty metres wide. A low wall ran along one side, on which a hundred or so people squatted, the high garden walls of houses forming the other boundary with the goals (not marked in any way) at either end of the street.

The afternoon was beautiful and sunny, the mountains blue and grey in the distance over the rooftops, and golden sunshine dappled through the green leaves of overhanging trees. The game had started and the spectators were very knowledgeable. One side wore blue and the other a motley collection of various different colours; the Civil Service and the Army were playing the Police.

All organization ended there.

They played with a ball, but the head of a goat – better an enemy – would have done as well. There was no referee, no rules, and like all truly violent sports, between plays everything was astonishingly gentlemanly. The ball was hit at all angles and at all heights, bouncing off garden walls, piles of straw and overhanging trees.

The spectators scattered whenever the fury of play swept into them. One rider had a new and unstoppable colt. He schooled the mount by riding him at the centre of the mêlée, emerging the other side unable to brake or turn. Each headlong gallop was stopped only by aiming the colt at a stone wall until he skidded to a snorting halt.

A local dandy arrived and made much of adjusting his white shirt and jodhpurs, pony held by several doting friends. He took to the field and turned instantly into a dervish like the others.

A blue Datsun driven by a uniformed army officer drove through the game the length of the pitch, hooting wildly when the ball was hit under the car. The players surrounded the vehicle, slashing wildly with heavy, iron-wood mallets. Towards the end of the game, a very foolhardy youth drove a motorbike through on a short cut to the main street.

I had avoided the Dutch girl, who was standing on the other side of the pitch with the polo player. She had told me of her desire to go riding, and how she had been trying to get the polo player to borrow a horse for her.

At the end of the match he put her onto one of the more manageable ponies. In the crowd, heads were shaken, an amused consensus that she would not be back.

The wise lookers-on were correct. She vanished into the dust. A happy crowd dispersed chuckling, leaving the polo player, hands on hips, standing in the centre of the battleground, looking hopelessly to the east. After ten minutes, when all but I had gone home, he trudged off in the direction the pony had taken, his smart leather riding boots grey with dust.

The word from the bazaar was that the army had cleared the road to Soust. I hired a van. In the meantime we moved hotel; there was a grave risk of undernourishment if we remained where we were. Andy and I made the journey, Henry having decided it would be an ideal opportunity for filming. We faced an eight-hour round trip, so that opportunity was slight.

With the owner of the pickup, the three of us crammed onto sunken seat springs and listened to Pakistani versions of Kissy Blossom-Tips. The cassette box covers showed them to be large ladies, adorned with vast quantities of jewellery.

The drive was exciting. We shut our eyes frequently.

It proved too dark and miserable a day to even take the cameras from their cases. On the return journey, buttocks aching unbearably, we developed a fixation about getting back to our new and very beautiful hotel for the evening buffet. Pressing on without pause, we made the meal by minutes. The others were wolfing down second helpings. Eating was still our main recreational activity.

From the hotel balcony, we could look down on planes coming in to land at Gilgit airfield. The roads south – and out – were completely blocked, with no hope of clearance for some time. It was said that the Pakistan Airforce would use C130 Hercules transport aircraft to get people out.

We decamped to the airfield to try our hand at getting onto a plane. The scene was confusing. As hundreds of tourists clamoured at the airport building, a large military and police security cordon was placed round the runway.

A silver C130 landed (they are usually olive green). The cordon bristled with weapons and senior officers. Soldiers were everywhere, smartly turned out in British Army-style 'woolly-pullys', shaped berets and old-fashioned swagger sticks. Large, khaki groups chatted as if at a cocktail party. Prosperous-looking Arab VIPs strolled across the tarmac and we were ordered to put cameras away.

Outside the terminal building queues formed as officials called for names. A list of those wanting to fly to Islamabad was compiled several times by different people, loose rucks forming in seconds. Actively curious locals swelled the crowd, enjoying (and contributing to) the rising tensions.

It seemed hopeless to expect that we would get onto a flight with our huge pile of freight. Straws were drawn for who would stay until the road was cleared.

I had a chat with the police inspector guarding the door into the terminal lobby, calling him 'Inspector', then 'Sir'. He reciprocated and called me 'Sir'. We shook hands and exchanged more pleasantries – as the crowd around us pushed, pulled, elbowed and agitated.

Robbo came thrusting through with a huge box on his head. The Inspector shoved the crowd out of the way, then pulled Robbo from the sweaty throng and through the door.

With this splendid policeman's help, in fifteen minutes we got our equipment through the crowd, into the terminal, and were at the head of the queue – to understandably menacing comments and attempted obstruction from fellow travellers. On the transport plane, our equipment comprised two-thirds of all the luggage aboard – and the fares being charged were for seats only. The Air Load Master had been trained at RAF Lyneham – which could have had something to do with our good fortune.

From the moment the plane took off, we climbed the ladder to civilization several rungs at a time. By four in the afternoon I was lying on a hotel bed in Rawalpindi watching televised cricket. England were getting beaten by Pakistan, Emburey finishing his quota of ten overs, at one for thirty-four.

Some of Wednesday, 21 October and most of Thursday, 22nd were spent getting Liquor Licences from Punjab Customs and Excise. Finding the right building took time as those from whom we sought direction sucked teeth and clucked with disapproval. We could only be after one thing.

Echoing corridors bustled with clerks carrying dog-eared sheaves of paper, amid a pervasive smell of unflushed lavatories. Finally reaching the Holy of Holies, we met He-Whose-Signature-Must-Be-Upon-Everything lest the rotation of the world be jeopardized. 'He' was enormously fat, a black fountain pen constantly in hand. The phone rang. He muttered confidentially into it:

'Tractors . . . diesel fuel . . . motorcycle . . . OK.'

Acolytes respectfully slipped papers under the pen, murmured, and he signed – an elaborate swirl, carefully dated. With decisive thumps of stamp, another deed was done.

We sat before his desk on a long, hard, wooden bench, infidels desperate to pour alcohol down our throats. The forms stipulated, in litres, exactly how much we wished to consume each night to satisfy our craving. His round head looked up for a moment.

Scratch, thump; scratch, thump . . . ten times and it was done. The culmination of many hours of interesting, bureaucratic orienteering.

That evening we went to the British Embassy Club – no disco but a 'Casino Night'. We were of mild interest as 'fresh blood', but not as travellers, because many of the people there had been to China on previous tours of duty.

Before she became too drunk, Sheena told me about her two years in Beijing, during which she was allowed once to take the train to Xian and back. Living and working in exotic places is very different from travelling through.

Henry and I left the others in Rawalpindi. He had to get back to work and I needed to get the film processed. Although the idea was to stay in Pakistan for two weeks and have a relaxing holiday, most wanted to go home.

Henry had been very short with people who asked to forego this holiday and take the next Tristar out. He regarded leaving early as an act of disloyalty to the team, a rather dishonourable renegation from the whole concept of the trip. The faithless would in any case have to pay a share of bills run up in their absence by the others. Bob Woods in particular was quietly fed up, wanting to get back to see his fiancée.

The last moments of fear were at Islamabad airport; Pakistan has a serious internal terrorist problem and security at airports is severe.

'What do you have in these round tins?'

'Cine film.'

'You must put it through the X-ray machine. It will not hurt the film.'

'It is special, very sensitive film.'

'The machine will not hurt it.'

'I have done this before. It will hurt the film. I have been making a television film about Pakistan for the British BBC, a very beautiful film about your very beautiful country.'

'You must put it through the X-ray machine.'

'May I please see the officer in charge?'

Thirty kilos of cine film in a black bag, four months' work about to be wrecked by some poorly adjusted Third World X-ray machine.

'How do I know there is film inside all these cans?'

The spectre of having each can opened and ruined spun before my eyes. I quickly thought about the chief customs man's position. He needed to be able to say to his boss that he had done something, and it probably didn't matter what.

'Why don't you select one of the tins and X-ray that?'

'What about the X-rays?'

'I have coded all the tins and some are less valuable than others. If you choose a valuable one I'll tell you. For safety, one roll of film cannot be important.'

'All right.'

There was a long queue at the check-in desk and our plane for Karachi was due to take off. As dumb Englishmen with no cash, only credit cards, a large excess baggage charge was waived. We made it onto the plane. A passenger failed to show up after checking his bags onto the flight. In a well-practised operation, the security people unloaded every bag from the hold, lining them up on the tarmac for identification, reloading after a bomb disposal team had removed those that remained.

I arrived at my flat in Clapham, expecting, as I always do after being away for some time, to see a blackened hole at number 3A where the gas main has exploded and the building burned down. Amazingly this had not happened, nor had the place been burgled or vandalized. The kitchen table bore four months' mail, mostly bills and some official-looking letters. The personal ones I opened immediately.

The official letters told me what I would be doing. The Army had mapped out my future: comfortingly boring expeditions to exotic places like Salisbury Plain, Sennybridge and Surrey Commons. Five months of steady living were just what I needed, wandering around military training areas on exercises – or windsurfing in Chichester Harbour as my new regiment was based on Thorney Island.

In the event, after a number of telephone calls, I found myself taking up another, very different appointment, commanding an artillery battery re-trained as an infantry company in County Armagh – on the Northern Ireland/Eire border. My battery were to leave England in a few days, having completed their three months' Northern Ireland training. I had to get what training I could – as fast as possible.

My time at the Army Staff College three years earlier had been lonely and miserable – memories of wandering through echoing corridors hounded by virally-induced depression. My friends had rallied round, keeping me going and trying to cheer me up when it all seemed too much.

I lived in the Staff College mess and my next-door-neighbour was Major Andrew French, a chunky, effervescent infantry officer with a lovely, gentle sense of humour. He was an excellent staff officer and made sure I kept up with the course work.

I first met Andrew on a German language course; there was much extra-curricular language laboratory training in the Bier Kellers and Wein Stubes of Mulheim. In the evenings he was to be found in the vortex of beery choirs, performing like an unsupervised sophisticated dancing bear. The next morning, irritatingly, he invariably got full marks in the vocab tests – having tried out his new words on the locals the night before. At Camberley, apart from emerging as one of the rising stars of the fiercely competitive course, Andrew swiftly established himself as the mainstay of the college rugby club – both in the scrum at tight-head prop and socially.

A few short months after we dispersed at the end of the course, Andrew was blown up by an IRA land mine – in the area of Northern Ireland to which I was posted.

Every season, our year's rugby team, plus spectators, returns to

Camberley to play the current Staff College side for the French Cup. The game starts with one minute's silence and fourteen men on our side of the pitch – a space where the tight-head usually stands. Another prop comes on at the first scrummage. From then on, we have sixteen men on the pitch.

The first part of my 'crash-course' training for Northern Ireland involved examining past incidents, with photos and video film, and discussing how to avoid or deter any repetitions. It was very depressing to have the harrowing details of Andrew's violent death thrown suddenly at me from a bright screen in the darkness of a warm lecture theatre.

Once again, I was wondering how I would survive. Holding down the job without being sacked would not be easy – but more importantly, doing the job properly and bringing everybody back in one piece was my responsibility. I reckoned I was extraordinarily lucky that my five-man team had emerged completely unscathed from the Falklands War. Similarly, on Henry Morgan's expedition, we had escaped scot-free from the grim statistics of the Karakoram.

My previous luck introduced an added dimension to my worries. With supreme unfairness, might the probabilities somehow even themselves up on the soldiers of my next command? They did not deserve to have me descend upon them with my potential burden of unexpiated disaster.

Such fears are not helpful – mere superstitions from the dark watches of the night. Most people suffer from them, an unhelpful product of our intelligence; they express a dread of the unknown that is always much worse than the reality that stimulates it.

Beliefs of some sort are required, if only to counter the negatives that generate fear. Coping with one challenge followed by another when there is nothing but doubt in your heart cannot be done without belief in something – or you crack up.

In the mountains I had learned a lesson the hard way. Contrary to my previous (and for me unique) experience with my team in the Falklands, I learned that since you cannot rely on others, you must rely on yourself.

Before joining Henry's expedition, during my illness, I had been faced with this lesson but was not fit enough to be able fully to appreciate it. Only my absolute friends were able to cope with me when I was really down.

For over a year I believed myself to be like a machine that had broken down. I imagined that once the medics identified the parts needing replacement, I would be back to normal again. I was thirty-two when I became ill and thirty-four when I realized that there would be no sudden miracle cure. I was becoming middle-aged, so it was stupid to expect a return to the extreme physical fitness of my late twenties.

Regardless of how I felt, it was my life – with only the one shot at it – and I had to make what I could out of it. Compared with other people who really *are* ill, I was doing all right.

I still feel ill with the ME, only I try to ignore it and get on with living and working. Sometimes I miscalculate and overdo things – and wind up in black depression suffering sore throats, headache and exhaustion. But everyone can feel like that from time to time; at least I have a reason for it, a name for the condition.

Dragons are strange, unfathomable creatures, strong and constant, the impersonal protectors of those who enlist their help. They graze on sunlit hillsides, sleeping in caves carved from the rock. A wise man would never interfere with one; for if woken from sleep, a dragon eats whoever has disturbed him.

Dragons are above and beyond all worry and weakness, while people on their own are weak. We need dragons. The mystical animal represents faith itself, the inner spark of belief in ourselves that we all have – but which can easily be overwhelmed by the floods of unhelpful emotion and stress that we inflict upon ourselves.

I knew that I would need a dragon's help in tackling my new posting. Where excitement was concerned, I was washed out. Rather than another adventure, what I really wanted was six months of mundane, steady living in the same place to re-establish myself as a person.

To survive the opening few weeks in Northern Ireland, the most important thing was for me to get to know my one hundred or so soldiers. Somehow, from that process, I must emerge as a person whose judgement could be trusted.

Once I'd established myself with my soldiers, learning the ropes in a completely unfamiliar military environment would not be difficult as they would make sure I got it right. After that I faced five months of operations. On the one hand, this would be professionally interesting. On the other, the thought of grey streets, closed faces and the reimposition of the probabilities filled me with gloom.

However I was no longer, as I had done before going to China, complaining about being bored.

The clocks were striking midnight with the cracked tones of bells well used to the passing of the years. At one end of the Mall the women's prison stood empty, the fine stonework and slate-tiled roofs now depressingly dank in the soft rain of the winter's evening. The tall trees in the park were gaunt silhouettes against the orange of the street lights, the statue of a horseman black and shining. At the other end of the Mall, the War Memorial stood in darkness, the glare of white floodlights on the front of the court house drawing the eye towards mortar-proof chicken-wire screens and the television cameras that ringed an otherwise splendid stone building. At either side of the green park, where the Armagh City rugby club once played their home matches, were a crescent of Georgian houses with brass plates, museums, a church and a Protestant chapel.

The clocks finished striking midnight; Christmas Eve was slipping into Christmas Day. Second Lieutenant Helen Jones, my regiment's Assistant Adjutant, and I sauntered together, arm in arm along a puddled path beneath the trees. My suede shoes were soaking up water like blotting paper. The bars and pubs were closing and the streets were noisy with drunken singing and other couples lurching home after a seasonal skinful. On top of the hill, in St Patrick's Cathedral, the Cardinal was urging his congregation to consider the evils of abortion and the famine in Ethiopia. We did not have long to wait.

Two four-men teams of soldiers slipped quietly from a side street onto the Mall, quickly setting up a vehicle checkpoint, stopping cars, asking the occupants where they were going and searching the odd boot and bonnet. Radios crackled quietly in the cold night air, the men's breath pluming white as sentries sighted along rifle barrels and 'chatters-up' stooped to peer in through car windows and pass the time of night with passengers.

We sauntered past. With Helen, I was trying to achieve a small degree of anonymity in a town where all outsiders are instantly recognized. We quietly wished each member of the patrol a happy Christmas. They smiled and nodded ruefully, thinking of their own families across the water.

There were no more cars, nothing more to stop. The patrol evaporated into the back streets as quickly as they had arrived, leaving us on our own. The Mall was perfectly silent.

We stopped for a moment in the shadows, beside a small rubbish bin which at first I did not notice in the darkness. Two years ago a policeman had been blown to pieces by a bomb hidden in a bin just like this one. We moved quickly away, back onto the road. A battered Golf Polo, with a scruffy-looking male passenger in the rear seat, pulled in beside where we were standing. My equally dubious-looking driver, Gunner Jeanes, leaned across and opened the door, the muted crackle of the military radio just audible.

'S'arnt Douglas's patrol have just left the police station,' he told me.

In an hour or so everyone would be safe behind the wire.

'Let's get back to camp, Jeano,' I said.

Helen got into the back and I sat in the front passenger's seat, closing the door and fastening the seat belt. I eased my 9mm pistol from its spring-loaded shoulder holster and slipped it under my right thigh, where I could get at it quickly.

'Did you do any carol singing?'

'Yeah, leaving out the high notes,' I replied.

From the back of the car Gunner Moor chuckled:

'You two just won the prize for the most miserable couple in Armagh City.'

I was back in the real world again, which seemed somehow to be a continuation of my journey. I am curious. When will the journey end?

EPILOGUE

On returning to Britain the expedition split to the four winds and has never been fully reunited. Being in Northern Ireland, I missed the official reunion in Plymouth, hearing the celebrations in the background when a lightly oiled Henry telephoned me in my Armagh Operations Room. On the occasions when I have bumped into team members, it has always been a great pleasure to see them again, despite a degree of shyness on both sides. We never knew each other as normal people before going – which was a significant omission from our preparations for the trip. Now, with the rigours and difficulties in the past, we know each other extraordinarily well, and enjoy, rather than endure, each other's company.

Today Henry Morgan is a civilian, working for a company that sells ancillary equipment for (amongst other things) heavy goods vehicles. He was offered a place on the Army's Everest expedition but turned it down, marrying Catherine instead. John Day finally settled down to more everyday life at the Royal Engineers' School of Survey at Thatcham.

Jerry Slack has become a helicopter pilot and is set to join the crack 3 Commando Brigade Air Squadron. Bob Wood continues to pass on his expedition leadership wisdom and mountaineering expertise to soldiers and is based at Dover.

Andy Aspinall, in the Royal Engineers' Regiment near Cambridge, injured himself badly whilst ski-mountaineering in the Alps. After a year of intensive treatment he still suffers ankle pain but nevertheless plays basketball for the Corps team.

Ian Roberts is forging ahead in the climbing world, working in Plymouth as a member of the Training Team at 59 Commando Squadron RE. Nick Moore is an adventure training instructor at the Army Apprentices College at Chepstow.

Conrad Ainsley has become a Physical Training Instructor. He is on an advanced course in Aldershot with the Army Physical Training Corps. Robert Nelson has been promoted to Lance-Corporal and returned to Chatham after a tour in the Falklands to learn a new trade.

I returned from Northern Ireland, unscathed and, more importantly, without any of my soldiers having been killed or injured. So far, there hasn't been much time to knock on many doors, so as I write I'm still looking for a producer for the film. It's a ripping yarn and would make a jolly good television documentary . . .

INDEX

INDEX